THE
GREY
MEN

THE
GREY
MEN

PURSUING THE STASI
INTO THE PRESENT

RALPH HOPE

ONEWORLD

A Oneworld Book

First published in Great Britain, the Republic of Ireland
and North America by Oneworld Publications, 2021

Hardback ISBN 978-1-78607-827-8
Trade Paperback ISBN 978-1-78607-951-0
eISBN 978-1-78607-828-5

Typeset by Tetragon, London
Printed and bound in Great Britain by Clays Ltd, Elcograf S.p.A.

Oneworld Publications
10 Bloomsbury Street, London, WC1B 3SR, England

Stay up to date with the latest books,
special offers, and exclusive content from
Oneworld with our newsletter

Sign up on our website
oneworld-publications.com

MIX
Paper from
responsible sources
FSC
www.fsc.org
FSC® C018072

For those who cannot fail to remember,
and to those who would have us forget.

'Next year we celebrate the seventieth anniversary of the creation of the Ministry for State Security!'

FORMER STASI LIEUTENANT COLONEL, 2019

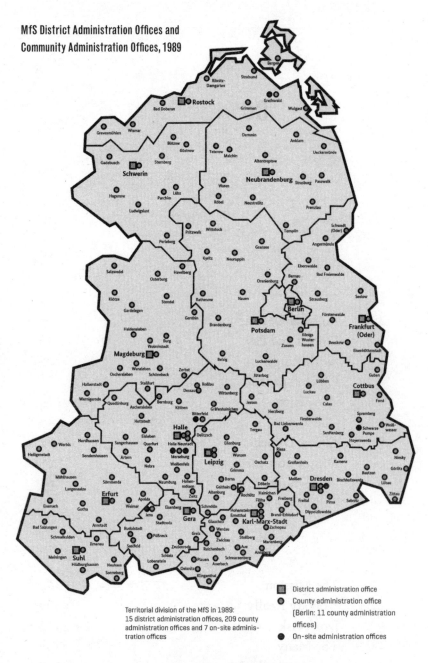

MfS District Administration Offices and Community Administration Offices, 1989

Bergen

Ribnitz-Damgarten
Stralsund

Rostock
Bad Doberan
Greifswald
Grimmen
Wolgast

Grevesmühlen
Wismar

Bützow
Güstrow
Demmin
Anklam

Gadebusch
Sternberg
Teterow
Malchin
Altentreptow
Ueckermünde

Schwerin
Waren
Neubrandenburg
Strasburg
Pasewalk

Hagenow
Lübz
Parchim
Röbel
Neustrelitz
Prenzlau

Ludwigslust

Pritzwalk
Wittstock
Templin
Schwedt (Oder)

Perleberg
Gransee
Angermünde

Kyritz
Neuruppin
Eberswalde

Salzwedel
Havelberg
Oranienburg
Bernau
Bad Freienwalde

Osterburg
Nauen
Strausberg
Seelow

Klötze
Stendal
Rathenow
Berlin

Gardelegen
Genthin
Brandenburg
Fürstenwalde

Haldensleben
Burg
Wolmirstedt
Potsdam
Königs Wusterhausen
Beeskow
Frankfurt (Oder)

Magdeburg
Zossen
Eisenhüttenstadt

Wanzleben
Zerbst
Belzig
Luckenwalde

Oschersleben
Schönebeck
Jüterbog
Lübben
Cottbus

Halberstadt
Staßfurt
Roßlau
Dessau
Wittenberg
Luckau
Calau
Forst

Wernigerode
Quedlinburg
Bernburg
Köthen
Gräfenhainichen
Jessen
Herzberg
Finsterwalde
Spremberg

Aschersleben
Bitterfeld
Torgau
Bad Liebenwerda
Senftenberg
Schwarze Pumpe
Weißwasser

Hettstedt
Halle
Delitzsch
Riesa
Hoyerswerda

Nordhausen
Eisleben
Eilenburg
Görlitz

Worbis
Sangerhausen
Querfurt
Halle Neustadt
Wurzen
Großenhain
Kamenz
Niesky

Heiligenstadt
Sondershausen
Artern
Merseburg
Leipzig
Oschatz
Bautzen

Nebra
Weißenfels
Grimma
Löbau

Mühlhausen
Naumburg
Borna
Döbeln
Meißen
Dresden
Bischofswerda

Sömmerda
Hohenmölsen
Geithain
Hainichen
Freiberg
Freital
Pirna
Zittau

Langensalza
Zeitz
Altenburg
Rochlitz
Flöha
Sebnitz

Erfurt
Apolda
Eisenberg
Schmölln
Hohenstein-Ernstthal
Brand-Erbisdorf
Dippoldiswalde

Eisenach
Gotha
Weimar
Jena
Glauchau
Karl-Marx-Stadt
Zschopau

Bad Salzungen
Arnstadt
Stadtroda
Gera
Werdau
Stollberg
Marienberg

Schmalkalden
Rudolstadt
Pößneck
Greiz
Zwickau
Annaberg

Ilmenau
Saalfeld
Zeulenroda
Reichenbach
Aue
Schwarzenberg

Meiningen
Schleiz
Plauen
Auerbach

Suhl
Hildburghausen
Neuhaus
Lobenstein
Oelsnitz

Sonneberg
Klingenthal

Territorial division of the MfS in 1989: 15 district administration offices, 209 county administration offices and 7 on-site administration offices

■ District administration office
◉ County administration office
(Berlin: 11 county administration offices)
● On-site administration offices

To Know Everything
Stasi operational offices in East Germany – a country smaller than Florida.

CONTENTS

PART III

AUTHOR'S NOTE

This isn't a history book, as I'm not a historian. But like all true stories, it begins with and is carried forward by the past. More than that, it's a product of real events and circumstances that are still hard to believe, the lingering effects of which confronted me daily during my years serving as an FBI agent in Eastern Europe and other places around the world that were traumatized by tyranny. These real dramas deserve far more than a printed page, and are deeply personal to people whose lives were forever altered. They were confirmed by my many formal and informal conversations with police and intelligence services of those countries and my own.

Where the story will end remains to be seen.

PREFACE

Dresden, East Germany
Tuesday

What would happen today, Siegfried would never be allowed to forget.

He stood on a street corner with a group of more than a hundred young activists who were giddy with excitement. It was December 5, 1989, and tyranny's half-century grip on Eastern Europe was breaking apart in front of them. The Berlin Wall had fallen less than a month before and anything now seemed possible. Communism was reeling and a new world seemed nearly within reach. After demonstrating in the streets for weeks, frequently clashing violently with security forces, they all now sensed that something had changed. Word quickly circulated that the inner sanctum, the offices of the East German secret police, the feared Stasi, were being occupied all over the country.

Why not then also here in Dresden?

The group fragmented and rushed down Bautzner Strasse and along the Elbe River, before finally crowding together again near a grey compound that they all knew housed the regional Stasi offices. For forty years before that day, and even a month or a week before now, this place would have been avoided at all costs. The block buildings complete with prison cells symbolized the iron grip that the Ministry for State Security had wielded over the city for decades, and that the Soviets had before that. It was a place of nothing other than misery and fear. Never somewhere any of them would have gone voluntarily. Until today.

The crowd grew much larger and the winter night had already come by 5pm when they made their move. Gathering courage and sweating in spite of the wind from the river blowing damp and cold, several hundred activists pushed their way inside the iron front gate, determined to prevent the destruction of whatever files were there. They hoped not to get shot in the process.

To their surprise, no machine-gun-carrying Stasi guards in grey uniforms stood in their way. The few occupants inside appeared confused and accommodating, and the place was largely empty. They opened office doors, and looked in drawers. They were there to protect the files, they announced. Nobody stopped them. The fear of a dictatorship had lost its grasp, and everyone there could smell death.

Now more emboldened, and quite sure something monumental had taken place, Siegfried and part of the crowd clustered at the entrance and quickly descended the stairs. On a whim they rushed together across the wide boulevard, chattering nervously, their eyes now focused on a pale yellow house within sight on Angelikastrasse. Everyone in Dresden knew the KGB was headquartered there. This time without any hesitation they confronted a lone guard at the gate and repeated their demand to be let in. The crowd seethed with energy and stared impatiently as the guard rushed inside the building, returning with a young, small officer dressed in the green uniform of a Soviet lieutenant colonel. This Russian officer appeared agitated as he approached the gate, speaking fluent German.

'My comrades are armed, and authorized to use our weapons in an emergency.'

The group withdrew. The face of that Soviet officer remained burned in Siegfried's mind, and also the name when he later learned it. It was Vladimir Vladimirovich Putin, the future Russian president. Putin was then assigned to Dresden on his first foreign KGB posting. On that day a Stasi-issued identification card was in his pocket.

Throughout the chaos on the streets that week, Putin and the three other KGB officers sitting on the second floor of the house on Angelikastrasse that evening naturally assumed they'd receive ample protection from a nearby Soviet tank regiment that was based in the city. The tank commander was close and indeed fully prepared to intervene with brute force. He only waited for the call from Moscow, which they were all sure would soon come. It never did. 'Moscow was silent', they were all told. Many of those in the know believe this incident, and the resulting rapid fall of the secret police and communist East Germany, had a profound impact on Putin. He was soon forced to hastily drive back to his hometown of Leningrad, which had suddenly become St Petersburg again, in disbelief, with little besides his wife and a twenty-year-old washing machine that he'd received as a gift. It was over. On arriving in St Petersburg his colleagues at the KGB even started referring to him by a new nickname:

Stasi.

This was the end for a young Vladimir Putin, and for the ruthless Stasi. Everything was finished.

Or was it?

PART I

1

PERSONAL DESTRUCTION AS A FINE ART

It was a crisp fall morning in 2008 and dawn had barely arrived. The sort of day that warned of yet another early and brutally cold Baltic winter. I was driving a vehicle with diplomatic plates on a deserted road, speeding to a location very near the Russian border.

As the deputy FBI agent responsible for liaison in the region with criminal or terrorist investigations involving all of the fifty-six domestic Bureau field offices, I was in yet another unusual job. Next to me that morning riding shotgun was an ethnic Russian police officer from that Baltic state. I knew Anatoly well, having worked with him on cases involving organized crime and cybercriminals that touched his country and the United States. As is usually true, many found it irresistible and not so difficult to steal from America. Computers made it dramatically easier to do so from the safety of St Petersburg or a Moscow suburb. But sometimes they crossed a border, and sometimes they waited a little too long to cross back.

As a rule, while working overseas I always carefully avoided mentioning politics or history with any of my contacts. That was especially true in formerly occupied countries. There was tragedy of many kinds everywhere in Eastern Europe, and it was frequently unclear which type someone had borne. The people here were warm and genuine, but also hesitant and somewhat formal. It was still odd enough to come across an American, besides the occasional adventure-seeking tourist. However, law enforcement people worldwide share two things: one is wanting to get the bad guy, and the other is talking when bored.

Anatoly leaned back in the seat and sighed, fingering a cigarette with obvious regret since he knew he couldn't smoke it for another forty-five minutes. 'So, many in America think that we all are happy here now?'

'You mean you're not? But why?' I paused, noticing him staring at his hand. 'You can smoke that – no problem for me. Just roll down the window.' He grinned but shook his head, instead tucking the wrinkled cigarette into his breast pocket. 'My parents are not doing well now. Before... they knew that a loaf of bread and liter of milk were fifty kopecks each last week, and would be the same next week. They had a free flat, too. Now that all changed, and they're pensioners. And since we are in the EU, when we convert to the euro it will be worse! My father tells me things were not so bad before...'

I nodded. It was a Cold War legacy, sudden inflation and loss of status of the ethnic Russians. 'But, Anatoly, you weren't really free, right? Could you leave the country back then, before 1991?'

He stared at the road and rolled the window down a crack, breathing in the icy air. 'No. Of course not. But I was young and didn't think about it. My father said that was okay anyway. We were so happy that our number had just come up to finally let us buy a Lada. We would have a car! He liked to tell us we were birds in a gilded cage.' I sat quietly, knowing such candid comments might not be well received by many non-Russians in Eastern Europe I knew and worked with, who had lived for two generations as second-class citizens.

The trip that day, and Anatoly's calm efficiency in pursuing Russian criminals, paid off. A tip was checked out, and soon a special police team silently lined up late in a dim upstairs corridor of a drab block of flats on the edge of town. They stood in the shadows and against the wall as the point officer lightly tapped on the door and waited. When the dead bolt turned and a crack appeared, the officer's boot jammed it open and shoved – 'Politsiya!'

As the door sprang open, the surprised man inside grunted and spun without comment, scrambling for the dining table where a laptop lay open. He didn't make it.

After he was taken away, a search team began their methodical work. They found two encrypted thumb drives – identifying an international network – hidden in a picture hanging on the wall, bundles of cash stuffed behind a wall panel in the kitchen and a confused girlfriend. That man – a high-level cybercriminal whose organization stole nearly $10 million from a US bank in twelve hours over a three-day weekend – was the first such Russian to be extradited and sent to a federal prison in America.

In the United States, the Federal Bureau of Investigation is both the primary domestic intelligence organization and the principal federal law enforcement agency.

J. Edgar Hoover created the first overseas FBI office in 1941, then needed to combat the Nazi threat. Others soon followed, as they proved essential to increasing liaison and reach, which were crucial to the global nature of all major investigations, especially terrorism. After the fall of the Soviet Union, a forward-thinking expansion of these offices took place in newly liberated Eastern Europe, where most countries had been closed to Western contact for half a century. It was a new frontier.

With this new access came tremendous opportunities and many surprises, but it also required navigating the deep divisions that lingered from the years of occupation in police states. For those who have new concerns of possible intelligence abuses in the future, there are clear lessons to be learned.

When the Soviet empire crumbled in 1991, the loss of status of those with privilege was universal, as the rest savored new freedoms. In the years I lived and worked in Eastern Europe, I became accustomed to stumbling on surprise and tragedy. The idea that the very recent past of fifty years of occupation had been wiped quickly away was mostly an illusion, a veneer. Sometimes less than that. I had attended meetings in buildings that had once belonged to the Soviet state, visited empty file rooms, former basement execution and detention cells. More than once I even had revealing conversations with old women selling cigarettes and candy from small kiosks on the street, as they always had. In most places, you could see it in their faces. The pain in the eyes of the older generation, confusion in the middle-aged and the eagerness and tentative hope in the new. It wasn't uncommon for those in the recently freed police and intelligence agencies to whisper to me with a quiet gesture while nodding at someone else seated at a meeting: 'He was KGB!' Or, they pointed out a German – 'He was Stasi!'

Many times, it was true.

Less than three weeks after my trip with Anatoly, I stood in an office in Berlin that had been occupied for twenty-eight years by the most feared man in Germany. The desk was now carefully wiped clean except for two black telephones neatly arrayed to one side. It still had the well-worn chair in which the head of the Stasi, Minister Erich Mielke, had sat for nearly three decades. His huge, thick wall safe stood open and empty. Mielke was called the *Master of Fear* by East Germans for good reason – he created and ran the secret police with an iron hand and was also the person who oversaw the construction of the Berlin Wall in 1961. Although I was on an unofficial visit, it was hard not to notice the irony of an FBI agent being here, in this place. I turned and stepped into the adjacent room in which stretched a long, gleaming conference table, and thought about the old men who had sat there.

The stated goal of the Ministry for State Security (MfS), Staatssicherheit, or Stasi, was simple: *To Know Everything.* The proud slogan, used with their red crest depicting an outstretched arm gripping a rifle with a bayonet, was the *Sword and Shield of the Party.*

Unlike other Eastern European security police agencies, their responsibilities were very different. They combined the agencies of state security, foreign espionage, police and judicial ministries. They were an intelligence service, secret police, public prosecutor and elite military all at once. In addition, they were charged with monitoring the churches, all aspects of the cultural sector and the news media;

prosecuting those who tried to escape to the West; and gauging the population's mood. They weren't accountable to the German Democratic Republic (GDR) legislature, the Volkskammer, but only to the Politburo – of which Minister Mielke was a senior member. He also had a dedicated and heavily armed motorized rifle regiment at his disposal, the Felix Dzerzhinsky Guards Regiment, some 11,000 members strong.

In private, Mielke liked to call himself fondly a Chekist in honor of Dzerzhinsky (aka 'Iron-Felix'). In 1917 Dzerzhinsky founded the Cheka, the predecessor to the Soviet Narodnyi Komissariat Vnutrennikh Del (NKVD) and the Komitet Gosudarstvennoy Bezopasnosti, better known as the KGB. In fact, at Mielke's order the Stasi crest was designed to be similar to the Cheka's.

With Mielke firmly in control, the Stasi grew exponentially. Formed only in 1950, by 1953 the organization already had more employees than the Nazi Gestapo. That number then doubled each following decade. Even the KGB, which during the Cold War had an estimated one officer for every 600 citizens, fell far behind the East German Ministry for State Security average of one officer for every 180 persons. If you add the Stasi informers, called *Inoffizielle Mitarbeiter*, Unofficial Employees, or IMs, that number grows to one per sixty-three persons. The Stasi created reams of detailed reports. Of the sixteen million citizens in the GDR as of 1989, the Stasi had files on six million. *The Firm*, as it was more commonly referred to by those within, had more than 90,000 full-time employees and 189,000 active informants at the bitter end in late 1989. They operated from one of 209 offices solely designed to scrutinize and take actions against their own population, each and every day. Their sole mission was to protect the leftist dictatorship. During the four decades that the Stasi operated, they dedicated 250,000 employees and 600,000 informants to this task.

They were known collectively to many East Germans as the Grey Men. Those to be avoided and not spoken about, as if they didn't exist. If ever seen on state television, they were guessed to be those in the background, wearing grey suits. And exist they did. By the mid-1980s, every day special machines were steaming open 90,000 pieces of mail for their inspection, 5,000 officers were engaged in physical surveillance, and 6,000 were busy with wiretaps and hidden microphones. Their seventeen secret prison facilities, scattered across the country, were always occupied.

As an average East German, many things could and frequently did cause your destruction by the Stasi. A casual conversation that was somehow reported and a tick placed in your file, a family member who was perceived to be disloyal, your expressed wish to travel to the West or dutifully applying for a permit to do so, a refusal to report on others, a letter you wrote or one you received, a political enemy, receiving too many packages in the mail from West Berlin, an opinion you voiced in your school classroom, or any number of other minor ways. Sometimes it was a report filed by your spouse, brother, sister, child or even parent who you didn't know was an IM. Most East Germans never knew why they didn't get that exit permit to visit family in the West, or that job they applied for, or even why they were refused entry to the prestigious Humboldt University in East Berlin, or another school.

If you were in Berlin, the answer might have come on a street corner with a hand on your shoulder, or an unexpected early morning rap at the door.

'State Security.'

You would be thrust by two or three men into a small delivery truck idling at the curb, perhaps appearing to be from a flower shop or a neighborhood bakery. Inside you would be summarily locked into one of two tiny metal compartments with no windows. Before the door to the tiny cell slammed you might glimpse a uniformed guard with a small machine pistol seated outside. For long hours, the truck would then drive randomly around the city to disorient you, before finally halting at what appeared to be a faraway place.

It was at that place, and within a walled compound called Hohenschönhausen, which officially didn't exist on any map until

1990, and surrounded by an otherwise unremarkable residential neighborhood, that you and every new prisoner would stand alone and blinking under bright lights and in front of a high desk. A green ledger would be opened. Next to each prisoner's name, and the name of the arresting Stasi member, which was neatly entered into the book by the uniformed duty officer, was a simple sequential number. It was that number by which the prisoner would be referred to, from that moment on. Personal identity was over. You were a number, and only a number, to you and everyone you would see. Even the fact that you had been arrested was a state secret. It was then that the twenty-four-hour interrogations would start. Many would disappear for years here, or at facilities like it, never hearing their names spoken or even seeing another prisoner.

Perhaps you were lucky. You were thought to be a dissident, but not dangerous enough to the state to be imprisoned in one of the remand facilities. In that case, they would employ *Zersetzung*, which loosely translated means decomposition – to degrade, subvert and render ineffective. It was for them a fine art.

Some found out only years later while reviewing their Stasi files how their life had been ruined. It turns out it doesn't take much to destroy a person. A quiet 'not recommended' to a diligent company or government agency vetting applicants, or just a mere pause during the conversation when a routine call was made to a university, was enough to sidetrack the course of lives.

Between the commencement of the Cold War in the late 1940s and 1990, two entire generations of East Germans were trained in this way to please the state. It was roughly in the middle of this period, during 1977, that the GDR stopped recording statistics on suicides. It became embarrassing and inconvenient to do so.

Then on November 9, 1989, the Berlin Wall ceased to effectively keep the East in, or the West out, and the communist state fell. To the credit of the new German Republic, the Office of the Federal Commissioner, known as Der Bundesbeauftragte für die Stasi-Unterlagen, or BStU, the official custodian of the Stasi Archive, was swiftly created in late 1990 to allow affected persons and researchers access to the more than one hundred kilometers of recovered Stasi files. That decision wasn't without controversy. At the time many, for their own reasons, called for the records to be destroyed. Thankfully, others prevailed. It was, after all, a singular opportunity. The people had a right to see their files, if they had the nerve to look. Many never have.

———

More than a quarter of a century after the GDR and the Stasi unraveled, going to the Records Agency to review the files, even if they're not your own, can sometimes be an unsettling experience. I discovered that when making a routine request to see certain organizational records. It was a spring day, and I received official notification that files I'd requested were ready for viewing.

Arriving at the appointed time at the Berlin BStU office, a government-appearing building just off Alexanderplatz and deep in the former Eastern Sector, I was ushered into a room resembling a school classroom, complete with rows of small desks. About half of them were filled by people who had arranged themselves apart from each other. Facing the room at the front was a stern-looking woman who seemed ready to ensure we kept quiet. That seemed hardly necessary, since unlike a school classroom no one in this room was in any way acknowledging anyone else. To the left of the minder there sat rows of files stacked neatly against the wall, each separated by a slip of paper that matched the number given to you. After displaying identification and your letter of appointment, and signing a book, you sat at your desk and reviewed what they brought you, one file at a time. It was a tense collection of uneasy people.

Looking to the back, I noticed an elderly woman, wearing a worn grey sweater pulled close, get up and shuffle to the front. With her eyes averted, she carefully replaced a volume in her row and took another, barely denting at least five thick volumes that remained. It was the story of her entire life, and maybe that of her family as well.

She appeared to be what they collectively call in Eastern Europe a pensioner. No doubt it required a great deal of courage for her that day.

I later asked my contact, an efficient woman at the Records Agency, about the close monitoring that went on there.

'The assistant is needed in the records inspection room for two reasons,' I was quickly told. 'One is to offer aid to those who sometimes physically break down when reviewing their files' (they are removed to special counseling rooms). 'The other is because there have been attempts to destroy or remove the documents. Even to tear out pages and stuff them in their mouths.'

The Stasi files, filled with shocking deceptions and human weaknesses, even years later remain pools of tears.

In Germany, years after unification, people hesitate to mention the Stasi. For those longtime Berliners on either side of the faint marks on the streets and sidewalks that mark the Wall, virtually all family histories have been touched. Families from the East always doubted the West could understand, and remain afraid even now what secrets are contained in the kilometers of detailed records now carefully cared for by the Records Agency. Those in what was once West Germany are embarrassed to have it as a combined legacy that refuses to die. Many of them were also impacted, either by divided families, guilt over their success or perhaps collaboration. To many of both of those groups, there remains a very real Wall in the mind.

So where did they go, the successful and senior Stasi officers who designed all of this? Asking that simple question to many, it seemed apparent that nobody really knew the answer.

I wasn't a stranger to government intelligence or police agencies, by then having served more than twenty-five years as an FBI agent, including years running offices in Eastern Europe and Africa. I first stood in Germany shortly before the Wall dramatically fell in 1989. I had seen first-hand many times, and in many places, the twisted impacts and bizarre remnants of the Cold War, a war that was never very cold. I'd been on the front lines of the rapid increase of cooperation between intelligence agencies made necessary by the upsurge in global terrorism. I have no illusions about the necessity of that fight, or of the need to be on guard against spies within. Even so, the unprecedented depth and influence over society by what many insiders still call the Firm was chilling.

While no serious comparison can be made between the intelligence service of a dictatorship, such as the GDR, with those services found in America or Europe today, there are valuable global lessons to be learned and questions that must be asked and answered. Among rumblings that we're now poised on the brink of a new Cold War, that Russia and China are becoming increasingly restless, are concerns that intelligence abuses may once again be tolerated. China, the largest repressive state at the moment, is busy further perfecting surveillance and detention of millions of citizens, while extending technological repression globally without regard to state borders.

Clearly, being worried that an externally focused intelligence agency like the National Security Agency (NSA), which is mainly concerned with foreign terrorists, unfriendly or rogue governments, and spies, poses the same risks as an inwardly directed agency such as the Stasi is without merit. Regardless, it's true that Europe and the United States, and the rest of the world, are quickly changing to confront our new threats. Not having the recent lessons learned from the excesses of a leftist communist government close at hand would be unwise.

2

PRESENT AND PAST

Two hundred thousand travelers passing daily through the crush and bustle of the world's largest airport are oblivious to a decades-long struggle that rages close by.

Just north of Atlanta today, in a suburban town of maybe six thousand people, an aging but still neat and trim man well past seventy runs a German car repair shop. It's a family business, held together by passion, sacrifice and long hours. The cars that litter the outdoor lot hint that business is good. The owner's house is just down the street. By day he repairs and restores Audis and BMWs. Late at night he's on a special phone line at the shop, calling Germany well into the early hours of the morning, determined to prevent the reemergence of communism and to speak up for its victims.

When I saw him, Christian Lappe was sitting erect and on the edge of his chair placed just out of the hot Georgia afternoon. He was gesturing at a picture in front of us, and his passion was undeniable. Hearing him excitedly describe his restored vintage BMW Isetta supercar, it was hard to believe this man had been an enemy of the state. I doubt if his neighbors even now suspect. But it's clear that's how the East German Ministry for State Security saw him. Arrested by two MfS officers the first time when he was nineteen, he was held and interrogated for four months. The Stasi was intent on ridding the German Democratic Republic of him and everything his family stood for. They were, after all, the children of a Lutheran minister, who placed God before government and thus wouldn't be tolerated by a state that was focused on eradicating what it considered the threat of religion.

Christian paused from waving the car picture and turned it over on the table, his sharp eyes and face darkening as he rummaged through papers strewn all over the floor.

'Communists are just Nazis painted red,' he repeated. It was one of the first things he'd said to me on the telephone months earlier.

'A famous German said that. It's true.'

He stood and stamped his feet while rubbing his arms as if trying to warm himself.

'Yes, the Stasi arrested me. More than once. I wrote political poetry. Then I wrote a letter to a friend in West Germany telling him I planned to escape, and asking for help. Of course, I knew better than to mail it.

'My mistake was giving the letter to someone else to deliver. They gave it to the Stasi instead. The last time they didn't let me go – they kept me in jail, in Halle, at their prison.'

He reached over and grabbed a huge bound stack of papers from the shelf, his MfS file he had received later from the Archive.

'It's all here!' He dropped the stack on the chair with a thud. 'Two thousand pages on me.'

I flipped through hundreds of pages of interrogation records, all neatly typed and signed.

'I was called only *Prisoner* when they spoke to me. Those first four months with the Stasi, I never saw another person – just my interrogator.

'Wait, except for one day.' That was when a medical person came in and smeared both of his arms with a sort of chemical, without explanation. 'Some sort of medicine they were testing, I learned,' he said. 'At the time I was told not to touch it but to tell the interrogator if there were reactions.'

Finally, at age twenty-six, and after having been arrested four times, Christian was sentenced to two years in prison for trying to escape to the West. After some time, he was assigned to work in the prison's small workshop in the basement. It was across the hall from the room, the Stasi guards reminded him, where the Nazis had executed prisoners. Where he worked every day, the guards said, had been the waiting room for the condemned. After a year and half, he somehow ended up on a list of prisoners ransomed to freedom by the West German government. He was free!

But by then, imprisonment, interrogations and uncertainty had altered his life forever. Next, the identical thing happened to four others in his family. One of them committed suicide as a result.

Arriving in West Berlin confused and blinking in disbelief, Christian sought a trade, eventually working as an engineer, and years later marrying an American woman.

'She tells me all the time to forget this stuff. But how?' he said, the sad look briefly changing to a smile as his wife appeared and then disappeared back into the rear of the house. 'I cannot.'

He glanced toward the family pictures hanging on the wall, and stepped nearer to look closely at one of them.

'The first time after that I returned to East Berlin was in 1991. I had to see it for myself, that it was gone. That they were.'

'And was it? Were they?'

Shaking his head, and staring at his working man's hands, he peered back at me over reading glasses.

'It was confusion then. Confusion and hope. I work with other victims of communism there even now, and return maybe once a year or so. I just came from Düsseldorf.'

He dropped back down into the chair and scraped across the floor as he moved closer, threading his way through stacks of papers.

'Was it gone, you say? I don't know. Sure, the border was open. But the Stasi...' He stared out the window toward the shop.

'Now there are those they call the *Antifa* there in Germany, and even in America now! In Hamburg recently, those that said they were Antifa, antifascist they claim, burned cars in the streets!' He paused and his face darkened. 'The monster of communism isn't dead! Ignazio Silone had it right!'

'Silone, the Italian writer…?'

'Yes! He had it right! He was a communist who became an anticommunist. He said that when the fascists return, they will call themselves antifascists! Those calling themselves antifascists are rising! Antifa, and the others.'

'And the Stasi? What happened to them?'

'They're there. All over Berlin, even now with their money and influence. Ask anyone!'

Sitting in middle America on a humid afternoon, I heard the same things I'd heard many times in Eastern Europe. Pain, frustration and a lack of resolution. This was a man whose entire life was permanently altered when he was nineteen. Such things were a common specialty of the Grey Men.

At the shop, we weaved our way through German classic cars in various stages of restoration. Christian showed me the 1957 Isetta, a perfectly restored and gleaming red-and-white micro BMW of a type I had never seen before. It's unique, having only one large door in front resembling that of a refrigerator. Produced in Germany in the fifties and early sixties, at the time it was credited with keeping BMW from failure and bankruptcy.

Christian volunteers as the US representative for a Stasi victims' group. 'From a phone in my shop I call Germany almost every night and day, to talk with the others. We can't let the communists return!' As he walked me out to the driveway, he held out his hand. 'Things don't look so good.'

He stopped and squinted in the sun. 'You know, I've started writing poetry again. Political kind. They didn't win. I even had some published in a magazine once. I'm still working on the rest. One of them is posted on the wall in Berlin at the victims' association. I'm working on more, but they won't publish them in Germany now.'

The Isetta had been perfectly restored, but Christian wasn't there yet.

———

East Berlin
May 1959

The man pacing nervously had no way of knowing that in only two years the Berlin Wall would be erected in the dead of a single summer night. Yet he and many others he spoke carefully with knew something bad was going to happen. And soon.

For now, travel from the communist East to the West was as easy as walking across the street. That was the problem. A huge problem for the East German government, as all the wrong sort of people were leaving – the productive, educated and those inclined to take risks. Something must be done, but even the Soviets were resisting the kind of drastic action that the SED Politburo had planned. The Socialist Unity Party, or SED, were the leaders of the nine-year-old East German communist dictatorship. They called it the German Democratic Republic, the GDR. There was in reality nothing democratic about it.

To the Grey Men, who were busy adding thousands to their ranks, all the people planning to leave only meant there were even more troublemakers to be dealt with. They called them criminals. Officially at least, there hadn't been and never would be any politically motivated arrests in the GDR. Publicly claiming otherwise could get you arrested. The laws could easily cover anything that the state didn't like. But at the moment all they could do was watch as educated and productive citizens stepped into the West, most never to return. Others tried to maintain a life, crossing to work in the West for hard currency, and returning to families in the East on evenings or weekends with scarce goods and West German marks.

It was late in the evening, and the lanky thirty-six-year-old walked back and forth in his tiny East Berlin flat, making up his mind. Wilhelm Knabe was one of seven children and knew the value of a family and sacrifice. His mind raced; there was a tough decision to make that night. He was one of many who'd survived the Second World War in Germany by sheer luck, and since then he couldn't avoid the thought that someone had been watching over him. As a result, he had become a pacifist and developed a Christian faith. Barely making it through the closing days of the war in Dresden, he survived the Allied carpet-bombing, only to be nearly shot by the Nazi SS. They assumed that a young man riding a bicycle through a burning city to see if his mother might still be alive must be a deserter or spy. He somehow talked his way free and then survived postwar imprisonment by Stalin's army. But then fate and bad luck dictated that he would find himself in the Soviet part of Germany as the Cold War descended. He already understood tyranny: his father had died during SS interrogation when Wilhelm was only sixteen.

By ill happenstance he was now an East German subject. Not a good future for him or his young wife and three small children, with yet another child now on the way. He heard Soviet premier Nikita Khrushchev announce on the radio that the 'Berlin problem' would soon be 'solved'. He had watched what the Nazis, and then Stalin, had unfurled in Europe. Now he was seeing worse things with the Stasi, and had a front-row seat for the escalation of the Cold War. The last straw came the day he received the letter. Ripping open the official envelope, he read the notification. He was expected to join the reserves in the NVA, the National People's Army. Wilhelm refused, a very dangerous thing to do. He was employed in a decent job at the time, but could sense things were rapidly closing around Berlin and his family. Like most people in the city at the time, he wasn't sure how the ax would fall or when. He decided not to find out.

'We're going,' he told his pregnant wife. 'Tonight. Gather just a few things for the children.'

Late that May evening the family of five merged with the usual daily crossers to the West Berlin side. Wilhelm abandoned his job at Humboldt University and they left behind virtually all their possessions. Maybe his decision was finally made by what his wife had said late at night the week before. She had told him that she sat and wondered every day if her next child would be born in a Stasi prison. Born as an enemy of the state.

A few steps over and the family with the pregnant woman stood in West Berlin. To avoid suspicion and possible questioning by onlooking State Security officers, they carried few possessions. They had become refugees. Now, where would they go? There was nobody to greet them that night; crossers at odd hours were common then. And so, the Knabe family started to walk. Eventually they stopped in the town of Unna, long enough for his wife to give birth a couple of months later. They named their new son and fourth child Hubertus Wilhelm Knabe. Forced by the descending Iron Curtain to abandon relatives and the family home, Hubertus had been victimized before he was even born. But he was one of the lucky ones. They were all surely safe in West Germany.

His parents raised him in the Christian faith and often spoke of the evils of the communist dictatorship from which they had escaped. Hubertus, described by teachers as a bright and intense boy, quickly became restless in Bremen, a town north of Berlin in which he spent his childhood. It was a restlessness that's common to young men. He grew up his whole life seeing the Berlin Wall and the soldiers, but lived in freedom as a citizen of West Germany. Or so he imagined.

In reality, by the time Hubertus Knabe was nineteen he had already been targeted by Department XX of the Stasi, who had opened an operational file on him. More than twenty years later he would learn that Department XX specialized in taking actions against churches and those who attended them.

3

AWAKENINGS

By late 1979, Hubertus Knabe was barely twenty and active in the Peace Movement in West Berlin. He began visiting the communist East frequently on weekends, his West German identification tucked safely in his pocket. As matters of the heart would have it, he soon met a special woman in a gathering of theology students at East Berlin's Humboldt University. But she was a citizen of the GDR – meaning things were quite different for her. Annette was a captive.

The two of them were renegades, asking far too many questions, and as such they had much in common. They had long discussions about their frustrations with the communist system. He sensed that she was the one. Hubertus did well with his studies, especially those involving history, but wasn't content with that. He began to write while sitting safely in West Berlin, recording his thoughts about the realities of the communist system in East Germany. On weekends with Annette they shared everything, talking forever. He was careful not to stand out and wrote about those things under assumed names, random ones such as Klaus Ehring, just in case.

One of his early writings was simply an open letter to Erich Honecker, the East German president, posing a polite series of questions. Not daring actually to mail it, he printed the questions on stickers, which he smuggled in the lining of a torn pocket of his old coat when he crossed to meet Annette. Sometimes, he brought banned religious materials over the same way. They attended a church together and such materials were of interest to the pastor.

Information, he learned early, is what matters. It's a very effective weapon against tyranny, and what dictatorships fear. As a West German, he was permitted to travel to East Berlin and stay for up to three days, thirty days per year. It was a good way for the GDR government to ensure some much-needed hard currency would be left behind, forcibly exchanged at the unfavorable official rate. Over months of such trips, he was always alert to try to detect any watchers, and to have political conversations only in private places. Political gatherings in public were banned anyway. He was doing well, he assured himself, acting like an East German. He soon became even bolder – or maybe it was the foolhardiness of youth. Hubertus next began to bring prohibited books with him, also hidden in the lining of his tattered jacket as he passed through the checkpoint at Friedrichstrasse. It was a small thing, a further little act of defiance. He doubted anyone would care.

He had underestimated the Stasi.

Just before Christmas 1979, Hubertus received some bad news from Annette. State Security had knocked on the door of her flat in East Berlin's Pankow district. Two men with persistent questions. Questions about him and her. He always safely and easily crossed back to West Berlin after a weekend, something she couldn't do. He was worried, and had to see her.

A few days after a restless New Year's Eve, he presented himself in the crowd at the crossing at Friedrichstrasse as always, and slid over his West German identification card. Something was different. The border guard sitting at his high desk looked closely at him and the card. He glanced down and hesitated while thumbing through a document that was just out of sight. This time, the reason this crossing place was best known to East Berliners as Tränenpalast, or the Palace of Tears, became clear.

'Your entry is not allowed' was all the border guard announced before thrusting the ID at him and pointing back the way he had come.

'Next!'

Hubertus stood on the platform, identification clutched in his hand. There was no one to ask why he had been turned away. Helplessness, and a sick feeling, washed over him. It was devastating to a young man in love. He later chanced a guarded telephone call with Annette, but what now? Would she be arrested? He could do nothing about it!

Carefully, over months, they began to plan to meet in Budapest, where they could safely talk over her applying to visit the West. Who knew how long that process would take, or if it would succeed at all? They both realized that even the action of making such a request would be a stain for life in her file. *We must!* There was no other choice but to give it a try. In a brief meeting in a Budapest hotel they carefully crafted her exit application. Then they separated, to nervously wait and wonder.

Hubertus returned once again to the refuge of his studies, to work on a PhD from West Berlin's Freie University. Just being there was historic, he supposed. Famous US Army general Lucius Clay originally founded the university to be a place 'free' from communist influence in 1948. Two months later, Clay gave the bold order for the biggest airlift ever, which rescued West Berlin from a Soviet stranglehold.

As those first months turned into a year, and then two, it ate away at Hubertus. He was banned from returning to Annette and East Berlin, but that only made him more determined. He knew he had to go back.

His father tried repeatedly, and vainly, to discourage him.

'Your life is good!' he would say. 'Why take such a chance?'

Hubertus nodded and decided he would wait for the right moment.

So, he studied some more, wrote and waited. After two years, Annette was unexpectedly approved to visit West Berlin. Like many others who managed to get out by asking to 'visit relatives', she knew she wasn't going back. Being together again and safe was a relief, but something more still spoke to him from the East.

Hubertus slowly began to realize how much he had to thank his parents for saving him from a life under the communist dictatorship. That didn't change his decision, however. He was going back. The more he wrote about the leftist dictatorship, understood what the Nazis and the communists had done to Germany and considered what he and Annette had been through, the more convinced he was that he had something to accomplish there.

Something else consumed his thoughts and sleepless nights. He'd been so careful on those trips! Very careful. Somebody he knew had informed on him. Who could that informer be? He was determined to find out. How, or when? He had no idea.

———

A wall would naturally make things easier for the Grey Men of State Security, which was a primary goal. Officially, the Stasi and the communist leaders of the GDR preferred to call the project the *Protective Barrier*. It was, they insisted, needed to keep antisocialist elements out of East Berlin and thus not taint the socialist paradise called the German Democratic Republic. In reality, it was desperately needed to stem the flow of people constantly streaming away from socialism and to the West. There were no refugees going in the other direction. To build it they needed approval from Moscow, which they finally received.

GDR president Walter Ulbricht made a clear and forceful dismissive statement designed finally to put the rumors to rest:

'Nobody has the intention of building a wall!'

It happened two months later. The Wall was swiftly rolled out unannounced one quiet Sunday morning in August 1961 under the watchful direction of State Security minister Erich Mielke. Ida Siekmann, a nurse, was the first person to be killed there only nine days later while making a desperate last-ditch attempt to escape the day before her fifty-ninth birthday.

The Wall was reinforced and perfected over the years, becoming in reality two walls with a mined no-man's-land in between. The final version, a well-developed death strip, was patrolled by dogs and had machine guns placed in key areas, set to fire automatically at any movements. The standing order to the patrolling border guards was to shoot without warning. The causes of death of the at least 136 persons killed there over the years tell the story:

Shot dead while trying to escape. Drowned under fire. Shot as an escape helper. Committed suicide after failed escape attempt. Died as a result of injuries trying to escape. Drowned in border waters.

Perhaps five thousand more were arrested for planning to escape over or under it, or for being found hidden in vehicles at tense checkpoint encounters.

Now that East Berlin was satisfactorily contained, the Stasi could much more easily concentrate on running down their enemies. The embarrassing flow of productive elements to the West, damaging the image of a socialist paradise, could be all but stopped. Everything inside the GDR could then be dealt with by the most omnipresent, intrusive and ruthlessly effective secret police the world had ever seen.

The Stasi dealt with things by turning their own population inward against itself, adapting old Soviet detention facilities and constantly improving on their methods. Training materials for new officers announced the enemy:

Every citizen is a potential security risk! That was the message drilled into each and every recruit.

There was much to be done. Massive hiring of officers, all possessing unquestioned authority. Perfecting the means of decomposition, rendering troublesome persons ineffective and sidetracking their lives as needed. Improving the seventeen special prisons scattered throughout the country. Next, expanding reach far beyond the borders via the intelligence section, deploying officers to other border areas, improving the arms and heavy mechanized equipment of the motorized rifle regiment. The Dzerzhinsky Regiment would need tanks and better automatic weapons. And all of them naturally must always be on the lookout for means to acquire hard currency. The Party must be supported and protected.

———

Hubertus and Annette, now finally together in West Berlin, realized they were lucky. Others told them that, and they told it to each other. After all, it only took two years to get her out. Hubertus busied himself as the years went on, with his writings and completing his PhD studies. But the man who the Stasi was by then calling *Glue* was looking East, and he was becoming even more restless.

4

ENEMIES OF THE STATE

'Worse than the Gestapo!'

That was how famed Nazi hunter Simon Wiesenthal once described the Stasi.

At least 280,000 East Germans were imprisoned, terrorized, kidnapped, murdered or driven to suicide by their own government. Many more found their lives sidetracked, and most have never spoken about it. Families split by parents being hauled away, prison, expulsion for ransom, or perhaps turning one family member against another. And how many others never took that chance, never created passionate writings or art, or used their intellect to make a difference? It was best to take the safe road, take the dull job that the state offered, best not to stand out. Even if your telephone wasn't being monitored, your mail not being opened, your neighbor or close friend not reporting about you, better to assume they were.

By the age of eleven, schoolchildren were encouraged to tell their teacher if they had an interest in working for the Ministry for State Security. That would be dutifully reported and a note placed in a file. Mostly, though, the real recruiting for officers was done from within the ranks: sons and daughters of loyal employees. Much more predictable that way for the organization, they decided. But not too many of the daughters. In 1990, 85 percent of the MfS's 91,000 employees were male. The actual size of the organization always remained a closely guarded secret. The United States and allied Western intelligence agencies in the 1980s believed them to have 25,000 members, still a huge number for a small country. But they were all wrong, by a factor of almost four.

Nobody really knows even today how many informants, called Unofficial Employees, or IMs, they operated. Perhaps 500,000 people over forty years, or maybe double that. Wives reporting on husbands, brother against sister, children against parents. In 1989, more than 10,000 of the operational IMs were children. People were scrutinized everywhere. All apartment buildings in East Berlin had a person who kept a house-book, a record of all visitors who stayed in any of the apartments overnight. That information was routinely relayed to the MfS via a trusted local police officer. Whatever the actual number of informers was, there's no doubt that the Stasi, the self-nominated *Sword and Shield of the Party*, was close to achieving their ultimate goal: *To Know Everything*.

Their training showed preparation for an even stronger grip. Training of new recruits increasingly emphasized operational and practical aspects of surveillance, interrogation, selection of informants and scientific aspects of detecting threats. They operated departments at major East German universities for this purpose, including a complete law school in Potsdam. The 'cadre', as it was called, became much better educated than the general population. In reality, the so-called university law school was neither a university nor a law school. A glance at the long list of dissertation topics they submitted in the school shows what the interest was:

- *The Manifestation of Anti-State Activity*
- *Conspiracy and Secrecy by Members of MfS as a Prerequisite for Ensuring the Internal Security of MfS*
- *Detection and Processing of Offenses of Unlawful Leaving the GDR*
- *Investigation on the Facts or the Endangerment of Public Order by Antisocial Behavior*
- *The Repeated Interrogation of Witnesses and Accused Persons*

Humboldt University in East Berlin also housed a broad Criminalistics Section only for the Stasi, well known for their ability to analyze graffiti and identify the perpetrator. It trained generations of the organization, and was headed by undercover officer and doctor of medicine Professor Hans-Ehrenfried Stelzer. When the fog cleared in the early 1990s, Stelzer would be more commonly known to Germans as something quite different.

The MfS was organized into Directorates, called Main Departments, to parallel the KGB structure. By Western standards, then or now, their activities and sheer penetration of the general population were shocking. The actual number of direct employees and informants is one example. What they all did daily is another.

The Second Main Directorate, which handled counterintelligence, also opened all mail to or from any noncommunist country. Ninety thousand pieces every day were being carefully steamed open by 1989. There were other goals besides identifying subversive targets. Any small amount of West German marks being sent from the West to their hopeful relatives on the other side of the Wall was removed from the envelopes and sent to a special account. During the last three years of the dictatorship, the equivalent of US $4 million was collected this way. Packages of otherwise attractive goods were many times diverted to a warehouse for other uses, such as providing treats for Stasi generals and colonels, or favored Party officials, who frequently dropped by for that reason.

And then there were the large, round, clear glass jelly jars with tightly screwed-down tops, identified by only a number. Thousands of them arranged neatly on shelves, each with a piece of cloth inside. The MfS collected samples of body scent, secured from interrogated prisoners told to sit on their hands on special chairs, or instructed to place the cloth under their arms at police stations. Sometimes, special entry teams would break into houses and steal women's undergarments for the jars. This was all designed to allow tracking of these people with dogs, if and when required. The numbers on the jars were recorded in a name index for quick reference.

In the Third Directorate, six thousand officers were assigned to intercept and monitor the telephones and conduct microphone surveillances.

More than one thousand people were killed for political reasons in the GDR. The Stasi was responsible for fifty attempted murders and 650 abductions, including political kidnappings from West Berlin. Some of those targeted were drugged by a person they thought was a friend before being shoved into the trunk of a car. At least 200,000 persons were jailed for political purposes. More than 300 were killed at the GDR borders trying to flee the country. The last of these was a dark-haired twenty-year-old named Chris Gueffroy, who dreamed of becoming an actor in West Berlin. He was shot through the heart late in the evening of February 5, 1989, while trying to escape over the Wall. Less than eight weeks later, as the GDR began to unravel, the long-standing shoot-to-kill order was revoked. The communist masters had developed a new concern for their public image, and their own survival.

There were no pensions for the members of the Gestapo. But at present, Germany is promptly paying more than 350 million euros each year to former Grey Men who are living all over the world.

———

Lothar Schulz was standing and waiting patiently for me on a cold late afternoon on the steps of Hohenschönhausen, the main Stasi prison in Berlin. Now a frequently visited memorial, it was named simply for the district in which it was built, but didn't officially exist for decades. He offered to show me around, and though quick to say he had never been an inmate at this particular prison, he had volunteered at the Memorial. Now in his late sixties, being here somehow helped him.

'No. I wasn't here. But those other places...'

We sat at a table just inside the outer wall.

Lothar, a distinguished-looking man with carefully groomed greying hair and a professional bearing, was at one time a highly educated nuclear engineer in the GDR, and on the way up. That is, until the day he said, 'No.'

He was one of five selected to attend prestigious advanced training in the Energetic Institute in Moscow in 1976. This was the Harvard of the Eastern Bloc. As part of the process he was tested extensively on his engineering knowledge and experience and passed easily. He had, after all, recently been the coordinating engineer for the construction of a nuclear power station in northern Germany and also spoke fluent Russian. The final step was an interview with a Russian official in Berlin. Just a formality.

'Very impressive, Mr Schulz,' she commented after closely reviewing his file. 'I see no problems!'

'Good!' Lothar's eyes shone and his face beamed. This was a big career step!

'One more thing, Mr Schulz,' the woman said as she closed his folder and he stood. 'What would you say if you were invited to join the Communist Party?'

He thought about it, shrugged and answered honestly. 'I would say no.'

There was a brief, awkward silence and she stood also.

'Thank you, Mr Schulz.'

She turned to leave the room and stopped.

'One word of advice, Mr Schulz. Don't be too concerned about studies in Moscow!'

Lothar returned to his job at the central power station, but promotion opportunities had vanished. By February 1978, when he was twenty-eight, he had had enough and officially applied to leave East Germany. The next day, he was summarily fired. Frustrated, he attended a political event weeks later in central Berlin and was singled out and arrested. During his forty-hour nonstop interrogation, the officers continually drilled a vision of his new dismal future into his head. Since the protest event was covered in the Western press, they said, it was a much more serious crime. He would be subject to a sentence of seven to nine years.

Seven to nine years. The promised sentence quickly followed, and Lothar disappeared into the prison network. When released early, he was assigned a new job by the state. He would be a janitor for the rest of his life. After three years of doing that while living in a flat that he later learned had Stasi microphones installed and a State Security captain residing upstairs, he was allowed to depart to the West.

'What do you think those Stasi officers are doing now?' I asked. Lothar's response was odd.

'I'm not here now to talk of such things,' he said, glancing down.

―――――

The man stood and thrust out a hand as I walked through the door to a warm one-room office in a once modern high-rise near the Zoological Garden in Berlin.

'I'm Diederich. Hugo. This is VOS.' He pumped my hand and motioned to a chair in the cluttered office. Hugo was the only person holding together an otherwise dying organization, and he knew it.

VOS is the Victims of Communism, or Victims of Stalinism, depending on who's speaking. It's an organization designed to represent victims of both the secret police and communist GDR, and the Soviet machine that seized Eastern Germany before that.

Peering through square glasses at me was an affable man with an infectious, weary smile, sitting at the desk among overstuffed bookcases of binders. 'We had 26,000 members over the years, now perhaps one thousand are still active.' He motioned to his computer screen, turning it so that I could see. 'I keep them all in here!' He tapped the glass. 'See, they were all on index cards since 1951. I had them all scanned,' he proudly told me.

He leaned back and flashed a sad grin. 'Next time you come, I might not be here!'

He pecked something on the keyboard and turned the computer off.

'We will be forced to move from this office in a year. Building renovations and conversion to high-priced real estate.'

'Where will you move with all of this?' I motioned to the bookcases overflowing with documents.

He shrugged. 'Maybe to my flat.' He stood and looked at his watch. 'Let's go.'

He had invited me to accompany him to Chemnitz, a city south of Berlin, to meet with a group of survivors. Soon I was squeezed into his old blue Opel Corsa and speeding with him down the autobahn.

It was only then, as we weaved in and out, dodging other cars, that Hugo started to tell his own story.

'I was a victim of the Stasi myself.'

He was enrolled at Humboldt University in 1986, and by East German standards had a good future.

But he couldn't take it anymore, the mindless, constant control by bureaucrats, limits and worry, and decided that he had to escape communism.

As a young man he knew better than some about the value of keeping things to yourself, and said nothing of his plan as he grabbed his backpack and small tent and left Berlin for Budapest in August 1986. No problem, it was innocent. Hungary was still behind the 'protective barrier' then, a good friend of East Germany. A vacation, he casually told anyone who cared. But this vacation was different. He told no one, especially not his family or friends.

Hugo prepared as best he could, taking his small stash of illegally acquired West German marks and carefully folding the bills inside chewing gum wrappers and burying them in the bottom of his pack.

Upon getting off the train in Budapest, he hoisted the backpack and immediately headed for the Austrian border. Much too hard to go over the Wall in Berlin; lots of others had died trying that, he had heard. He was careful and quiet, slowly walking on the hiking paths through the woods with his rucksack, looking like any hiker, he imagined. It worked, and he gradually approached what he thought to be within a half-mile of the border. He was suppressing his excitement; he hadn't seen another person for some time. Freedom was now within easy reach! Around the next bend and over that gentle hill, he figured. Just fifteen minutes…

'Hände hoch!!' Hands up!

A green-uniformed German soldier pointing a submachine gun appeared from nowhere and blocked the narrow path.

Later he learned that the East German border guards were also posted in Hungary specifically for this purpose – to catch the ill-prepared and unsuspecting 'criminal border crossers' in the act.

He met his first two State Security officers at a small detention house nearby an hour later. They joked and laughed among themselves in front of Hugo and other frightened prisoners about the handful of young men they had captured that day. Young men whose lives they knew were now ruined.

'Didn't they hear? There is a hole in the Wall this week in Berlin! They could have just walked through!!'

Soon he was placed on an airplane with five others, all handcuffed and gagged. Five Stasi officers accompanied them on the flight to Berlin, but said nothing. Yanked off the airplane without words, he was taken to a cell somewhere. Then came several months of inter-rogation designed to get him to reveal the names of anyone whom he had spoken to about his plans. That was a special crime in the GDR, not reporting someone. They would also then be arrested. But Hugo had been a bit of a loner, and had nothing to say. He was sentenced to a fifteen-month prison term for attempting illegal crossing of a border. Within weeks he was placed on a special train that they used to distribute prisoners throughout the country. The night train, they called it. He sat in a windowless car silently with the others, having no idea to which prison he was headed.

Months later, while sitting in his cell, Hugo received word from his brother that a letter from Humboldt University had arrived at their shared Berlin flat within weeks of his arrest. It was signed by a supervising professor, whose name he never forgot. Professor Helmut Klein officiously informed Hugo that he had been summarily kicked out of school due to crimes against the state.

A year later, he had become a very different person. Living in a cell with murderers and filled with insecurity about your future does that to most young men. Each morning he would be bused to a factory to work for free for the MfS, lifting heavy metal parts and running a metal press. Once he dropped something big on his foot, crushing bones. Two days later he was finally taken to the prison doctor. The treatment was some cream for his foot, and a boot three sizes larger to allow for the swelling. His deformed toes are a permanent reminder.

At the end of each day, they all knew the routine. Hugo and the others would line up silently until the officer called their name. Only then could they board the bus back to their cell. One day, they never called his name. Hugo stood alone in the darkening yard, watching the bus drive away and wondering what he had done. Two Stasi officers shoved him into a smaller van without saying a word. The door was slammed shut and the van headed in a different direction. He knew better than to ask why. That night he was in a different prison. Over the next few days he pieced together that he had been on the latest list of prisoners for whom West Germany had paid a ransom. He didn't believe it and kept his mouth shut. Even if true, anything could happen.

It was only when he was unexpectedly given used but cleaner clothes and placed in a cell with three others wearing clean clothes that Hugo became optimistic. A guard snapped a new photograph of him, and the interrogators started asking a different question:

'Don't you really prefer to remain in the GDR?'

'Well, no, but only because I have a brother in the West.' He was much more careful now.

They were allowed a razor, and a small shop in the prison yard sold them ground coffee in exchange for some East German marks they pooled together. But there was a problem. There was no way in their freezing cell to heat water for coffee, and no radiator to make it even lukewarm. One of his cellmates, who had been an electrician, had a thought. They disassembled the light fixture and dangerously thrust the live wires into a cup to heat the water. Risking their lives for a cup of hot coffee didn't seem odd to any of them at the time.

'The guards had a certain way of slamming the locks and drawing the bolt at the door,' Hugo told me as he paused to spin the wheel of the Opel hard while stomping on the gas to pass a truck at breakneck autobahn speed.

'When you heard it, we instantly jumped up and stood, waiting for whatever would follow, and for whoever might be led away.'

One young man who shared Hugo's cell didn't come back at all one day. It had been discovered that he was the son of an East German scientist, and thus ineligible for ransom. Too risky to let the West have that opportunity. He was sent back to another prison to finish his sentence.

After three more weeks, it was Hugo who was led away when the cell door clanged. Down the steps from the special cellblock that inmates called 'the Birdcage' and out the door into the yard. He stood blinking in the sunlight. He had never been allowed outside to see the sky at this place. With a grunt and a gesture he was told to board a waiting bus. Other prisoners were already there, all sitting silently, faced by two Stasi officers. By its modern look, the bus appeared West German. The motor coughed and they headed west. He still had no idea where he was. After hours that lasted a lifetime for a young man, they stopped at what seemed to be the border. They were led out briefly and the bus was searched carefully. Hugo and several others watched as the GDR plates were changed to those of West Germany. Another gesture and it was time to climb aboard again. The bus was restarted and lurched forward.

'We all noticed then that the two officers had disappeared, but none of us spoke at all.'

Minutes later the bus stopped again and a uniformed West German soldier stepped on. He handed each of them a small paper sack containing an apple, a banana and a pack of Western cigarettes. They each clutched their bag and filed off the bus silently as instructed, instinctively standing in a line. It wasn't until an excited group of people obviously dressed in Western clothing rushed to greet them that the shouting and crying started.

Hugo learned moments later that two of the prisoners on the bus were husband and wife. They hadn't seen each other for two years before being carefully placed by officers side by side on the bus. Forced to endure the long, uncertain bus ride without speaking or touching, it was their final punishment.

Hugo remembers that day vividly, and is certain the other thirty-nine former prisoners do as well. He blurted out the date in the Opel at once when asked if he remembered it.

'Yes. It was the fourth of July, 1987.'

Thirty-three thousand prisoners were ransomed to freedom in the West in this way. Hugo had last been at the prison in the town of Chemnitz, which was where we were headed in the car that day. Most of the people were processed there before being turned over for an average ransom payment of 90,000 Deutschmarks, roughly $45,000. In the early 1970s, when this started, suitcases of cash were received by a Stasi officer. But that was quickly streamlined to the much tidier bank transfers. At first, more money was charged for an educated prisoner; the MfS thought them more valuable. Later the flat-fee approach became the norm, in hard West German Deutschmarks, of course – it was easier when you were dealing with tens of thousands of people. The prisoner ransoms were kept quiet on both sides, with West Germany paying from a classified budget. Only those sentenced to more than one year were deemed eligible by the West under the secret agreement. As a result, nearly every person arrested afterward for even the most minor political crimes was always sentenced to at least thirteen months in jail.

Over $1 billion for this project alone had flowed to the East German Communist Party coffers by 1989, none of which was ever accounted for.

Hugo Diederich couldn't forget the letter from Professor Klein expelling him. He thought about it frequently for years, waking up in the middle of the night, sometimes angry and sometimes shivering. I will confront the professor today, he assured himself repeatedly. *Today*. One day in 2004 Hugo saw an obituary notice – Professor

Helmut Klein was dead. He clipped the notice from the newspaper and pinned it to the wall in his flat, where it remains. He looked over at me as we raced down the autobahn, tightly clutching the steering wheel of the car.

'I won, I suppose.'

5

THE THIRTY

The blue Opel jumped the curb and slid to a stop as Hugo manhandled it into the parking lot of the Hotel Sächsischer Hof in Chemnitz. All the rooms in the place that night would be filled with survivors of communism, there to attend a memorial the following day.

We walked into the small dining room and thirty men and women stopped talking and looked over at me silently. I didn't seem German. Seeing Hugo smiling cheerfully, they greeted us both warmly. With a wave of a hand I was seated at one of the tables. The men next to me nodded and introduced themselves in turn. They all had a story, mostly about surviving but also about those who hadn't. To my right was a distinguished, younger-looking businessman with round glasses and a neatly trimmed beard. To my left was an eighty-nine-year-old man with tired eyes named Rolf. He spoke first.

Rolf was swept up by the Soviets and dropped into Sachsenhausen prison camp in 1946 when he was fifteen. His crime was that of being a teenaged boy, a possible threat to the iron curtain being rolled out by Stalin after the war. Like most of these camps, Sachsenhausen had been a Nazi concentration camp, closed and reopened again by the Soviets three weeks after they liberated it from the Nazis.

The older man leaned forward. 'Everyone was sure things would improve when the Russians left and we were all turned over to the new East German state in 1951. They were fellow Germans!

'We were all wrong. The Germans and the Stasi were far worse.'

For Rolf, the MfS took at face value the various confessions that the Soviet interrogators had made him sign. He had no idea what they said, since they were written in Russian, but as a fifteen-year-old boy he signed anything just to survive. Two-thirds of the teenage boys there died of hunger or froze to death. What difference was a piece of paper?

The Stasi used the Russian 'confessions' to mark him for life. When he was finally released they told him he had a choice: sign yet another piece of paper to join the Communist Party or not. If he signed, they said, he would be sent to school to become an engineer. If he refused, he would be assigned to work as a locksmith's helper for the remainder of his life. Rolf looked directly at me and lowered his voice to a whisper.

'I signed.'

Alex, the distinguished younger man seated on my right, was an inmate at Sachsenhausen when he was far younger. He was born there while his mother was a prisoner. They lived the prison life together; he thought that was the way life was supposed to be. When he was nearly three, the Stasi separated them without notice. He was sent to an orphanage to be 'educated in the spirit of socialism', while his mother was sent to West Germany to spy. He was the collateral to make sure she behaved. When he was twelve, two men grabbed him from the orphanage and put him on the train to West Berlin. When he got off at the station alone that night, a strange woman in Western clothing rushed up and squeezed him tightly.

'I'm your mother!'

She had done a very good job for the socialist state and was being rewarded, someone told him. In time, he got to know her.

Alex now runs an organization specifically dedicated to thousands of children born to those in political detention in East Germany.

Across the table, and over the plates of robust food, sat a quiet woman who hadn't spoken. She was drinking an especially dark beer. I pointed at her glass and ordered one of the same from the waitress. A smile emerged.

'It's a black beer, from Bavaria!'

'What was it like for a woman in the GDR and the Stasi?' I asked her as we raised our glasses. After taking a tiny sip, she waited politely until everyone at the table stopped talking.

'We lived two very different lives. One at home, and one outside. Outside we were very careful what we said. You just never knew…'

One day, her twelve-year-old son came home with a letter from school warning that he had been critical of communism.

'Written by someone who didn't even speak to the boy!'

She fought for a year to have the letter removed from his file.

'If I hadn't, he would never have gotten into any university with that in his record!'

Thirty former citizens of the GDR, the proud socialist state called the German Democratic Republic. And what was their message to a young person in Europe or the United States today who thinks that socialism isn't so bad? The response to that question was silence followed by hoarse laughter, and a sad shaking of heads.

Sometimes, when people were jailed for speaking out or trying to escape, their children disappeared.

In 1988, Andreas Ley sat in jail for attempting to flee. It was three weeks before Christmas and less than a year before the Wall fell. He was told that his three-month-old son had become ill and been taken to the children's hospital in Dresden. Ley, who was sentenced to five years but released immediately in 1990 after the GDR fell, has never seen his son again. He's been looking for him ever since. From his Stasi file he learned that the boy was given to a family loyal to the regime, an irreversible process even now. Some parents like him were told their children had died at the hospital, but were denied the right to see the bodies. Many have long suspected the children were instead given to Communist Party families. It was another program run by the MfS.

Uwe Mai has been searching for his parents even longer. He was six years old in 1961 when he came in from playing along the riverbank and found some strange men in the kitchen with his father.

'Your mother ran off, I can't keep you anymore,' his father said. Uwe was later taken aside by others who whispered that his mother went to the West. He never saw either of his parents again.

In 2014 an organization was formed in Berlin, Stolen Children of the GDR. There are currently 1,500 members, with 600 directly connected to a missing child.

―――――

For any dictatorship to survive there are two essential elements. One is to control all aspects of a society, and the other is to instill mistrust and fear. There's no dispute that the Grey Men had done well at both of these. They also excelled at a key part of the second element – making the general population assume the secret police were present everywhere, even in those instances when they really were not. With all of this, it still couldn't save them. Sixty-six days after the Wall was breached on a late November night in 1989, the most feared secret police organization in history would cease to officially exist. But the 91,000 highly trained and motivated people, and their loyalties, would not.

Stasi ID – issued to KGB lieutenant colonel Vladimir Putin.
Used to freely access Stasi facilities, it was identical to that of MfS
officers. Discovered in the former Dresden MfS offices in 2018.

Guarded main entrance to Stasi headquarters in Berlin, 1983.

Stasi minister Erich Mielke, the longest-serving secret police chief in Eastern Europe.

Minister Erich Mielke, head of the Stasi, at the
thirty-fifth anniversary of the GDR, Berlin, 1984.

Prisoner registration ledgers, Stasi Hohenschönhausen prison, Berlin.

Disguised Stasi prisoner transport truck.

6

DAY X

Sunday night
Thirty-two days before the fall

State Security minister Erich Mielke sat silently just after 9pm on October 8, 1989, in his spacious office on the third floor of Haus 1 of MfS headquarters. He was secure within the walled compound that stretched across four city blocks in the Lichtenberg district of East Berlin. Protected by four blocks and fifty-two individual, highly guarded buildings that didn't officially exist and were shown as a blank spot on city maps. But he was also eighty-one years old and angry. Not a good combination.

By all rights he should have been elsewhere this particular evening, basking with other SED Communist Party officials in the continued celebrations for the fortieth anniversary of the GDR. It had been observed in the usual grand way the day before. Fluttering flags, military pomp, commemorative medals, waving officials and carefully selected foreign comrades. There was his own private celebration planned also. He had seen the MfS through thirty-nine years personally since it was formed by unanimous vote in 1950, and was proud of it all.

Instead, here he sat, staring at his desk with disgust. *If it wasn't for them! The rabble!*

The increasing protests by the agitators in the streets of Berlin ruined everything. Embarrassing him and the Party in front of Soviet secretary general Gorbachev, the other foreign guests and even Western media. *How dare they?*

Tomorrow, another protest was expected in Leipzig, his colonels told him. Even bigger maybe. If only the weak ones in the Politburo showed they had a backbone, and simply let him proceed to do what should be done.

They were ready. His beloved Firm was ready. He had seen to that years ago, and smoothed and perfected the plan every year since. Directive 1/67, which he had himself carefully written and seen approved by the full Politburo, provided for the creation of internment camps throughout East Germany for political opponents in cases like this. Meticulous plans had been completed in all of the fifteen Stasi district offices more than ten years before. The constantly updated lists of persons to be screened for immediate arrest by 1989 had swelled to more that 85,000 – 14,000 more than just three years ago.

More is best!

Specific facilities were identified and readied in every district. Rules for method of arrest, and who might be liquidated, were written. Every one of the 209 Stasi offices in East Germany had also identified a temporary facility suitable to detain the thousands for the first few days, before the transfer to larger new prisons.

He and his senior staff thought of this moment frequently. Watching the Chinese shoot hundreds of protestors in Beijing's Tiananmen Square, ending that protest only months before, he was preparing for the same. But they would do it far better. The Chinese had waited too long to act. He wouldn't. Recently, Mielke had ordered the formation of enhanced anti-riot teams equipped with specially modified electrically charged batons to act as human cattle prods. It was up to him, and his MfS, to again be the Sword and Shield of the Party.

These enemies of communism, the street criminals, it's just what I wrote Directive 1/67 for. Hundreds of employees had been preparing for this day for decades. All mid-level and higher Stasi officers had naturally also long known about this plan, and their personal role. It was created by him, but all of them crafted and fine-tuned it. They made it real. If he weren't so angry at the moment, he would have instead been pleased.

They had no qualms about it. The state must be protected. It wasn't as if they would execute everybody like the Nazis did. They were better than the fascists, and it wasn't necessary anyway, in most cases. There were other ways.

Mielke reached out and snatched up the telephone to summon his secretary, who also was working that Sunday night. Today would be the first step toward implementing the response. What was always called *Day X* in the plan would be here soon enough.

Two orders went out that evening from the Minister and General of the Army, as he liked to be called, to all offices. The first emphasized to all officers that they were required to have their service weapons in their possession at all times. The second instructed all units to 'take appropriate measures to provide, in the short-term, delivery and arrest of sensitive-negative persons'. That meant also to prepare for the *Go* order. That final order from him would be a simple code word transmitted from his office, '*Schild*' (shield). *Day X*. After that the arrests would promptly begin, while rolls of razor wire were quickly rolled out to encircle all pre-selected places of imprisonment. It would be their finest moment! He looked forward to it.

After his orders that night, temporary detention facilities would immediately become the priority for supplies. Some were old Nazi prisons, schools, hospitals or convenient factories. The individual officers in the eight Main Departments and Stasi Berlin headquarters were responsible for compiling the lists, monitoring the locations of the 85,939 persons listed at the moment, and ultimately making the arrests by whatever method they saw fit. Everyone on the list, called *controlled persons*, were routinely being watched anyway, by physical surveillance, informants or technical means.

'Arrest at the slightest irregularity' was the Day X instruction. The usual artists, media people and others thought of as troublemakers, described as 'unpleasant citizens', were naturally first on the list, as well as those who were known to wish to travel to the West, or had close relatives there. Troublemakers within religious communities also. Those with any contacts with Western embassies. Immigrants, those expelled or who had resigned from the Communist Party, and members of peace movements. Leaders of any of these groups were top priority. Circumstances were specified that would prompt liquidation of certain subversive forces. Any attempted escape from arrest would be dealt with by a prison sentence of two to ten years.

Special attention was to be paid to foreigners and transit travellers. More than 850 foreign diplomats and correspondents in Berlin were included. No chances would be taken, no leaf left unturned. At Day X plus one day, the guard towers would be erected at the first thirty-five temporary facilities, which could hold twenty-two thousand people, and those to be held within them would soon arrive by the truckload. They shouldn't be called prisoners, Mielke had personally decided, but instead be referred to as *isolated people*. Words matter.

All *isolated persons* would be interrogated by officers from Main Department VIII, Observation/Investigations, which in 1989 was headed by someone especially favored by Mielke, Major General Karli Coburger.

He sat back in his chair and rocked impatiently. What of the Russians? They were always ready to assist, or at least publicly threaten to assist to help their communist brothers. But now with Gorbachev refusing to stand up for comrades in Poland and Hungary, would East Germany be cast out next? Mielke had modeled the MfS organizational structure after the KGB, after all, and they always knew to report first to the Russians about matters of significance, and to the GDR Politburo second. He was loyal! So, what did Soviet president Gorbachev do yesterday in front of the crowd? *Nothing! No show of strength, no small veiled threat of Russian assistance if requested by the German Democratic Republic! Nothing!*

Instead, he looked over at the GDR comrades on the podium at his side, and announced to the crowd:

'Life punishes those who come too late.'

Standing up, Mielke turned and dropped a folder into the large built-in wall safe behind his desk. He paused to contemplate two of his prized possessions he kept on the top shelf. A bronze head bust of Cheka founder Felix Edmundovich Dzerzhinsky sat alongside a large white plaster death mask of Vladimir Ilyich Lenin.

They had started it all, but *he* himself had made the Firm.

The minister couldn't help but momentarily smile at another special tool on the bottom shelf. There, next to the pistol and two boxes of ammunition. His square red suitcase – much more effective than the pistol. He frequently took the suitcase to Politburo meetings, where he would sometimes snap open the locks and appear to refer to documents inside. That's where he kept the secret files about all of them, the other Politburo members would guess nervously. He was rarely challenged in those meetings anyway, but if he was, placing the red suitcase within view was usually enough to shut them all up.

Mielke closed the thick steel door and spun the dial. He walked from his inner office, turning right into the massive conference room with its powerful, long and gleaming table. His face flushed, he could feel the anger. It was late and he would meet with a few of his generals before being driven home. The talking stopped as he entered the room and sat to take his place under a huge impressionist-style oil painting that he'd commissioned years ago to commemorate another of his successes – the construction of the Wall.

Coburger! Where are we with those protests?

As long as things held together just long enough to get the trouble-makers off the streets, all would be in order. By now, all of the fifteen district offices had his orders, which they would in turn relay to nearly two hundred other smaller offices in the country. The long-awaited Day X would soon be here. That calmed him a little as he took his seat at the head of the long table to review final details.

Thinking that it was finally starting, that once again, they would be the Sword and Shield of the Party perhaps calmed him.

The document sat on the table in front of each of them in the room, as they voiced final plans.

Supplies had been flowing to the detention sites since the protests started weeks ago. All elements were fully prepared. There were instructions on how to deal with every possible form of resistance, and even the prisoner sleeping arrangements:

Each cell should have benches suitable for twenty-five people, a transportable toilet bucket and ten square meters of floor space covered with straw for sleeping… guards should permit no talking…

Of course, the laws on the books of the GDR would be upheld in the process. Carefully laid out in the plan were the crimes that the tens of thousands would be arrested for:

Offenses against the socialist property and the national economy.
Offenses against the general security.
Offenses against the state order.

As always, the GDR legal system was designed to be flexible.

The carefully crafted plan was perfect in Mielke's eye. It would crush dissent and dissenters and save the GDR state.

Once he issued the final coded order, after the formality of approval by the SED Party chairman, the head of each of the fifteen district offices would open two sealed envelopes that they already possessed. Inside would be detailed instructions specific to their area. He expected the final approval from the Politburo within days. What choice would they have? The plans for Day X that lay on the conference table in front of the old men that night would later be described as nearly a carbon copy of the plan used by the Nazis to round up the Jews.

Mielke was certain his precise and brutal plan would work to seriously dampen the populist movement and maybe avoid the collapse that was coming. He didn't realize that he'd waited a month too long. The real Day X was quickly unfolding and it was quite different and unplanned by any central authority. Indeed, neither he nor the generals at the table knew that few within the organization would pay much attention to either of the first two orders he sent that evening. By then, most of the tens of thousands of officers could plainly see what was really coming and were worried about their personal livelihoods. Some managed to hold off their doubts and diligently returned to shredding documents in the basements. Others decided the time was right to plan to be away from the office for some excuse. Still others checked their pistols and locks in the buildings and prepared to barricade themselves behind steel doors, if it came to that. And they were all quite sure it would.

Those in West Berlin were also nervous. Sitting in the security of their flat, Hubertus and Annette were among them. Even though they had no idea about the desperate plans being unrolled for Day X, it was hard to keep to their routines. They worried for Annette's family in the East. Anything could happen, and it didn't seem that whatever it was would be anything but violent.

Yet instead of proudly issuing the final codenamed order *Schild* and teaching the unpleasant criminals a lesson, in thirty days Mielke would be forced to resign and the detailed plans for Day X would be lost for years in the chaos. And, just six days after that, private citizen and former Stasi minister Erich Mielke would become the star in the most famous broadcast ever in German television history.

7

CHAOS, DISBELIEF AND FEAR

International Press Center, East Berlin
November 9, 4pm
Seven hours before the fall

Günter Schabowski sat slumped in his chair that Thursday afternoon, waiting. He couldn't know that what he would soon do would redefine millions of lives, but was still uneasy for some reason. The worried look on his face was plain to see.

The nervous bureaucrat sat in a room on the ground floor of the officious grey building at 36 Mohrenstrasse. The press center was arranged carefully with a long table in front and hanging flags in the rear. The credentials of all who tried to enter were inspected and logged. Next door, a gleaming new showpiece of the GDR chain Interhotel was under construction, and both places lay within sight of a historic seventeenth-century cathedral. Power, knowledge, control and permanence, it all seemed to say. Essential elements of any dictatorship.

That November day none of that could conceal the stench of sudden death present there. In an odd twist to the common Western domino theory, in which one communist state creates more among its neighboring countries, the people crowding the room – mainly foreign reporters and government officials – seemed to understand they were witnessing the reverse somehow taking place. After all, Poland had just voted out the government, and Hungary had opened its borders. But nobody knew what would happen here, or when. Least of all the Stasi and the rest of the East German government. Those in the audience were restless.

Schabowski was tense and nearly alone as he sat at the long table wearing a light brown suit, yellow shirt and brown tie, clutching an unseen paper in his lap for support. He sat in between two men in grey suits. His silver rectangular glasses slid down his nose time and time again. He wasn't at all accustomed to the bright lights of the television cameras or the dozens of microphones thrust rudely in front of him. And why should he be? As a member of the East German Politburo and barely sixty, he was young in government circles. True, he had spent years in journalism, but naturally in communist style. Reporters were told what to write before or after an event, and dutifully wrote it. People listened when he spoke and didn't interrupt. Having been awarded the prestigious Order of Karl Marx just two months earlier, he liked to tell people he was a journalist as well as a politician. But these people here were the enemy.

There had never been free-for-all question sessions with Politburo members facing journalists, especially the aggressive, foreign kind. And not on live TV. Never. Until now. Looking out at the crowd, Schabowski saw countless Western reporters in the room. A tall one he recognized as Tom Brokaw from the American station NBC stared back with his brow furrowed, pad in hand. They were all shouting. He looked back down nervously at the note in his lap. It didn't help that he had missed a key meeting beforehand, instead just having had several Stasi-approved papers shoved into his hand on his way to the press center.

He cleared his throat again and stared into the back of the room.

'As I said, a new draft travel law was taken up by the government three days ago—'

'What of the 500,000 people protesting now in East Berlin?' the Italian journalist from ANSA shouted.

'What is the meaning of the new law? Why is it a draft?' another shouted from the back of the room.

'Well, the new law…'

This was something that Schabowski and two others in grey suits, sitting officiously but silently with him in front of the packed room, weren't at all accustomed to. Shuffling his feet, he glanced down at the two pages of notes that had been written for him by a Stasi general that morning. He knew the paper held no answers, but pretended it did each time a question was shouted from the audience. They were reporters and should understand how to behave. But there was a restless weakness in that room that evening that was infecting even the East German press, and everyone could feel it.

Schabowski repeatedly shook his head as he pushed up his glasses and tried to read from the draft law in front of him, which was also intentionally vague.

People who already had passports and visas could travel to the West. That was safe, since only a third of East Germans even had a passport, and only a tiny portion of those held a visa. Meanwhile, others could apply for exit. That was also good. Unstated was the fact that it would naturally take at least six to eight weeks to process any such applications – affording desperately needed breathing space. Should be enough to buy time until a permanent solution could be found by year end. That's what the East German leadership hoped for. Time.

The shouting resumed, silencing Schabowski again.

'You say it is possible for citizens to exit? With or without a passport?'

'It's not a question of tourism. There is a new law, only a draft really…' he began.

'Does this apply to East Berlin?' The Italian journalist kept pressing, along with a West Berlin tabloid reporter shouting, 'Everyone?'

'Of course, from all of the GDR.' Schabowski's eyes flicked to the clock. Nearly 7pm. This arrogant inquisition would end with the press conference at seven. Exactly seven.

'But when will this become effective?' the Italian shouted again.

Schabowski hesitated as he pushed the glasses up his sweaty nose once more. He looked to his notes, and then to his MfS minders, who sat stony-faced. He had no idea what he should say. Finally, under his breath as he fixated on the clock, he spoke while rustling his papers:

'Immediately.'

More chaos, and some journalists jumped up and rushed from the room.

'The conference is over.' Schabowski stood as he looked at the clock with gratitude. It was precisely 7pm. He wouldn't have been so grateful had he known he would be forced to relive that performance for the rest of his days.

The live feed was seen by millions of East Germans, including senior Politburo members watching from much more comfortable places. One member blurted out loudly, 'Is he crazy? They can *apply* but it will take weeks to process…'

Too late. The damage had been done.

Schabowski rushed from the room. He hoped to disappear but was stopped in the lobby by Brokaw, who, incredibly, convinced him to go live on NBC in the room upstairs. He did so, this time trying out his broken English with even more disastrous results. Minutes after, NBC's Peter Jennings stood at the Wall and announced to the world again that East Germany would allow citizens to pass through by morning.

Thousands of East Germans headed for the checkpoints, some climbing out of bed to do so. Pubs emptied out into the cold night air.

––––––

All points of exit in the GDR were routinely controlled by the Stasi's Main Department VI, then headed by Lieutenant General Gerhard Neiber, and more directly that night in Berlin by Colonel Rudi Einhorn. It was always too important to trust such things to the normal border guards. Many of the MfS men there typically wore border guard uniforms anyway, with the green shoulder boards, so as to blend in and conceal who and what they were really looking for. The main checkpoint at Bornholmer Strasse saw hundreds of people show up within an hour of Schabowski's comments. Lieutenant

Colonel Harald Jäger, deputy head of the checkpoint and also a Stasi officer, had just come on shift, and was buckling his belt when he heard about the press conference.

'Scheisse!!' He turned to find the television.

'What did he do?' Jäger stared at the rerun with disbelief.

Thousands more people were massing in the street at a cautious distance from the checkpoint within the hour. Lieutenant Colonel Jäger stepped out of the office and yelled for them to go home. One man instead pulled a piece of paper from his pocket and screamed back:

'Here's what the Politburo said tonight on TV. Immediately!!' Jäger went back inside and slammed the door, grabbing the phone to call his superior. Bornholmer was always the problem first, he knew. It was the nearest crossing to the Prenzlauer Berg district, what the Stasi called the troublesome place of the 'hostile-negative and decadent elements'. Artists and literati, in their disgusting cafés and bars.

'It's your call – but keep order!' he was told by his superiors. 'If they won't go away, let a few over but stamp their ID cards and warn them they can't come back! Relieve the pressure maybe,' Colonel Einhorn suggested to him.

Jäger had a Makarov pistol in his holster, fifty men at the station, many of them carrying submachine guns, and about one thousand reinforcements he could quickly call up. He could give the order to shoot, but decided they would run out of ammunition before any reinforcements could arrive, and they'd probably all be beaten to death with their own hard rubber truncheons.

It would be very ugly that way. And for what? He glanced out the window and estimated now that the crowd had swelled to at least five thousand people out there in the November frost. They were pushing closer to the station.

At thirty minutes to midnight he told his men to start stamping ID cards across the photo and let some cross. The first were warned:

'If you cross, you cannot come back!'

The crowd didn't care. His men looked to him and with another shrug he nodded.

'Raise the barrier.'

The border guards stopped stamping and just stood aside. Within forty-five minutes startled guards had let 20,000 equally shocked people stream over the bridge into West Berlin. Many of them ran, others walked uncertainly, all expecting to hear gunfire behind them at any moment. Perhaps they would be the first one shot. One shot could have started it. But that one shot never came.

The Wall fell gently. There was no going back, and the other Berlin checkpoints quickly followed, allowing unrestricted crossings over the next few days.

The mistake at the podium at 36 Mohrenstrasse that evening, and the later shrug of self-preservation by one East German border guard and Stasi officer had far more impact than anyone could have imagined. Throughout Germany, and the Eastern Bloc, the events were irreversible. Everyone was shocked. The Wall fell?

Soon in the neighboring Baltic countries even the KGB would beat a hasty retreat back to Russia taking everything they could carry along with them. The leftovers were for the soldiers, who would remove and cart off much of what was visible – bolted down or not – sometimes including toilets. But in Germany, the secret police simply had nowhere to go. And too many people were now watching. What none of them guessed while looking on with horror as the Wall fell on that cold November night was that their organization would be hastily renamed eight days later. Even through the fear and disbelief, none of the highly educated officers would have imagined that twenty-seven days after that, their beloved Firm – the MfS, the most feared and ruthless secret police organization in modern history for forty years – would officially cease to exist.

The seven thousand Stasi officers working at the East Berlin head-quarters went into full self-preservation mode after that chaotic first week in November. Many at the sprawling and walled headquarters complex scurried about working to destroy anything sensitive. The other 84,000 employees throughout East Germany followed suit. 'Bring anything sensitive quickly to the district offices, now!!' the order screamed. They had all been shredding since early October anyway, but it wasn't enough. There was just too much paper.

Within the more than two hundred smaller offices, the scramble intensified. The district offices could be protected better, they reasoned. It was also a better place to do all the shredding. While the basement shredders worked, groaned and failed throughout the nights trying to erase secrets, individual officers became consumed with their own futures. Some feared the same fate as the Gestapo. Back then, members had been imprisoned or lynched by the public. And they knew that, when you looked at how each organization treated its citizens, the things they had done to the German public for forty years were in many ways worse than in the first German dictatorship of the century. They only hoped that enough of the right files could be shredded or burned first.

8

DISSOLUTION, DISAPPEARANCE AND ANGER

Yes… in here. This place will do. Can you see it? Careful, get back!

It was an early morning four days before the fall, and two young activists in Leipzig, East Germany, had taken it upon themselves to look for the smoke. Opening the window on the fourth floor of their borrowed flat, and still breathing rapidly from the climb up the stairs and clammy with fear, they sat back from the opening and simply watched the place that everyone called Runde Ecke, or Round Corner.

They were in danger and they knew it.

They focused on the stately building with a classic red roof that sat on a street corner in the town center; it had a history of importance. It was built in 1912 on the site originally occupied by the first-known German castle, perhaps 900 years earlier. Its name refers to the structure's gently rounded façade where it sits, in a city of square blocks. Much later it became known as a place of fear, housing the Gestapo during the Second World War. At the end of the war, the building was briefly occupied by the US VII Corps after Leipzig was liberated by the American army, but very soon thereafter it fell to the domain of the Soviet secret police, the NKVD.

History wasn't on the two activists' minds that Sunday morning in November. They were there because of the current tenants. For nearly three decades, Runde Ecke had served as a notorious district office for the Ministry for State Security.

Even in the middle of 1989, when the surprising chatter started in informal channels that the communist GDR might be short-lived,

Leipzig residents took great pains to ignore the building on the Round Corner. They sometimes walked blocks out of the way to avoid the place or unconsciously ceased conversations if they were close. It was as if the building itself had ears. Lots of bad things happened near that place.

Nearby was the site at which all official executions in the GDR had been carried out under MfS direction. Until 1967 the guillotine was favored; after that the Soviet method of an unexpected shot to the back of the head was adopted. It was perhaps two such shots that carried out the sentence on Werner Teske, executed on Minister Mielke's order on June 26, 1981. The horrible offense by thirty-nine-year-old Teske was that he was one of their own – a Stasi captain who made sloppy yet unfulfilled preparations to defect. Per the normal practice, the trial was secret, his remains were quickly cremated, the death certificate was forged to state 'heart failure' and the family were lied to. Teske's widow thought he was in jail until she learned otherwise nine years later.

The two nervous citizen activists were there to watch for smoke plumes that could be a sign that the Stasi was burning files. If that happened, the young men had no idea what they could do about it, except to tell someone else. This simple act they knew put them at risk of arrest by the green-uniformed paramilitary police – the Volkspolizei, or Vopos – who would no doubt swiftly turn them over to State Security for interrogation. For this reason, they tried their best to be discreet, knowing that a window flung open in November was already likely to attract notice.

No one knew that the end for the communist dictatorship had already begun less than a month before, not even a kilometer from Runde Ecke, and in a church no less. St Nicholas Church, a soaring Romanesque structure, had stood since the twelfth century. Damaged in WWII, it seemed unlikely it could also survive forty years of a godless communist state. Yet it was here that a crowd of first hundreds, then thousands, were welcomed inside for political conversations. The crowd spilled into the streets and became hundreds of thousands, too big to brutally swat away. Communism was being crushed in Germany, and by people carrying only candles.

In other cities throughout East Germany, more citizen activists were given the same nearly impossible task as in Leipzig by the tense and informal network.

'Watch! They will try to burn everything!'

At that moment, within Runde Ecke and all other Stasi facilities, those whose main job was to prop up the government had their own problems. Suspecting the offices were being watched, and realizing it would be hard to hide evidence of large-scale file burning, time was running out. Instead, they set aside large basement rooms where staff worked day and night shredding documents. Unfortunately for them, they had East German shredders, which proved far less robust than their Western counterparts. One by one, the machines failed from overuse. Hundreds of burned-out shredders were later found. Unlike today, when millions of records can be easily destroyed with a few computer clicks, the Grey Men were prolific generators of paperwork in a pre-digital age. So they continued their work of diligent destruction nonetheless, ripping up the paper by hand, even after being jarred on the evening of November 9 by the unthinkable. The Berlin Wall had fallen.

On December 4, following weeks of demonstrations in Leipzig and after seeing no telltale smoke from the imposing Stasi office, it was time to gather courage and do something. But what? And who would do it?

'Who will sacrifice themselves?' A couple of the younger activists stepped forward, but many others shook their heads and quiet looks were exchanged.

'But we have no weapons, not even sticks. What if—'

A few more stepped up. And more.

After four decades spanning two generations of fear and control, a rather amazing thing took place that morning. Citizens' Committee members merely walked into Runde Ecke by the front steps. They passed confused members of the feared Stasi Felix Dzerzhinsky Guards

Regiment, who carried Makarov pistols and new Wieger StG-943 sub-machine guns capable of firing 600 rounds per minute, and peacefully occupied the building. Coincidentally, orders had just been sent out by nervous Party officials restricting the normally trigger-happy elite guards. The activists asked politely to meet with the management and announced they were there to 'safeguard the files'. This stunning feat was repeated throughout the GDR that week, an event later called the Peaceful Revolution. For the Stasi it meant they'd gone overnight from being the hunters to the hunted.

Perhaps it was only peaceful since by then most of the officers were no longer reporting to the offices, and most of the 11,000-member Guards Regiment was ordered to stay in their barracks. It was assumed a deal must be in the works. Best to avoid public violence at the moment, the Party leaders reasoned. They would, of course, negotiate and the Firm would survive. The new German government and foreign governments could be their allies, and shame and embarrassment their friends.

Even in those days before the internet, news of what happened in Leipzig traveled at light speed. The following day, December 5, ragtag groups of activists overran many of the other Stasi offices throughout the GDR. It was sometimes messy, as there was no social media or smartphones to coordinate things, and every place was different. Berlin happened last. It was in Dresden, a city near the Czech border and 120 kilometers east of Leipzig, that the group of brash activists including Siegfried Dannath encountered Vladimir Putin in front of the KGB office, perhaps changing world history as a result.

After the chaos, disbelief and fear, opportunity emerged. Suddenly, more than 91,000 loyal state MfS employees, many with insider knowledge and marketable skills to the intelligence community, realized they needed to seek work. Nearly 90 percent of these well-trained officers were under the age of fifty. Almost a third were under thirty-five.

Another blow to the Firm was symbolic, but certainly noticed by the proud and privileged officers. The Ministry for State Security was now openly toxic to the population. So, days after the mistake that caused the Wall to fall, it was officially designated as subordinate to the East German Parliament, the Volkskammer. That was both disconcerting and demoralizing to the Stasi rank and file; previously they were only accountable to the Politburo. An obvious demotion. In fact, Minister Mielke had never lowered himself to appear before the Volkskammer at any time during the past four decades. Soon he did just that, for the first and only time. It was memorable, in all the wrong ways.

In a televised appearance before the GDR puppet parliament on November 13, Mielke stood from the government bench and approached the podium at the Palace of the Republic in civilian dress. He wore a dark blue suit, pale blue shirt and carefully knotted patterned tie. His hair was slightly rumpled, giving him the appearance of an affable university professor. Peering above his glasses, Mielke strove to be strong, conciliatory and magnanimous. He began by describing the MfS.

'We are the sons and daughters of the working class, we represent all social strata. We represent the interests of the working people.' The rumbling started. 'We have extraordinarily high contact with the working people—' Laughter from the gallery began. 'Comrades,' he continued. The first heckler interrupted him.

'Not all members of this chamber are your comrades!' someone shouted.

Mielke wasn't a man used to being confronted, but decided to appear welcoming. He stretched out his arms.

'I love all people!'

Laughter and obvious derision filled the packed gallery. He stumbled further, appearing pleading and confused. Nearly everyone was shaking their heads or laughing now.

The East Germans watching on their televisions saw the face of a weak man and a weakened Stasi. We were afraid of *this*? The thousands of officers also watching were devastated by the loss of deference and respect. *This* was the man who had led them for thirty-two years? Morale plunged again.

Less than a week after his appearance, which generated the most-watched television segment in German history, and is still popular on YouTube, Erich Mielke was replaced. That happened one day after the agency was renamed the Office for National Security, AfNS. Perhaps this new name, which seemed a bit more like a Western agency, would enable the MfS to stay intact, many officers hoped. The Firm would survive.

No, said the East German public, suddenly realizing a new ability to speak out; they wouldn't accept a shell game. AfNS itself would be dissolved only weeks later, becoming perhaps the world's shortest-lived intelligence agency, and all hope of that kind of survival faded. It seemed that the Stasi had nowhere to go. But the shredders kept running anyway at the sprawling MfS headquarters on Normannenstrasse, well past the evening of Monday, January 15. That's when a huge crowd crashed through the gates and occupied the heart and brain of the Stasi. Television was filled with images of the crowd tearing through documents and desk drawers. There was now no disputing that everything was over.

In reality, it wasn't. The destruction of files continued for months more after that.

The MfS foreign intelligence section, called HV A for Hauptverwaltung Aufklärung, which translates to Headquarters of Enlightenment, saw to it. The HV A always considered themselves a cut above the rest. After all, they reasoned, they were protecting the GDR, not imprisoning tens of thousands of their own citizens like their colleagues in the Investigations Directorate. Operating from a separate building at Stasi headquarters in Berlin, in fact they were threatening, bribing and extorting East Germans and Westerners to spy. Sometimes it was with a few compromising photographs, hopes of romance or barely veiled threats about family members living behind the Wall. Occasionally, they even tried to appeal to communist ideology, but that approach rarely, if ever, worked with Westerners. Of course, the HV A knew they had two masters. The human intelligence, or HUMIT, they collected was shared routinely with the KGB station in East Berlin. The KGB rezidentura, or station, there was the largest in the world for the Soviet empire at the time. The HV A was also the routine conduit for State Security, as well as a proxy for the KGB, for the many dealings with terrorist groups like the Red Brigade and Red Army Faction (RAF). Both were left-wing terrorist organizations busy targeting American and NATO facilities in Western Europe with shootings and bombings.

The fear in West Germany of what was in the HV A files was the main reason they were allowed to continue to shred well into 1990, long after protestors occupied most of the Stasi offices. Even then, few in West Germany or the rest of Europe were that anxious to have Stasi foreign spies identified. Helpful Stasi officers told the occupiers from the Citizens' Committee it must be done, otherwise people in the United States who had helped Germany would certainly get the electric chair. The activists, mostly left-leaning themselves at the time and not especially fans of America, agreed. *The death penalty? No, that must not be allowed to happen*.

Nearly all Stasi foreign intelligence files were quickly shredded, pulped or burned. Computer magnetic tapes and backups were destroyed under the eyes of the officers. This destruction of the foreign intelligence unofficial employee files was a great relief to many in West Germany who were concerned about being implicated in cooperating with the MfS. A relief, unless someone, somewhere, had a copy.

Unfortunately, one brown folder looks a lot like another. It turned out that the friendly HV A officers had an even more important mission that they failed to share with the Citizens' Committee, who then in theory controlled the place. The files of foreign agents – those folders identifying IMs, which were quickly gathered and destroyed – were casually mixed with an even more important series of brown folders. Those folders, also quickly dumped by the HV A helpers into the shredders and pulping machines, were the officers' own official MfS personnel files – thousands of records of employment for all officers within the HV A. They could all start anew, and they celebrated among themselves. Nobody could identify them as having been Stasi officers, unlike their comrades in the other departments. The Stasi officers of the HV A took care of each other. Everyone else in MfS was on their own.

It almost worked. It certainly should have.

In their haste, and facing a rapidly narrowing window in which to protect their future careers, they overlooked something very important. There was another file that the prolific paper generators at the MfS kept for every officer. Something that most would never have a reason to see or even know about in the normal course of their duties; something that was kept elsewhere. They were called Central Card Files. These files were typically a four-page summary of the officer's identification, photograph, dates of service, career, assignments and commendations. All Central Card Files were later found intact, making it possible to easily identify and prove the employment of all Stasi officers, including those of the HV A. That oversight became very inconvenient to those who would at first rest easy as they boldly denied their Stasi history.

Even some outside the Firm argued for a complete destruction of all the files. 'Destroy them all! A fresh start for Germany!' they urged. But too many others were suspicious, and most of them wanted answers.

9

OPPORTUNITY HUNTERS

US Embassy – East Berlin
Tuesday

Deep within the tan, gabled five-story building on Neustädtische Kirchstrasse in the Mitte district, which housed the US Embassy to the GDR, it was the morning of January 16, 1990, and a grey secure telephone was ringing loudly.

The man who stared at it was the beleaguered CIA station chief. He was sitting on the X himself at the moment, much more than usual, and he knew it. Ground zero for disbelief from all angles that the agency, and the rest of the US government, failed to predict that the Wall would fall, and with it the Stasi. Just yesterday the nearby State Security headquarters itself had been stormed and occupied. It was even more shocking to the media elites who had witnessed President Ronald Reagan in Berlin barely two years before when he famously stood at the Brandenburg Gate saying, 'Mr Gorbachev, tear down this wall!' The brooding commentators at the time referred to Reagan as naive for saying such things.

The station chief, or chief of station (COS), knew that only a few weeks earlier, the CIA Intelligence Directorate had published a then-classified report speculating cautiously about the likelihood of East and West Germany possibly moving ahead with reunification steps 'over the next several years'. Instead, Germany would be reunified barely nine months later. It was one of the CIA's biggest intelligence failures, without question. To be fair, none of the other intelligence services guessed it either. But that didn't matter.

Now the Wall was suddenly a relic, the Stasi offices were mostly all overrun and the telephone deep within the embassy continued to ring. The phone's display showed that the call came from a known secure number in Washington DC. The chief of station finally sighed and picked it up. He knew what was coming. Some have claimed that on the other end of that call was President George H. W. Bush himself, having seen news reports of the takeover of the Stasi complex in Berlin and demanding to know what the CIA was doing to recover new reams of intelligence material. It's doubtful any president would personally make such a call, even one like Bush who had served as CIA director in the past, but that uncomfortable question was certainly asked. Likely it came via a query posed by the president to his CIA morning briefer, which trickled down rapidly. No matter – it was a hard question for the COS to answer.

There was certainly no denying that East Berlin was swiftly becoming like Budapest in 1945 all over again. A free-for-all. With the Wall gone, the GDR couldn't survive. Within months the three Baltic states would also declare independence, promoted by the imminent death of the strongest communist satellite state in the bloc. By December 5, CIA traffic started speculating that the regime was finished and not even creative attempts to reinvent it as a last resort by the GDR government were likely to succeed.

The truth was that the CIA's chief in East Berlin knew full well they hadn't been very effective against the Stasi at all over the years. The MfS always ran ruthless and effective counterintelligence operations with large surveillance teams whenever any CIA case officer hit the street in East Germany. Later it would be admitted that nearly all the sources the CIA had run in East Berlin were in fact double agents for the MfS. But the message delivered on the tense phone call that day in January, and by the representative from CIA headquarters who arrived in person shortly afterward, was crystal clear. 'Get to work!' So, they did.

It was an easy message for a Washington bureaucrat to deliver, but in East Berlin in January, the Stasi wasn't yet dead. Risky and wholesale cold-calling and door-knocking of key officers started anyway, throwing normal caution and intense preparation to the wind. With those who answered, the CIA hinted at cash payments and maybe relocation to the United States. Those efforts usually resulted in hang-ups and stark embarrassment instead of much success. But there was some good fortune. Cash was paid for car trunkloads of files, and, astoundingly, more than a year later a relatively small amount, which some say was $75,000, was paid for sixty-three rolls of 16mm microfiche purporting to identify those persons who were the foreign agents of the Stasi HV A. The images included thousands of index cards called F-16s and F-22s. When the two types of cards were used together, the identity of a Westerner possibly working for the GDR secret police was revealed.

One of the first foreign agents of interest to the United States found in the rolls of microfilm was codenamed *Schwan*. The information on both cards was passed to the FBI and *Schwan* was rapidly identified as an American named Jim Clark, a private investigator who had worked for a defense contractor. Clark and two others, Kurt Stand and Theresa Squillacote, who had foolishly named both their children after the founders of the German Communist Party, would be arrested in Virginia and convicted of espionage for spying for the Stasi since the 1970s.

Actions taken concerning other non-Germans identified remain classified until an undefined future date in the United States. Information on many British citizens was reportedly forwarded to MI5 soon after, although that has never been publicly confirmed.

The sixty-three rolls of 16mm film taken to Washington, later referred to as *Rosenholz* (Rosewood) files by West German intelligence, were held closely by the CIA for a very long time. After repeated requests for years by Germany at the highest levels were tactfully ignored, a copy on 381 CDs was finally returned to the reunited Germany, but not until 2003 – thirteen years later. The files the CIA sent back had had all non-German names removed. Even so, there were images of 293,000 cards identifying thousands of West Germans as possible Stasi agents, and some who also may have become Russian assets.

The Kremlin
Friday, January 26, 1990

As the CIA was scrambling in East Berlin, another frantic meeting was taking place in Moscow, deep in the inner sanctum of communism. The Central Committee of the Communist Party of the Soviet Union was meeting that morning in the secretary general's office. It was an emergency meeting convened to discuss the East German breakdown. Ten men were attending, all of them unhappy about recent events. One of them recorded the conversation. Secretary General Gorbachev started:

'We are now with the GDR like with our own Azerbaijan: no one on whom to rely, and no one with whom to have confidential relations.'

Vladimir Kryuchkov, head of the KGB, spoke up next, referring to the fate of the GDR Communist Party, the SED. 'The SED's days are numbered. Our people are afraid that Germany will become a threat again. It is necessary to actively support our friends, the former colleagues of the KGB and MVD [Ministry of Internal Affairs – USSR] in the GDR.'

Gorbachev paused to listen to the conversation among the others, before interrupting. 'Of course, the GDR must be singled out. This is a special case.' After a further furious exchange among the group about what should be done, he interrupted again:

'Don't give up on the SED. There are still two million members there. Let 700,000 be left now. It would be irrational to totally write them off. Some kind of left-wing force will crystallize out.'

———

Hubertus Knabe was in one of the first crowds of curious West Berliners who filtered over the bridge to East Berlin after those first few weeks of 1990, once they were all fairly certain that it wouldn't be locked down again. Until the end of January, that was a real possibility, and what most really expected. Slowly, over weeks and months, as more and more of the concrete structure of the Wall was chipped, beaten or pounded down by delirious crowds, it seemed Berlin was truly no longer a prison.

Stunned by the chaos and the crowds of happy East Germans streaming west as fast at their feet or their boxy two-cylinder front-wheel drive Trabant cars, called Trabis, could carry them, the Communist Party and their Stasi protectors were in survival mode.

Soon also, the streams of those headed west over the death strip diminished enough so that former East Berliners and others went in the other direction. Many West Germans went to see for themselves what life had really been like in a communist dictatorship, or to see long-lost relatives. Others had a very specific purpose in mind. There were Americans, Brits, Russians, French and nearly everyone else in the intelligence business mingling with the crowds.

Naturally there were still some ongoing and cautious intelligence operations, but whatever they were called at the moment, the Stasi remained very active on the streets in East Berlin well into January. They also were busy convincing the Citizens' Committee occupiers of their Normannenstrasse headquarters, and all of the district offices, that the destruction of files was a good thing and must continue.

Then there were the deals cut on quiet side streets for carloads of stolen files, tense conversations in small flats with those trying to make their own arrangements to go to the West, and Russians out doing damage control for their own purposes.

As Hubertus stood for the first time back in East Berlin since being refused entry in 1980, it was hard for him not to think of the past ten years. It was eight years since Annette had got out. What would life have been without her?

'Your entry is not allowed.' He could never forget. Five words that brought his life crashing down.

Now the unimaginable had happened, surprising everyone. Standing in East Berlin as the excited people streamed past, he had a plan and a mission. He would be a part of the reckoning that they all assumed was coming. A necessary and orderly accounting for the crimes committed in the name of communism that imprisoned hundreds of thousands and ruined or sidetracked the lives of countless thousands of others. By then, Hubertus had become known for his writings and his activism in the West German Green Party. With a PhD in politics nearly complete also, he was headed straight for the place where all the answers would be found. That must be the Stasi files. They must be preserved at all costs! He worried about what might happen. Some in both Germanys were calling for wholesale destruction at the time, for their own suspicious reasons.

It was a short trip for Hubertus Knabe to the East that day; he could see that things were not yet ready. There were no decision-makers, only dangerous confusion. Stasi people were still there with the files, talking with Citizens' Committee activists who were trying vainly to understand what was important. He realized that the real decisions about the fate of files were being made somewhere out of reach. It was a battle being fought in negotiating rooms of the West and East German parliaments.

There would be no wholesale destruction of the files, it was finally announced. Minister Mielke was summarily arrested and symbolically locked up in his own Hohenschönhausen prison. But that feeling turned to uneasiness. Mielke would soon be transferred to the much more comfortable Moabit prison in West Berlin. Hubertus was impatient. Every day that passed meant that further files would be destroyed, stolen, lost or sold.

With the rush to unify Germany speeding forward like a freight train, in spite of warnings from Great Britain and some others about the dangers of that happening, it was clear it would happen anyway. And fast. History had twice seen a reemerging Germany – the last time National Socialism, the Nazis, was the result. No, no, everyone was assured. We will apply West German laws, and transparency will be the priority. That did little to calm anyone's nerves.

Hubertus, now a driven and idealistic thirty-year-old, wasn't at first overly worried about any of that. He saw opportunity. A chance to right the wrongs of forty years of a repressive dictatorship, to create a new Germany with all tyranny of every sort in the past, to prosecute the many perpetrators. As talk of a new authority to be created as the guardian of the Stasi files that would make them available for research and to every victim became a reality, he was determined to be part of it. It would be called the Office of the Federal Commissioner, and be led by Joachim Gauck, a well-known and respected member of the East German resistance movement, who would later be called Germany's Nelson Mandela.

Gauck's new agency, now called the Federal Commissioner for Records of the State Security Service, Der Bundesbeauftragte für die Stasi-Unterlagen, or BStU, was officially placed in charge of the files on October 3, 1990, the day of Germany's unification. Three days before the end of 1990 the Stasi Records Act was passed, making use of these explosive documents possible. The BStU's first objective was to once and for all secure what they guessed to be about one hundred kilometers of files that were scattered around Germany. Next was to make sense of them. Finally, they were tasked with making them available to those who filed a proper request. To do all of that they would need to hire a lot of people, and fast. Hubertus raised his hand eagerly. It was a path that would consume his life.

While the CIA in East Berlin was trying to do what they could, by February 1990 in Dresden, the young KGB lieutenant colonel Vladimir Putin was nervously packing up to head for home. His assignment there had been comfortable but lackluster, and his then wife Lyudmila had reminded him frequently that the Stasi men of similar rank made more money and had nicer furnishings. The events in Berlin started KGB officers all over the Soviet Bloc packing up as well. They could and did leave, unlike their MfS colleagues.

Soon after, the International Press Center in East Berlin, in the now dull and tired building at 36 Mohrenstrasse where Günter Schabowski accidentally brought down the Berlin Wall, would have yet one more important role to play for history. Here, at another press reception staged by the new and also the last ever East German prime minister, Lothar de Maizière, journalists gathered. In barely six months Germany would officially become one country, after more than forty-five years of division.

At the back of the conference room that morning, and standing alone, was a young woman with recognizable East German clothing and hairstyle. She had just been appointed the deputy East German government spokesperson, perhaps the last who would hold that position. Her selection was odd, since her background wasn't public relations or government, but chemistry. She had no experience with such political matters, and appeared so out of place and uncomfortable that she was approached by one of the foreign journalists who simply felt sorry for her.

'Hello, I'm Ewald König, correspondent from Austria.'

The young woman nodded and stared back across the room.

'What do you think of all these journalists from West Berlin?' König asked, smiling, trying to make conversation.

Turning quickly, she stared at him. 'I find them… arrogant.'

Surprised at the response, he smiled nervously. 'And you are…?'

'Angela. Angela Merkel.'

The future chancellor of the soon-to-be united Federal Republic of Germany turned back to watch the crowd.

———

For the Stasi, preparations for the worst had actually begun well before the chaos, disbelief and fear started. It was even before 1985, the year Mikhail Gorbachev assumed power in Moscow, when billions of East German marks started to be converted to more usable currencies and flee from East Germany. That process was handled under a de facto section of the Ministry for State Security called the Commercial Coordination Unit, or KoKo, and under the careful direction of a Stasi lieutenant general. To those within the senior ranks at the time, that general was affectionately known as Big Alex.

10

FOLLOW THE MONEY

The massive change that rumbled with excitement and fear through the formerly divided streets of Berlin, a city that preferred to avoid such emotional displays, had barely faded. The large numbers of people now moving unhindered back and forth, while oddly paying little attention to the death strip, was less of a shock. Late-night chaos in the streets had quieted, and people were attempting to return to some sort of normal existence. It was less than a month after the breach of the Berlin Wall, and after 8pm on the evening of December 6, 1989. Already well below freezing and getting colder, the Western Sector shivered undeniably under the surface as a place both hopeful and apprehensive about the future.

A well-fed and tall East German man in his mid-fifties, with carefully groomed dark hair and bulging eyes, stood on a dimly lit deserted street corner near the Kreuzberg neighborhood of West Berlin. For forty years this street existed barely a tantalizing stone's throw into freedom. Wearing expensive Western clothing and concealing a small briefcase under his light overcoat, he was sweating profusely. His face reflected the pale, soft complexion of someone who spent little time outdoors and was accustomed to living well. The man stood for some time, away from the glow of the street lamp as the light snow slowly fell, and stared hard at the front of a tan, traditional block of residential flats across the street. They were the type of worn and unremarkable buildings that filled this working-class area. He had crossed into West Berlin nervously at the Invalidenstrasse border checkpoint after midnight three days earlier, to prepare himself. As he stood in front of the border guard, he knew he was at the site of many escape attempts – that had all failed. Six people had died trying. But he had the right documents, and hopefully a face that few people yet knew.

He stood on the corner looking for a particular number on a block of flats, and mumbled under his breath as he squinted at the numbers on the worn brown doors. *There.* The door he sought was otherwise identical to the others, and bore a typical scuffed dull metal kick plate.

He was about to do the most dangerous thing he had ever done in his privileged life.

The address was one of many known to the Stasi to be operating as a safe house for West German intelligence. Except to the common folks in both East and West Berlin, their existence was no particular secret. With the thousands of East German spies active in the West by 1989, including many well placed in government jobs in Berlin, things like this were hard to hide for long. Maybe that was one of several reasons why the man who stood on the corner this evening was sweating in spite of the sharp chill. He'd been living the last few days in hiding, even though he had long planned for this moment.

Finally, glancing in both directions, he stepped quickly from the curb and crossed. Striding to the front portico of the brown door, while keeping his head lowered and being careful not to slip on the fresh snow, the man peered at the nameplates next to the dulled brass buttons, looking for a certain name. *There.* He thumbed the buzzer and waited. There was no response. He produced a handkerchief and wiped his face before pushing the buzzer again. And again. A lone car appeared, moving slowly in his direction down the quiet street, and he tilted his head down casually, trying his best to hide his face in the shadow of the alcove. Staring at his hands, he noticed that they were oddly trembling. After a few agonizing seconds, the sedan passed by and turned east toward Lindenstrasse. He pushed the buzzer a third time and held it.

Ja! What do you want?

The man bent close to the intercom and whispered.

I'm Schalck. Let me in, please.

What? Who do you say?

He drew a breath and straightened up. *Schalck! Hurry! Do you know who…*

Yes, of course! The lock buzzed open. *Wait just inside.*

Gratefully, he stepped into the dark lobby and leaned against the heavy wooden door and exhaled, confidence returning. He mentally composed his final thoughts and his plans.

The two West Germans occupying the flat that evening were placeholders. They were members of the West German domestic intelligence agency, Das Bundesamt für Verfassungsschutz (Federal Office for the Protection of the Constitution), or BfV, one of many meet-and-greet teams deployed rapidly and instructed to receive and evaluate and report on the surge of defectors that the overnight collapse of East Berlin had brought.

The man calling himself Schalck knew that also, and he composed himself and, once safely in the flat, spoke to the two as if they were subordinates.

'I am Alexander Siegfried Schalck-Golodkowski, head of GDR Commercial Coordination Unit… KoKo…'

The older of the two young men raised his hand and gestured to the kitchen table.

'Hold that. Sit here. Identification, please.'

Schalck slipped an identification card from his coat, presenting it with a flourish.

The BfV man studied it carefully, and his eyes flicked up.

'Yours also, if you please!'

The man looked irate, but flipped open his official identification anyway with a snap.

Schalck nodded – he knew the display was meaningless if something was wrong. The Stasi had better fakes than the original. But, then, they would have taken him at the curb, drugged him and stuffed him in the trunk of a car.

'Um, MfS colonel? I see. Do you have something for us?'

'*Lieutenant General*. For you no, but for your superiors quite possibly.'

The officer shrugged and nodded at the other.

'Please sit... General, may we offer coffee? My colleague will leave to notify the appropriate people, and we will enjoy our coffee together. You will have someone to talk with until then. Good?'

Schalck looked around and noticed there was no telephone in the small flat, but didn't need to ask why. He was relieved.

'Yes, fine,' he snapped. The younger man grabbed his jacket and headed for the door.

'You! Wait! I have a critical message for your chief!'

Both men turned, and the one near the door slipped a notebook from his pocket. 'Go ahead.'

'Don't transfer me to detention in the Eastern Sector like some others were. I assume that I will survive a pre-trial detention in the GDR for a week at most.'

There was silence until the older of the two nodded, and the other rushed out.

'Now, please, some milk with my coffee!'

By all counts, Alexander Schalck-Golodkowski's defection to West German authorities should have been celebrated as an important first step in a long road to the healing and reunification of the two Germanys. He was, after all, a hated figure who had helped prop up the communist dictatorship for decades with his skills in financial subterfuge and his network of international contacts. These had made international weapons trading and terrorism support for the communist GDR routine. He had arranged the procurement of technology for the National People's Army, even under-the-table deliveries of spare parts for key companies. Money had flowed in – lots of it.

When asked, he was quick to brag about making plenty of hard currency for the GDR in those early days. Ah, he had been so young then. He was most proud of that. All the while his face was unknown to the typical German on either side of the Wall.

He was far less interested in discussing his close ingrained alliances with the Soviet state, his grandfather having been a Russian taxman and his father an officer in the tsarist army. The BfV and the Federal Intelligence Service, or BND – the exterior intelligence agency for West Germany – and their colleagues at the CIA knew that and much more about him.

Over the next few weeks, the interviews headed by the Federal Intelligence Service confirmed much of what they all already knew. Recruited into State Security in 1967, he had been a rising star and marked for success. That had been evident as far back as 1970 when he was awarded a PhD at the University of Potsdam for an interesting thesis titled *Avoiding Economic Losses and Generating Additional Foreign Exchange*. His doctoral supervisor then was listed as 'Mielke, Minister of State Security'. That was strange enough since Mielke had not even finished high school, let alone college. Schalck's dissertation read like a calm primer on money laundering and economic crime.

He ensured that plenty of hard currency was always available to Party officials to buy technology under the table, and to keep the favored ones supplied with everything from weapons to antiques, and to enable them to support the radical terrorist group of choice. He presided over more than two hundred cover companies and in excess of one thousand bank accounts throughout the world. He personally administered the program whereby large cash payments of hard currency were made to GDR accounts by West Germany for release of hostages over the Cold War years. The man they called Schalck, or Big Alex by his close colleagues at the Firm, was always treated as a hero and a provider, especially by the top political rulers of the communist GDR. He was twice awarded the prestigious Order of Karl Marx.

The East German mark, the Ostmark, was a so-called island currency: it was nearly impossible to directly exchange it for another. It stood no chance alone on the international market, and couldn't buy anything there. But he made transactions easy, and good things happened anyway for the Stasi, the Central Committee and other favored souls.

Once, when GDR general secretary Erich Honecker decided that the common people should be tended to, Schalck easily procured 5,000 tons of apples to distribute to the citizens, while also stocking up on caviar, champagne and diamonds for the favored class, and fresh orchids for their ladies. Rumors swirled in late 1989, as he was then also operating as trade secretary, that he had been approved by Moscow to perhaps take over as prime minister in a hoped-for new GDR. A stronger version of the communist state, they hoped, rising as a phoenix from the ashes. It was a brief, grand idea that instead was promptly swept aside by fate and circumstance.

He confirmed all of that to the questioners and more, and swiftly corrected them when they intentionally referred to him as 'General' or, worse, 'Colonel'.

Lieutenant General. I'm also state secretary and a member of the SED!

His interrogators naturally assumed it would be only a short time before the whereabouts of billions of hard currency would be revealed. Soon it became obvious Big Alex had his own plan.

By week three of the interrogations, which really were more like gentlemen's conversations during bankers' hours and closely overseen by West German authorities, Schalck was upbeat. This was nothing like how his beloved Stasi would have handled things. In return for information, he had first demanded and received assurances that he would not under any circumstances be sent to East Berlin. He was well cared for and everything was so civilized. He chatted endlessly, but his final position remained always unyielding when pressed by frustrated questioners. He had done nothing wrong and was merely serving his country, after all.

'What of the money?' they demanded. 'Where's it hidden?'

'I gave you a list of GDR accounts in Germany – everything else is in the records! You have the KoKo records now, yes?'

'Where is the rest of the money? What was converted on the black market and sent out of the GDR? Where are those secret accounts?'

'Check with the records! You know that KoKo is an organization separate from State Security? Do you understand they have more

than a hundred senior employees, and thousands of others? I don't
have it!'

It was late on a Friday afternoon, and the interrogators moved on
to other matters.

'What do you know about financing of terrorism by the GDR
with hard currency? Such as funding for that assassin for the Popular
Front for the Liberation of Palestine, Ilich Ramírez Sánchez, better
known as Carlos the Jackal?'

A sigh. 'What? Nonsense!'

'Oh? And what of the program you designed to steal art and
antiques and sell them?'

'Those were tax matters we handled; those people couldn't pay
their taxes.' Just routine for any government, he assured them. 'May
I have another coffee?'

He smiled softly; he had always counted that one as a lasting success.
It was actually the art program that demonstrated his genius to many
in the GDR and caused him to be noticed by Moscow when he started
it in the early 1960s. The government coffers were so desperate for
hard currency; they depended on him and his projects. They didn't
care how he did it, and neither did those he dealt with in the West.

Now he was in safety and quite enjoying the game once again.

Meanwhile, a frantic review of documents and interviews with the
few people who still reported for work at the KoKo offices in East
Berlin proved of little use. Receipts and records had in many cases
been destroyed 'on authority from above'. Nobody could say whose.
Suitcases full of cash didn't leave many trails either.

Frustration from interviewers mirrored rising elation from Schalck
when December ended, and it became clear that the position of prosecutors was that Lieutenant General Alexander Schalck-Golodkowski
couldn't be prosecuted or jailed in the West at all. At least, not for
now. He had carefully admitted only to being a good servant of East
Germany.

Peter Przybylski, a prosecutor in the unraveling East, was to the
point. 'Schalck? He's the jack-of-all-trades of GDR corruption.'

Officials on both sides shook their heads at the big Stasi fish that had already slipped the net. Gregor Gysi, a well-known East German lawyer and destined to be a member of the unified German Parliament and much more, was told of Schalck's defection and laughed harshly.

'He will never be prosecuted. He knows too much about Western officials!'

Some, like Rita Garcke, a woman aged by life well beyond her years, certainly would have spoken up, if asked. Sitting alone in a tiny, drab flat in East Berlin, just across the River Spree from where Schalck was enjoying his coffee and conversation that Friday, she would never have been satisfied with such answers. She lived each day with the trauma of being widowed suddenly and ruined because of *him*. Given the chance, she would have repeated her story about being jarred awake at six o'clock on a February morning in 1978 by loud raps at the door. Rising that morning with her husband, they glanced at each other and instantly knew. In East Berlin this could only mean one thing, and it wasn't good.

'State Security,' the men said, pushing their way inside.

One produced a notebook and started to list all their possessions. Another announced that taxes equivalent to 90 percent of the value of all their personal property were due and demanded summary payment. Confused, the couple said they had little savings. With a nod, the Stasi-led squad cleared out the entire flat, even emptying the sugar bowl and dumping flowers from a vase. The antiques her husband Peter, an East Berlin doctor, had meticulously acquired since before the war, were seized. 'They didn't leave me a chair to sit on!' she would later cautiously tell her friends, some of whom undoubtedly reported on her later.

'Then they took Peter away.'

She never saw her husband again.

Recovered records years later showed Peter had died in custody after months of imprisonment and interrogation. The official cause of death was listed in the files as suicide: 'strangulation in bed'. Rita never found out what really happened.

Records found in the Archive also detailed that the seized Garcke property was promptly sold by Kunst & Antiquitäten [Art & Antiques] GmbH, a shell company set up by Schalck. Most of the sales were to Western buyers, Dutch and Italian, but also Japanese – whoever offered cash.

Seizure and sale, and sometimes incidental death, were usually only part one of this project. Next would come a suitably long detention of the property owner in a prison, or in some cases a psychiatric hospital, to keep them quiet and help extort other funds from friends or family. Finally, for the lucky ones with wealthy connections, the Stasi would arrange a ransom in hard currency from the West. After payment, they would be expelled to West Berlin. Schalck fondly called the project *the Art Investigators*.

The same story was repeated more than two hundred times, and touched victims who died or fled when the GDR finally fell. Families are even now coming forward. More than one son is still fighting today from the United States to recover valuable artworks. Gilbert Lupfer, the lead researcher for the Dresden state art collection, would years later describe to a *New York Times* reporter what had happened as being reminiscent of the Nazi lootings from the Jews before the Holocaust.

The art project was just a gateway to something much bigger. In his quest to provide the thirsty GDR government with cash, Schalck discovered early on in his career the value of ransoming a variety of other persons to the West German government. They would always pay, and in nice, usable Deutschmarks. It became routine. More than 33,000 prisoners arrested for minor offenses such as political graffiti, or being too vocal about wishing to leave the GDR, or unfavorable writings, were sold into freedom in West Germany. Schalck arranged a special account at KoKo to receive these payments, which over twenty-five years totaled nearly 3.5 billion DM, US $1 billion. The last ransom payment was deposited into the special KoKo account at Deutsche Handelsbank only days before the end in November 1989.

But with the final decision made by the prosecutors in the first week of January 1990, little more could be said. It was a Tuesday morning, January 9, when the always cooperative Big Alex stood up and walked out onto the streets of West Berlin a free man after four weeks in custody, and promptly disappeared.

German intelligence officers had more pressing concerns at that moment. The Wall was effectively gone, and within days the Ministry for State Security would be technically disbanded, leaving the other 91,000 employees with secrets and grudges out and about, looking for work. The Russians and the Americans would be busy, too. Berlin would soon be an even richer hunting ground for all the intelligence agencies. And an even more dangerous place.

As the formal financial investigation was started by the unified Parliament, and professional money trackers were retained, rumors persisted about what had happened to Schalck-Golodkowski. Some said he was with Mossad in Israel, others were convinced that the CIA had spirited him away, and still others swore he had been seen living the high life in Yugoslavia. While all of those may have been true, the ultimate reality was far stranger.

Nearly everyone was unprepared for what happened next. A routine inventory found a surprise hidden in the cellar of the KoKo building in East Berlin – twenty-one tons of gold bars and crates of precious artwork. The gold was controlled personally by Schalck and surpassed the official reserves of the GDR State Bank five times over. It was valued at more than a quarter of a billion dollars. And there was the nearly empty safe in his office. Office personnel swore there was $660,000 in crisp notes in there only weeks before he fled. Where did it all go?

It seemed almost logical, then, that one of two agencies hastily set up to take control of East German assets would be called the Trust Agency, or Treuhand. It took up residence in a block building near Alexanderplatz labeled with the harmless name of the House of Electrical Industry. Located in the business center of East Berlin, there was much business that had to be done. They were to be the official failed communist state demolition team. Nobody really wanted the job, knowing they would be instantly hated or feared by the Eastern

half of the population, and disbelieved by the rest. The new organization was immediately swamped by the sheer volume of real property
and failing businesses from the fading GDR that they had to do something with. Not only all the property holdings of the Stasi, but more
than eight thousand commercial state enterprises employing over four
million people. At the time, this made Treuhand the world's largest
industrial enterprise. The job would depend on reams of paper, the
telephone, shoe leather and making lots of people unhappy.

Any doubts about just how much unhappiness the wrecking ball
of the GDR was causing soon came to an end one evening the following April.

It was late in the evening Easter Monday, a holiday in Germany,
when a serious-looking man walked along the Rhine River in
Düsseldorf. He was carrying a canvas bag and a white plastic chair.
Squinting across the street at a large home facing onto the river in
this affluent area, he stepped back off the sidewalk and carefully
placed the chair in the shadows on the grass before producing a pair
of binoculars and holding them up. Satisfied, he quietly got to work
with the contents of the bag. Finally, he removed a white towel and
unrolled it. Then he waited in the darkness.

It was nearly 10:30pm when he slid his 7.62 mm rifle from the bag,
draped the towel over the scope to dampen reflections and waited.
He had his eye in a comfortable practiced position as he embraced
the rifle, exhaling slowly. Then he casually fired three quick shots
over a clipped hedge and between the branches of two trees. All
passed within two seconds through an upper-floor window of the
well-kept brick house across the street. The first shot made a neat
hole in the glass, striking a man square in the back as he rose from his
desk. Treuhand's director, Detlev Rohwedder, was killed instantly.
The second shot hit his wife, who was entering the room. It nearly
severed her arm.

Responding police found the chair, three shell casings, the towel
and a typed note condemning 'attempts to subjugate the people'.
The Red Army Faction claimed the credit, the same German leftist

terrorist group, frequently supported by the Stasi, that only weeks before had conducted a sniper attack on the US Embassy in Bonn. The assassination of Rohwedder was never solved.

A calm and competent, yet aggressive, prosecutor named Georg Reinicke was engaged at about the same time to collaborate with Treuhand and head a more direct-action recovery team comprised of prosecutors, investigators and judges. Named the Independent Commission and called the UKPV for short, they were empowered to conduct searches of premises and issue judicial orders to reclaim funds. It was their job to follow the GDR money.

One of the first things both organizations noticed was that cash in large quantities had continued to be mysteriously withdrawn from East German government bank accounts for many months after the GDR shutdown. Suitcase money, they called it. Their first move was to freeze all remaining accounts of the GDR that they knew about. Was it too late? A staff member at the UKPV made a preliminary tally of how much hard currency was believed to have gone missing in recent years, and laid the document on Georg Reinicke's desk. Reinicke stared in disbelief. Their best guess was the equivalent of $11 billion.

———

As the miles of Stasi files were being quickly cataloged and made available to Berlin prosecutors, it seemed that Schalck had been less than forthcoming about many things. He forgot to mention that he was number 14 in rank of the organization's 91,000 employees, and reported only to its head, Minister Mielke, as part of a special division kept off the organization charts. Officially listed in MfS records as a colonel to avoid identifying him as a top leader, while being paid as a lieutenant general, he remained a shadow. The KoKo organization he led was hardly separate either. Of its employees, about half, or 113 senior staff members, were identified in the retrieved records as direct employees of the Ministry for State Security. Schalck was a secret within a secret, and so was KoKo.

The news media frantically searched for him, dispatching report-ers on wild-goose chases to far-flung destinations, without success. There were too many easier targets of opportunity at the time. And there was no shortage of endless other intrigues every day to cover and distract.

It was a scorching afternoon in the early summer of 1990 when a dull blue Trabant sedan wound its way slowly through the outskirts of Munich. Passing by trendy homes and shops of a type unknown in East Germany and turning up one residential street after another, the young woman driver appeared to be a tourist. By now, West Germans had become accustomed to the hordes of newly freed Easterners who were intensely curious and envious as they savored their surprising new freedoms. The locals likely did find the car funny. A twenty-five-horsepower East German sedan with no air conditioning, windows rolled down and loud, straining engine would have been at odds with the more typical BMWs, Audis and Volkswagens that populated the streets.

The Trabant swerved right onto a tree-lined, dead-end road and parked at the curb. A woman got out. She held up a piece of paper and looked closely at the small houses, before finally speaking to an old man out walking his dog.

'Excuse me. I am looking for the home of the Pastor Rüchert's widow.'

'Yes, yes! You can find her at the white house with the gate there,' he replied, pointing.

'Danke.' She nodded, tucking the slip of paper into her small handbag.

The tiny, neat home was what would be expected of the wife of a deceased pastor, and the driver pushed open the gate. A woman bent over, tending the garden, straightened and stared, hands on her hips.

'Is the pastor couple Gutmann from the GDR staying here with you?'

'Why do you ask?'

'I'm the pastor's daughter.'

A large man holding a newspaper appeared at the door, smiling broadly, nodding to the older woman.

'Father!'

Schalck-Golodkowski stepped back to allow his wife, Sigrid, who also held a Stasi rank, to embrace and pull their daughter inside.

'Your older brother is already here!' Sigrid said excitedly. 'Come! Sit!'

The family reunion went well through lunch, until the usually docile son blurted out the question.

'Well, Mr Currency Procurement, where are the billions?'

The awkwardness in the room was response enough, and Schalck turned to his daughter.

'Please keep silent – my life is in your hands!'

Within days, Schalck, hiding under the identity of Pastor Gutmann, had moved on.

In Berlin, a frantic UKPV had managed to assume control of bank accounts in East Berlin and transmit preliminary notifications to a few foreign banks elsewhere in Europe and Scandinavia, at least those that they knew about. Nothing could be done about the suitcase money. It was too easy to pass out of Germany and into neighboring Eastern Europe countries, all of which were struggling with similarly chaotic conditions.

While both Treuhand and the UKPV scrambled to look at past KoKo and other GDR financial transactions, Schalck was continuing to secure his future. Surfacing months later in the calm and serene surroundings of a lakeside villa in the beautiful Bavarian village of Rottach-Egern in the Tegernsee valley, he was again being exceedingly cooperative.

The Federal Intelligence Service reconnected with him and continued a series of conversations that would span some thirty meetings over the next several years, giving him the rather unlikely code name *Snow White*. He would talk of almost anything at length and did, except about where the money might be. His request to them for a new identity to protect him from prying media and others who would like to find him was summarily denied.

It seemed obvious to his interrogators, and certainly to him, that there was another problem. As one of the highest-ranking Stasi officers at the abrupt end, and also an SED party secretary and the keeper of the money, he was an image to most Germans of everything that was bad and corrupt. Though this is not at all inaccurate, it was not in his plan to end up the most hated GDR official next to Communist Party secretary general Erich Honecker and Stasi minister Mielke. The initial shock of German reunification had worn off, and the people were now demanding justice.

Lake Tegernsee seemed to suit Schalck and Sigrid quite well; it was an idyllic and discreet place. Even as he quickly became the latest infamous resident, villagers didn't seem to care. It was known as a spa region with a healing climate and was home to wealthy elites, who could usually be found minding their own business on sailboats or in the cafés. For years it was amusingly called *Bonzo See*, Lake Big Shot. This place on the lake also had a history of being lucky for survivors, even before May 1945, when the Nazi Waffen-SS chose it as the place for their final stand against a rapidly advancing US Army. Saved then from being shelled to quick oblivion by happenstance when an injured soldier limped from the hospital waving a white flag, the small community returned to taking all things and all people in stride.

As the years ticked by, Berlin prosecutors opened up dozens of preliminary investigations targeting Schalck-Golodkowski, charging him with everything from terrorism, corruption, tax evasion, espionage, drug trafficking and gunrunning. Most went nowhere; others were stalled and delayed by his full-time and well-paid Bavarian lawyer, allowing him to enjoy his lake villa in peace.

As he walked alone on the shores of Lake Tegernsee on a fall day in 1995, unneeded money from his insultingly insignificant Stasi pension in his pocket, he was still in the game, and officials in the West remained afraid of him. Now more than ever. He stopped and looked toward the looming façade of St Quirinus Abbey, a Benedictine monastery that had stood along the lake since the Middle Ages.

Endurance.

He reviewed his recent accomplishments. 1992 – attempted prosecution for narcotics trafficking... *discontinued*. 1993 – attempted prosecution for misappropriation of billions of GDR funds moved to foreign countries... *discontinued*.

It wasn't unusual for him to pick up the phone and make a friendly call to the Berlin prosecutors, inquiring if he was the subject of any new investigations. That was a bold move, since if not done properly it could have increased their motivation to try to understand the myriad of very odd KoKo financial dealings. Maybe not so risky, he decided, since he was the only one who knew all the answers.

And his future seemed bright. He would soon form yet another new company in Upper Bavaria. There would be media interviews and maybe even television appearances and a tell-all book for many to worry about. Taking a comb from his pocket, he ran it carefully through his hair.

Returning from his morning walk, Schalck had a spring in his step, as the first sailboats of the day were moving out on the lake. Nearing his villa, he mulled over what the day would bring. A few calls with old GDR colleagues? Of course, he knew that the Federal Intelligence Service was watching. It was to be expected. Even that was now fading, he thought with satisfaction. There was a statute of limitations on missing money, and so time was his friend. Sometimes he would be asked how he could afford a 4,000 DM monthly payment on the large house, when his pension was a pittance. With a wave of his hand he would talk of loans from friends or of consulting work. Once, when 420,000 DM, worth nearly $480,000 in today's dollars, appeared in his local bank account, somebody did notice. They also noticed another instance when an unsecured credit line from another supporter for 500,000 DM appeared. Naturally, he had a duly signed promissory note from one friend or another specifying 4 percent interest, to wave if needed as documentation for something that would never be paid back. A judicial officer had recently commented to the media about how easy it would be to get such large personal loans, 'if you had fifty million in a Swiss bank'.

Yes, perhaps he would start the day cheerfully, with a few phone calls to friends in Berlin. Life wasn't so bad. A lifelong communist, atheist and senior-ranking member of the Stasi, he would now end such phone calls with his new trademark salutation:

'God bless.'

The UKPV and their money trackers meanwhile continued frustrating attempts to wade through more than one thousand bank accounts in Germany and other countries, and make sense of KoKo's more than two hundred shell companies. With foreign accounts, inquiries were often turned away, since money laundering wasn't then even a recognized crime in Hungary, Switzerland, Liechtenstein and Luxembourg.

For these reasons and others, for years the focus was on the recovery of domestic assets found in the GDR. That was scoffed at by many as low-hanging fruit, officially explained away by reference to the slight UKPV staff. Money and property were recovered, and reports promptly written for Parliament. An amount of 1.6 billion euros reclaimed certainly seemed significant. Ultimately, only 600 million of that total was retrieved from outside of Germany. They claimed a victory nonetheless. Time was not the investigators' ally, and neither were the strict Swiss banking laws, refusal of other countries to cooperate, or political fears.

Many of the KoKo companies were quickly sold off by liquidators at Treuhand at bargain prices, with some mysteriously ending up back in control of Schalck's old business partners. Some changed hands even faster – before the liquidators even knew about them. The political will to turn KoKo and the Stasi upside down just wasn't present in the new Germany. Best to move forward and avoid uncomfortable questions. One UKPV member complained to a persistent reporter at *Spiegel* that there were simply far too few investigators to pursue the money with more vigor, adding with a sigh, 'Nobody really wants to know anyway.'

Schalck, taking his coffee each morning in the fresh air at the villa, surrounded by newspapers and his telephone, couldn't help but be entertained when he was referred to in the media as 'Germany's Goldfinger' or 'Alexander the Great' for his success in frustrating prosecutors. Time was also allowing the dust to settle, and a quiet network within members of the Firm was forming. One morning, with fall drawing to a close, he put down his cup and picked up a sheaf of papers. Maybe it would be a good day to call his lawyer and issue instructions on the new Bavarian business to be formed. He'd decided it would be called Dr Schalck & Company.

Yes, things were going very well indeed as seen from the shores of Lake Tegernsee.

All of that could well end in a blink of an eye, no matter how smoothly he worked his Berlin and global contacts. It seemed that Lieutenant General Schalck-Golodkowski was also destined to earn yet one more distinction. He could soon be one of the first members of the Stasi to ever be charged with a crime. Presided over by the serious, seasoned and no-nonsense Volker Neumann, the KoKo Investigation Committee quickly learned that for Schalck the art business was just the beginning. They were dumbfounded as documents revealed much more. Evidence surfaced of traffic in blood and death, all for hard cash. It was a billion-dollar business.

The line of mostly students in front of Humboldt University one April day in 1984 reached out to the sidewalk and veered left. Perhaps a hundred people stood patiently as the front of the line disappeared into a canvas tent. The tent bore a medical symbol and the employees within were from the Ministry of Health. A sign hanging at the entrance read *Donate Blood, Save Lives!*

The students knew they were doing the right thing. Similar blood drives were common throughout East Germany. Helping their neighbors.

Earlier, hours before the dawn, a train sped up as it departed the East German port of Rostock, on the Baltic Sea. Three of the freight cars bearing locking seals had been offloaded from a freighter from Sweden earlier in the day, and were en route to Finland. The Deutsche Reichsbahn or DR, the GDR rail system, wasn't so efficient by Western standards. It was a leftover from Nazi times, when it was made infamous by transporting millions of Jews to the gas chambers of Auschwitz and Dachau. But now it had another special role. The cars rattled through East Germany, pulled by a dependable black steam locomotive. The drab train cars were accompanied by GDR border guards on the trip south until they reached the West German frontier, after making a brief stop along the way. At the frontier, the border guards stepped off, all the freight cars were compared against manifests and the seals checked. The three cars in the back were destined for Finland, it was noted, and would be separated once in Austria.

When the three cars arrived at their destination days later, the seals were cut by a representative of a large Swedish defense contractor, Bofors Konsern. The train cars were all empty, which was fine for him. He expected as much.

Volker Neumann, leader of the investigation into KoKo, sat in his Berlin office in 1993, confused. What did files marked 'Blut' have in common with rail shipments to Finland? Blood? Then he suddenly understood. He was looking at two more very profitable projects designed by the Stasi's Lieutenant General Schalck-Golodkowski.

The investigators were dumbfounded as documents revealed traffic in blood extracted from GDR citizens and sold in the West as 'untainted' by the quickly spreading AIDS epidemic, and how starting in the mid-1980s Schalck and KoKo became a critical middleman for explosives and weapons destined for the Middle East. It was just another part of the billion-dollar business.

The Stasi art investigators seemed at the time to be an easy and low-risk way to earn half a billion dollars for the KoKo coffers and the Communist Party over fifteen years. Previously, they had emptied the GDR museums of any extra paintings. Who would complain? Not a museum director, and certainly not a lowly citizen, even if their spouse disappeared. And if they did, who would care about the rich hoarders? The ransom of thousands of East German prisoners to the West was another stroke of genius the SED leaders acknowledged privately. That alone brought in over $1 billion. Whereas the art and antique seizures and sales were well known in the West, at least among the always interested prospective foreign buyers, the ransoms were kept secret in both East and West for different reasons.

The GDR, like most communist states, never admitted any bad news. It didn't exist, just as there were never officially any political prisoners. Being seen to receive cash in exchange for freeing citizens would simply have been incompatible with that strategy. To admit that the government itself was just as desperate to get hard currency would likewise have been the acknowledgment of an embarrassing weakness.

In West Germany, care was taken not to use either of those facts for political gain, as the flow of freed political prisoners would have been shut off.

At first, they thought to use the chance to offload some real violent criminals. That ended quickly when the West scrutinized more closely who would be accepted. The Stasi next tried to set higher ransoms for those prisoners they deemed more valuable, those more highly educated. Under the sheer volume of the thousands of human transactions over the years, that stopped also in favor of the flat-fee method: 90,000 DM each, equivalent to about $45,000. Sometimes, goods would be exchanged instead, crude oil, or diamonds. KoKo easily converted those to hard currency.

Two KoKo projects, $1.5 billion hard currency brought in. But there were many others. Schalck's Stasi-run KoKo also sold blood to the West, harvested from regular Germans under false pretenses, and they sold weapons to fighters in the ongoing Iran–Iraq war. It was most effective when they sold to both sides at once. Of course, the GDR couldn't buy arms from the West; there was an embargo on sales to all communist countries of the Eastern Bloc. KoKo made a quick arrangement with Bofors Konsern, which solved the problem. Bofors would buy the weapons, explosives and other materials for delivery to a southern Swedish port, with the final destination listed as Finland. No problem for the embargo watchers. Since everyone was worried about a possible Soviet invasion of Finland, military materials were needed and expected. To save money, the heavy shipments would be forwarded by rail. That route involved a freighter to Rostock, and the sealed train cars would then travel through the GDR for a few hundred kilometers before crossing into West Germany and Austria, and routing to Finland. Somewhere along the way the train would be briefly stopped in a quiet place in the GDR by the Stasi, and the special cars offloaded. The seals would be replaced and the train would continue, much lighter. KoKo would make a nice sum as a middleman and weapons would reach their actual destination. It was yet another very profitable business.

It's not known who first came up with the idea to sell the people's blood, but Schalck and KoKo enthusiastically made it happen. Demand by the communist government for hard currency was insatiable as the GDR was teetering on the brink of insolvency.

As the 1980s began, the new and deadly disease of HIV was killing people around the globe, and it wasn't yet understood. People not in the high-risk groups of gay men and IV drugs users were getting it anyway, when receiving a blood transfusion at the local hospital. Clean blood was scarce, and valuable. With no reliable way to test the blood supply, people in Europe and America were deathly afraid. There was a perception that blood from East Germany, a tightly controlled and closed society, would be safer than blood harvested in the West. Price was not an issue to a wealthy European or American lying in a hospital bed. Blood from an estimated 40,000 East Germans a year made its way to a broker in Switzerland. Each year, the price went up.

In the GDR, citizens were strongly encouraged to donate blood, for their neighbors and countrymen. It was patriotic to do so, the campaign went. Seemed to be an easy way to please the state, without sacrificing your integrity or agreeing to spy on your neighbors.

The thought even appealed to those ever-increasing numbers who couldn't care less about the state's approval. Many of them could see the intrinsic value in donating blood to save lives. They had no idea it would be immediately packaged and rushed to Switzerland to be sold at top prices, with the money being deposited in Stasi-controlled accounts. It's likely that other donors were prisoners who weren't given any choice.

Maybe not as profitable as selling stolen art and antiques, people, or arms and explosives to the Middle East, but as creative as it was shocking.

The people's blood, a commodity like any other.

Celebration of the fortieth anniversary of the GDR in East Berlin, October 7, 1989, just before the fall. Mikhail Gorbachev and GDR leader Erich Honecker (front, center) are present. Numerous Stasi officers are also pictured.

Berlin press conference November 9, 1989, that brought down the Wall. Günter Schabowski, seated center right, is about to make the mistake of his life.

Stasi prisoner photo of a young Hugo Diederich taken before he was
ransomed to the West and his citizenship revoked, 1987.

Hugo Diederich, speaking at age sixty-five for VOS, Victims of Communism, 2019.

Some of the remaining thousands of bags of torn Stasi files waiting to be reassembled.

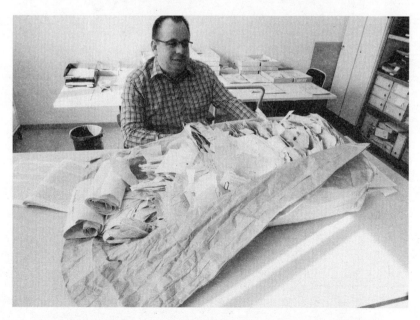

Hopeless state of the manual reconstruction efforts, thirty years later in 2019.
Nine people are assigned to the task, 95 percent of the torn files remain untouched.

PART II

11

THE MISSION

A secret and surprisingly bold operation was taking place one day in August 1990. It was nearly five months since all employees of State Security had finally been dismissed and eight months after the MfS was announced to be disbanded. They certainly weren't gone, and many of them knew that in less than two months the two countries would be unified and this chance would be lost.

A Stasi officer emerged from a building at the Normannenstrasse headquarters complex in Berlin, lugging a heavy bag. He paused at the top of the steep stairs for a second or two, to visually sweep those loitering in the courtyard outside, looking for any of the enemy that might get in his way. Descending while ready for trouble, he weaved his way around some suspicious Citizens' Committee activists. They still occupied the entire place and were on the lookout for anything unusual, but lacked discipline. At the curb he hefted the bag into the trunk of a waiting car and jumped in. By then, he no longer prominently used his folded MfS identification, but likely instead carried a plastic card identifying him as a member of the transition team or possibly the West German Federal Criminal Police (BKA).

The driver didn't speak or hesitate, but hit the gas. It wasn't a long drive from Lichtenberg to the East German military base on the outskirts of Berlin, and it was safer there to do what had to be done. The car slowed only briefly as the driver's Stasi ID came out as they approached the gate. It was still good here. The sentry waved them in. The car passed by mostly empty barracks and stopped at a long administrative building. The driver killed the engine, and they both slid out, the passenger retrieving the bag. Both glanced at each other for an instant before heading inside. They didn't need to say it.

The comrades must be looked after.

It was a heady time, when the reality had finally hit home. Many officers who retained access to the files and offices through jobs in the interim government finally realized that the Firm wasn't going to be reincarnated and continue on with a new name. The alternative idea to merge it with the West German services en masse had also been shot down months ago, and in weeks the GDR itself would cease to be.

That's why the unlabeled magnetic tapes in the bag taken that day were critical. They contained identities of all Stasi employees, dangerous information to possess at any time. A year earlier, the CIA would have paid millions for the information in the canvas bag, and those attempting to remove them from headquarters would have faced a violent and immediate fate, if caught.

Instead, the officers rushed inside and handed the bag safely over to other waiting officers, who had the right equipment standing ready. They got to work at once. In hours, the information on the tapes was safely converted into a suitable format. All the Firm's officers would have proof of employment, salary and the pensions due to them. They would not be denied compensation for their years of faithful service to the state.

It was done! Now, to distribute and hide copies…

They all heard the commotion in the hallway outside. And footsteps, lots of them. Frantically scooping up the tapes and copies, they froze as the doorknob in their workroom started to rotate. The door crashed open.

You there! Citizens' Committee! We will safeguard those files!

One of the citizen watchers at headquarters had received an anonymous tip. They were all on alert for those trying to remove file folders of records or property, and were enraged at what the officers had boldly and successfully taken. Angry activists raced over to the base, and were let in by confused soldiers. Their tip, the source of which would never be known, was surprisingly accurate, and they immediately found the cluster of former officers packaging up the tapes and new computer disks. They intended to seize them when they burst angrily into the room.

An argument ensued.

People will be killed if these records get out, they were told solemnly by the officers. That was usually an effective strategy, but this time it didn't work. The activists seized the processed tapes and disks anyway.

Since none of them knew what to do with the information, or really what the tapes actually contained, everything was driven to the East German Parliament building and handed over to one of the trusted members there. He locked them in his safe. After hearing and ignoring more warnings from former officers and other East German officials of widespread violence that would happen if everyone knew who the Stasi people were, but not knowing what else to do, the Parliament member sent everything to West German authorities. In a West German state office, a comfortable distance away from Berlin, data on nearly 100,000 Stasi officers was converted into the more common dBase format and more copies made. Soon after, the leaks started.

Bits and pieces, including names from the list, started to filter out, but no widespread violence occurred. There were no angry mobs tracking down Stasi men. Why is an interesting question, considering what two generations of living in a police state had done to the victims.

It was less than a year after the Wall had fallen, and many Germans weren't sure what the result was going to be. Those with violence on their minds hesitated. Focused on new freedoms, few were shocked at first upon learning who the Grey Men were. If you lived in the East, you assumed that everyone worked for the Stasi, and that every telephone was tapped. Safer that way. As odd as that may seem, fear of that nature was one of the Stasi's most successful accomplishments, and one of the saddest aspects of their legacy.

Early one morning more than twenty years later, the same list landed in my email inbox with a digital thud. A German source, living outside Germany, had sent it. It was titled only *Stasilist*, and was a huge file. I soon understood why.

A thick report of more than four thousand pages, it listed the names, birthdates and final salary of more than 90,000 official employees of the Ministry for State Security as of January 1990. I had heard it existed, of course, but people didn't like to talk about it. The MfS wasn't behind the technology curve in 1989, and they were routinely using computers and magnetic tape, and had dozens of twenty-megabyte hard drives. That was more than enough in the 1980s, especially for personnel uses. Traditionally, payroll applications are among the easiest and most immediate tasks to be automated. Repetitive and predictable, perfect for those relatively early days of computing.

I scrolled through the pages randomly and did some simple searching of names I was already familiar with from my time circulating in the police and security agencies. Other than a few of the very top people, who I wouldn't expect to be present on such a list, others appeared neatly organized in alphabetical order. Some months later, I received a second list, from a different source. This one showed the identities of more than 2,000 Stasi officers who had been placed undercover in various institutions throughout Germany. The OibEs, Officers in Special Employment, who were all earning two paychecks, showed up in nearly every part of government, education and industry. Some of them were on both lists.

The lists, which were repeatedly validated over the years, are nearly impossible to find within Germany these days. Many Germans hold private copies, yet few will admit they do. Publishing the list on any German website results in exposure to a huge government fine under a German privacy act. Anyone who posted the 4,022 pages, even in part, or linked to them publicly, was relentlessly pursued in Germany by officers turned lawyers or others financed by former officers, emboldened by new privacy laws in the reunited country. Pursued not because the names on the list weren't accurate, but because they were.

When parts of the list do pop up, or a name from it, it's frequently disputed by those lawyers who claim that it's inaccurate. It might include non-MfS people, they say, maybe vendors or others and not necessarily employees, and so on. Enough smoke and mirrors to sometimes scare off the casual website owner or small publication. Inevitably, if it's important enough for a newspaper to visit the Stasi Archive to check, they will confirm a name from the list as having worked for the Firm. I conducted my own further validation, comparing the information in the file with known information from the official Stasi personnel files, and to the work of serious German researchers and media accounts. The Stasilist checked out every time.

It's fascinating and unprecedented reading. Nowhere else in a former communist dictatorship will anything similar be found. The same is true about the existence of 80 percent of the secret police files. In other countries in Eastern Europe, small numbers of files did exist, but generally were not made available to the public. In 2019, Latvia made news by announcing the new availability of informant files left behind by the KGB. But names of official employees? Never.

More than 90 percent of the 91,000 MfS employees were under the age of fifty in 1990, and a third were under the age of thirty-five. So, maybe they weren't all old men who went quietly off to collect their meager pension, as some would have us think. More than 60,000 Stasi officers went out looking for work in 1991. By the salary listed, it was possible to reliably infer the final rank of each individual.

The level of education of the younger generations of officers had been steadily increasing over the years. Comparing the names to their actual personnel files at the Stasi Archive, it's obvious they were generally well educated, many with advanced degrees, and all well trained.

The early years following unification were critical to reestablish confidence in the German state and head off possible security risks and divided loyalties. As an investigator, my immediate thought was: why hadn't both lists been immediately compared in total to employee information both inside and outside government by 1991, to quickly identify where the problems could be moving forward? There was really no good answer for that, and still isn't, other than many people didn't want to see the answer. Certainly, in government it was an extremely uncomfortable question, and a new influx of skilled people was blindly welcomed in Western industry. Merely having been an officer of the Stasi might not be an issue, but not having transparency about who was where and doing what certainly was. At best, and only when applying to work for German government organizations and certain public institutions, applicants were politely asked to check a box on a form:

Have you ever worked for the Ministry for State Security? Yes or No.

Not surprisingly, nearly everyone checked *No*.

Private businesses throughout Europe usually never asked at all, and were generally forgiving of vague references or gaps in the CV of a German candidate. No such question was asked of applicants for the new EU passports, or on visa applications. As a new German passport enabled visa-free access to America, some former officers took advantage of it and traveled to see the enemy.

Now, the Stasilist has disappeared into the internet underground. Of the people listed, the current estimate by a German expert is that approximately 71,000 were employed as Stasi officers as of January 1990, with the remainder being staff. And that doesn't include the thousands of other officers who counted themselves lucky to have retired from the MfS shortly before the fall, many who already had safe and fictitious CVs. In most cases, those in both groups were never later identified, except if by happenstance.

12

NOBODY REALLY WANTS TO KNOW

More than a year passed while Federal Commissioner Gauck got things in order at the Stasi headquarters and scrambled to secure all 111 kilometers of files in some fashion. Twelve suboffices of Gauck's Records Authority had to be opened to control files at the district offices, and hundreds of qualified people found in Berlin. More hiring was needed at once for the massive task.

Gauck quickly recognized one particular name on the stack of applications, and in January 1992 Hubertus Knabe received word that he had been hired as the lead researcher. That day was monumental for him. The timing was perfect as he had finished his doctorate months before. But he wasn't at all prepared for what he saw on his first day on the job when he entered the former MfS buildings at the Normannenstrasse complex.

'The Stasi ran the place! They decided what you could see!'

For Hubertus, seeing the new Records Authority still overrun with State Security employees when he walked in the door was a bitter shock. At the actual Archive building, located in Haus 7 where the files had always been, he had to make his requests to the Stasi workers. It was surreal. The Ministry for State Security had been officially disbanded for a year and a half. They weren't called Stasi employees anymore, but there were many of the same people controlling the files. Everybody else knew who they were. They were the ones who didn't need to display their identification to enter the building. His requests for documents as lead researcher were often viewed with open suspicion, questions or disdain.

He charged ahead anyway and immersed himself in his work. New procedures had been implemented to allow citizens to access the records, and there were many questions to be answered and research was needed to assist in investigations of the federal prosecutor. It was a new era in Germany – he sensed it.

Sitting at his desk early one morning at the BStU office in East Berlin soon after, Hubertus immediately formally requested his own Stasi file. One of the first to do so, he had waited twenty years for his own answers. After carefully filling out the form and sending it through to the Archive supervisor, all he could do was wait. As he plunged into his work at the File Authority, he couldn't help but be both excited and worried about what his own brown folder might contain.

Since he was a West German, and had never lived in the East, maybe there wouldn't be a file at all. Many of his colleagues from the West later learned they had none, and some others were mysteriously given empty folders.

Weeks passed, and he was now immersed in several projects. Then the phone on his desk rang.

'Your own file has been retrieved. Would you like an appointment to view it?'

So there was something after all. Hubertus tossed and turned the night before his day at the place they were calling simply the Reading Room. His stomach churned over what he might find there, or what he might not. He woke up in a sweat after dreaming of a woman wheeling in a zinc coffin filled to the brim with files.

Instead, when he walked into the room early that morning, he was handed one brown file folder containing 121 pages and bearing the name 'GLUE' on the front cover. That's when he learned the name the Stasi had given him. The monitor pointed to a desk and turned away.

Hubertus sat down and tentatively opened the cover, impatiently skipped the contents listing and turned to information first received from the informer:

18 June 1979:

Excerpt from the IM Klaus meeting. At our request the IM once again described the information provided.

On 6 June 1979, the person Hubertus KNABE, born in Unna, 19 July 1959, address Lübecker Str. 19, Bremen, phone 501463, celebrated his birthday with Annette.

He wants to come again to Annette on 16 or 23 June. He plans to bring banned materials hidden in his coat.

A few days later, IM Klaus again provided information and a detailed sketch of Annette's apartment.

It was an Operational Process, or OV, file that had been opened, a main investigative file that required a plan. Lieutenant Heinrich, Department XX, was assigned and immediately began writing reports detailing antisocialist activities. He suspected Glue was planning an 'enemy action'.

The detailed reporting by IM Klaus continued over the next months: '... Glue and Annette have become intimate...'

'Glue is a supporter of Rudolf Bahro...' Bahro, someone Hubertus looked up to, was a well-known dissident who developed a Christian faith while being held in prison.

Surveillance reports followed his every visit to East Berlin, all carefully prepared by Department VIII – Surveillance and Investigations. Department M, which handled mail interception, was tasked with providing special collection from the mailbox near Annette's apartment.

The final straw apparently came when IM Klaus reported that Glue was arranging for two suitcases of banned religious books to be provided to a church for distribution in October 1979.

Hubertus remembered that he and his friend and Pastor Frank Rudolph, who had offered to distribute the materials when received, did indeed drive to an address in East Berlin and received the two suitcases late one October night. They parked the car at Annette's apartment, leaving the suitcases in the trunk, and went upstairs. Hours later the car was mysteriously stolen.

He remembered fear as he huddled with his friend. 'What should we do? What does this mean?' It means *Run*, they agreed.

The three were in a panic and went in different directions. Hubertus returned uneasily to West Berlin, afraid for his friends. By December everything was still quiet – until Annette told him of two strange and unidentified men, whom she suspected were Stasi, who had knocked insistently on her door.

'Will Mr Knabe soon return? Will he bring more pamphlets?'

'I don't know when he will come,' Annette responded. She seemed terrified as she guardedly spoke to Hubertus on the telephone about the next visit when they planned to meet just after the New Year. But then, all seemed normal once again.

The file in January 1980 describes Glue as a 'courier for an enemy organization' and provides the plan. It was titled 'measures of decomposition'. The stated goal of the operation was simple:

'To prevent enemy activities.'

There were many possible solutions discussed. One might be simply separating him from the *citizen*, or *the theology student with a negative attitude toward socialism*, as they referred to Annette. But not quite yet.

The first step was to keep the books off the streets. It was the 'securing of the materials in the car' for which the credit was once again given to IM Klaus. The second was an immediate entry ban on Glue, which was already in place. The third was continued following by IM Klaus as needed. But it wasn't finished, and it wouldn't be closed. The file would be transferred to Department X, who handled liaison with other socialist intelligence agencies. Glue's activities, every movement on future trips to Prague and Budapest, would be tracked by those services and dutifully reported back to the Stasi in Berlin.

The OV file on Glue remained active and occasionally collected more documents for the next ten years. He'd been monitored even while in West Germany.

Hubertus walked out of the file room that morning shaken. The file contained intimate details about his relationship with Annette and her apartment. How?

There was a process in place at the Records Agency to learn the identity of an informant. He now had to make a different sort of request: to learn the identity of 'IM Klaus'. That would take more time. The possible answer bothered him.

Should he let it go? Perhaps yes, move on. What if...

No!

He stared at the brown folder on the desk in front of him. For some reason, large parts of his file appeared to be missing, as if someone had removed them. But why? Would he ever learn the answer to that? He returned the folder and filled out another form, this time requesting the file of IM Klaus.

Meanwhile, he plunged back into his work at the Records Authority, researching and writing reports. Would anyone ever read them? At the same time, it was hard not to be enthusiastic about the thought of justice in a reunited Germany. As head of research for the new authority he was busy hiring people and having long discussions about what should be done first. Sometimes there were arguments. The Stasi people roaming around looked at them all with suspicion. It was an awkward and uncomfortable time at BStU then. Besides his previous work at a publishing house while finishing his PhD, this was his first big job and had lots of possibilities. Possibilities not just for recording history, but for providing real transparency to those who had targeted hundreds of thousands of their own countrymen. It was a pivotal moment for all of Europe, he knew. Hubertus was so busy in fact that he didn't even realize two more weeks had already passed when he received the call.

The requested IM file is ready to view.

He had been one of the first to review his own Stasi file. Maybe he was also one of the first to see who had secretly reported on them.

After another sleepless night, he lay awake next to Annette before the second visit to the Reading Room. This time, a file stamped 'IM Klaus' was laid in front of Hubertus. Trembling, he opened the cover and immediately felt physically sick. He clutched the file, took a deep breath, paused and opened it again. The person responsible for him being investigated and banned was none other than his close friend and confidant, Pastor Frank Rudolph. Rudolph was 'IM Klaus'. Pastor Rudolph, who wanted the books. 'I need books!' he had told Hubertus. So, he smuggled the books for Pastor Rudolph. The banned books, hidden in the lining of his old coat. A twenty-year-old, taking risks far greater than he knew at the time.

Hubertus would soon learn he had also been reported on by at least three others close to him, including an East Berlin university professor who was also secretly employed as a Stasi officer. Only one of these people ever later called to apologize. For him it was that silence that was even more painful.

At least it wasn't Annette. It couldn't be. He wouldn't have survived that.

But both of them had confided everything to their pastor and were devastated to learn about the deception.

Hubertus saw clearly at that moment, sitting trembling in the Reading Room, the true evil of the Stasi, how easily they turned everyone against each other. He never forgot that lesson. It influenced his actions, and focused his determination. In fact, years later he would point to the bitter deception as something that made him who he had become. This was the true face of the Stasi, how easily they turned friends and family against each other!

But he would never consider himself to be a *victim* in any way. He hadn't served years in a jail and had his life destroyed, unlike hundreds of thousands of others. They were the ones now crying out for justice, he told anyone who asked. He might have been among them, if not for the courage of his parents. They gave up everything that day in 1959 when they grabbed their children and rushed across Berlin to get to the West before the inevitable happened. He didn't fail to thank them for that, for giving him the chance to be born in and grow up in freedom.

Hands shaking, he closed the file that was stamped *IM Klaus* and stood up. Now he had work to do.

13

DON'T ASK

'Yes! What do you want?'

It was eleven months since the Wall had fallen, and the busy director of personnel for Brandenburg Plant Engineering GmbH, a large and previously unknown commercial builder in Berlin, was sitting at his desk when he snatched up his phone on the first ring. It was a pesky reporter.

'Of course, we are new and did much hiring lately. What of it?'

The reporter scratched some notes, and had more questions. It seems that two months after the GDR collapsed, this particular new West German builder acquired 120 new employees overnight. They were unusually skilled in communications equipment, antennas, security systems and various other crafts. The company appeared delighted as they immediately gave them new uniforms and new clean personnel files and put the 120 to work installing telephone equipment in government offices.

The curious reporter pushed further. It seemed that nine months earlier, in March 1990, that particular company had been formed and swiftly spun off by the East Berlin Foreign Ministry. It was the same month that the MfS was dissolved. Until then the 120 employees had all been busy as officers of the Stasi, Subdivision NX, responsible for the penetration of security and telephone systems of foreign embassies in East Berlin.

The personnel director for Brandenburgische Anlagenbau, a company name that seems innocuous even with the name in English – Brandenburg

Plant Engineering – was dismissive and expressed irritated indifference. 'Business is booming now, and our people are highly qualified! Lots of work to be done!'

The useful chaos of 1990 enabled computers, vehicles, buses and specialized equipment of all sorts to vanish from MfS offices in those last days, mostly showing up in new companies. That was true especially for the people. A major Western real estate development company in Berlin, Olympia Construction, acquired a new managing director in the first few months of 1990. Hermann Mecklenburg had been a senior Stasi colonel until that January, and immediately went back to work leveraging his usual industry and government contacts as he had always done.

Another company popped up at the same time with even grander plans. Wigeba, a developer of automation technology, went from zero to nearly 1,200 employees in one day. Several hundred of those were transferred directly from the Firm's Operational-Technical Sector (OTS). The OTS and their 1,131 employees had been charged with providing covert technical surveillance equipment, false documents and chemical and photographic equipment among other things. The Wigeba managing director was silent and unhelpful when a reporter called and asked about it. 'I cannot spy on people based on what they did in the past,' he said before hanging up. Wigeba, which still operates, was later determined to have been created by two Main Departments of the MfS.

Immediately after the GDR ceased to exist, which officially was unification day, October 3, 1990, most Western companies cared even less to know anyone's past. The number of these people who spread out through Europe, the UK or United States in this way is unknown. What is known is that the rollout of the open borders of the European Union, which started in 1993, only made that far easier.

It was uncomfortable to ask such things anyway, especially in Germany, and if too many questions were asked a good recruit might well be scared off. Just because the Stasi no longer existed as an agency, and the GDR was also dead, it didn't mean the skilled people and their networks went anywhere. On the contrary, both networks were very busy. Rainer Engberding, the chief spycatcher and counterintelligence chief at the West German Federal Criminal Police, was clear about it when asked.

'One must assume that the foundations for many of these companies comes from the looted war chest of the MfS.'

While Treuhand, the agency set up to locate property and dissolve insolvent GDR institutions, toiled to uncover the shell companies, the Stasi-run businesses frequently took care of themselves. The Department for Foreign Intelligence – the elite HV A, which was already operating more than seventy front companies – set up a second network of more companies in 1990, weeks before the MfS ceased to exist. Business certainly was booming. When members of Treuhand finally received permission to enter the offices of the HV A at the Stasi headquarters in Berlin, which only months before had been filled with technology stolen over decades from the West, they found empty and bare rooms. Almost empty. One reporter found a discarded Russian-made camera.

———

Sometimes, not asking wasn't enough.

Mid-September, two weeks before unification, an urgent communication arrived at the West German Embassy in New Delhi. The message came from the Indian Ministry of Foreign Affairs and sought their comments. The trade attaché at the just-dissolved GDR Embassy there, Volker Gafert, had requested a long-term business visa in India for himself and his family members. They wished to stay in India. His stated reason was to 'conclude ongoing arms deals between India and the GDR' that, according to Gafert, were now being handled by a newly formed German company, Engineering-Technical Foreign Trade GmbH. The new company would see to the efficient and continued processing of five outstanding contracts with the GDR, including one for the delivery of 13,000 submachine guns.

A few gentle inquiries to Bonn by the West German Embassy determined that two of Gafert's business partners were former Stasi officers, also with their own new Berlin company, Vercoma GmbH. One of them, Klaus Ullmann, who is shown plainly on the Stasilist, had been most recently the liaison officer to the Palestine Liberation Organization (PLO). The other, Rainer Lehmann, had departed just in time. He retired in 1987 after serving last as the Stasi representative at the GDR Embassy in India. It appeared the soon-to-be unified German Foreign Office had unfortunately stumbled upon part of the MfS-led network aiming to sell off equipment of the NVA, the heavily armed GDR army. Gafert's company, ITA, was soon linked to a sister company in this effort and both were operated under the KoKo empire of another now well-known name – Alexander Schalck-Golodkowski. Everything was for sale, including weapons, ammunition, protective equipment and even tanks and aircraft. One company in the network was said to have been founded in the United States by former MfS officers.

The official response by the West German Embassy to the Indian Ministry of Foreign Affairs in New Delhi suggested they temporarily delay a long-term visa for Gafert. After unification, officially then only days away, many of the arms deals would be illegal under German law. Nonetheless, it's believed much of the military arms and equipment made their way before or after this to ultimate destinations such as Warsaw Pact countries and Cuba. An investigation was attempted and indications were that the network had developed new contacts with West German arms dealers also.

Many of these companies formed in 1990 can still be found. Today, Vercoma GmbH, established by former officer Ullmann, remains listed in Berlin. Its business is described vaguely as 'import and export'.

It became exceedingly easy for the Grey Men with connections, marketable skills and access to equipment or insider knowledge to disappear into this network of old friends. So, quite naturally, the most determined and ambitious of them did just that.

14

THE MANY

Yes, yes! I can help you. Come in!

It was almost too good to be true. More than 20,000 German political prisoners of the GDR were soon seeking legal advice to have their Stasi arrests removed from their records. Without that, it would continue to be hard to get jobs, passports and foreign visas. They needed help.

After unification, overnight there were many more lawyers around in Berlin to choose from. Few realized just how many of these new arrivals had been employed by the Stasi, and were not trained to represent people at all.

Even fifteen years later, in 2005, some 700 former officers were practicing as lawyers in Germany. The majority had received their legal education at the Stasi University in Potsdam, officially called the Law University of Potsdam, or JHS. The training received there was oriented fully toward facilitating the mission of the Stasi, their lifelong client. JHS was dissolved with MfS in 1990, as it no longer had a reason to exist.

The 700, who had numbered more than two thousand in the early 1990s, didn't advertise their backgrounds, and many clients may not have even known whom they were dealing with in their criminal or civil actions, or in whom they confided with private family matters. It's likely that some of the former political prisoners, who frequently paid for legal advice to have their records of political arrests rehabilitated, would have appreciated knowing whom they really had hired.

So how does someone whose only legal training was provided by the most repressive state security apparatus in modern history practice law in a free society? That's a very good question, more than one German lawyer later said to me.

More than 2,500 MfS officers were pronounced lawyers over the years at the Stasi law school. It was by what some say was a quirk of fate, and others insist was carefully planned and inserted into the unification treaty, that they all became entitled to immediately become lawyers in free Germany following unification. The legal systems were hardly similar. But in the rush to unify it was agreed that all college degrees awarded in the GDR would be accepted. More than 300 Stasi officers had also received doctorates, after completing dissertations that in no way corresponded to scholarly standards. Just like Alexander Schalck-Golodkowski, lieutenant colonel and head of KoKo – the MfS-led money-laundering operation – they could refer to themselves as *Doctor* in the new Germany.

On October 4, 1990, the day after German unification, Stasi officer Frank Osterloh was ready. He was well aware of something that most of the German public was not. As long as he was on the rolls of the MfS when it was disbanded at the end of the previous March, after unification only six months later, he could fill out some papers and easily transfer his Stasi law degree to the new Germany. He planned his new career to be more successful, and much more profitable than his last assignment as an interrogator at Hohenschönhausen prison. There he was known as a particularly relentless interrogator whose trademark was shouting at the prisoners in the small bare rooms.

He waited quietly those six months, and after October 3 signed the papers with a flourish and swiftly turned them in. It would be automatic. Only later would the public in both East and West Germany become aware of this clause in the rushed unification agreement that had been carefully negotiated by Stasi and SED officials. Another successful operation. Maybe the phoenix was already rising from the ashes?

Osterloh couldn't wait to start. He was well known in the ranks of scattered officers, and now the promise in the media of thousands of prosecutions meant money and attention for him. That would be followed by more money and more attention from the thousands of now former officers who had every reason to be concerned about being one of the targets. But Osterloh, and many of the other then more than two thousand Stasi-trained lawyers, knew something that was another quiet secret of the unification agreement. It would be extremely difficult to prosecute any officer for nearly anything. But prosecutors would try, the people were crying out for it. He knew that most cases would be unsuccessful, but meanwhile he would make a name for himself while earning a lucrative living, and be seen as a savior to his colleagues.

By the mid-1990s the loud and flamboyant Osterloh was becoming one of the most popular of the former officers turned successful defense lawyers. He found fame defending many Stasi officers, border guards who had shot young men at the Wall, and Communist Party officials against all sorts of criminal charges. He was very good at getting them off, mainly by claiming they had only done what the East German government demanded of them. They were following orders when they destroyed that person's life, or warehoused them in a prison. After all, it's not a crime under German law to have been an officer for the Ministry for State Security, he would say. In fact, under the GDR law, there were officially no political prisoners at all, he argued – they were all criminals. Therefore, any claim to being jailed as a political prisoner should also be dismissed.

Frank Osterloh had been a loyal member of the Communist Party for nine years before swearing the oath to the MfS on February 1, 1972, and held identification number 430039. He quickly achieved the rank of major, and went back to school at the Stasi University. His name appeared on a joint dissertation submitted with two other officers, a major and a lieutenant colonel, that concerned the fight against underground political activity.

He worked for Main Department IX – Investigations, the core of the Stasi's domestic apparatus, where he rose to the rank of lieutenant colonel while ultimately assigned to Hohenschönhausen.

For at least a dozen years to follow the end of the GDR, Osterloh the interrogator kept busy. He defended a half-dozen leading Stasi officers, including Lieutenant General and Deputy Minister Gerhard Neiber, who was charged in cases involving Red Army Faction terrorists, kidnapping and murder. In 2000, he was the lawyer for Manfred Ewald, the former head of the GDR Sports Ministry and Olympic Committee, who was charged with secretly administering anabolic steroids to more than a hundred children.

'I request the procedure to be terminated immediately!' Osterloh demanded loudly in court. 'Doping of minors wasn't a crime in the GDR!'

Ewald, formerly a member of the Hitler Youth, was convicted anyway in a rare loss for the popular lawyer, but received only probation.

Osterloh the interrogator continued his profitable new career as the defender of choice for Stasi officers and former political operatives of the SED Communist Party until his death in 2004.

———

Hubertus Knabe and many others saw some positive early signs of a reckoning coming from the legal system of the unified country.

The Berlin prosecutor general's office initiated 15,200 cases. In the five years following 1990 more than 52,000 investigations were started throughout Germany into allegations of murder, attempted murder, manslaughter, kidnapping, election fraud and perversion of justice. These investigations involved not only Stasi officers, but SED officials and border guards. There were even investigations of those judges and prosecutors who had arranged more severe sentences than normal to allow the MfS to ransom the prisoner to the West at a profit.

Maybe there would be some justice for the victims after all. Justice like that was generally absent following the Holocaust, when only a handful of Nazis were tried and convicted. Hubertus and his generation had seen many other former Nazis prosper in German society.

Since the statute of limitations for all Stasi violations except murder was five years under the law of the newly unified state, in 1993 a special law was passed extending the statute for the more serious crimes by another five years. But as part of that law, all nonmurder prosecutions would be banned after 2000.

Plenty of time, thought Hubertus Knabe and others focused on justice. There will be justice, victims were assured. Believe!

Klaus Kinkel, the minister of justice, had made it clear to Parliament in 1991:

'We must punish the perpetrators. This is not a matter of a victor's justice. We owe it to the ideal of justice and to the victims. All of those who ordered injustices and those who executed the orders must be punished; the top men of the SED as well as the ones who shot [people] at the Wall.'

Quickly, a problem emerged. Should these people be tried under the laws of the old or the new Germany? Since West Germany never recognized the GDR as a sovereign state, and considered West Germany the government for all of Germany, West German standards must be applied, many said. That conversation was over almost before it began, when someone pointed out yet another little-known clause in the unification treaty which stated:

The penal code of the GDR, and not that of the Federal Republic of Germany, shall be applied to all offenses committed in East Germany.

In most cases that was the 'get out of jail free card' for those Stasi officers who would have been convicted under West German laws or according to European and international norms. The state system of the GDR had been crafted, and fine-tuned, to allow the MfS to do virtually anything without worry and without the normal checks and balances that protect against abuse of police powers. The rationale used for that standard could easily have been used to protect the Nazi leaders following the Holocaust.

Other problems surfaced. The Stasi still had lots of secrets, and many in Western governments were wary. The enthusiasm of the victims soon began to falter too as many had the focus instead turned on them if they dared to tell their stories. They frequently became the ones who were scrutinized as many old comrades came up with increasingly familiar excuses.

When the dust settled, out of the 91,000 employees of the Stasi just 182 were charged with a crime committed under the communist dictatorship, and only 87 were ever convicted. Of those 87, just *one* was sentenced to prison. That former officer received only four years in jail for providing explosives to terrorist Ilich Ramírez Sánchez, who used them to attack the French Consulate in West Berlin in 1983. Today in Germany, most people don't know these numbers; it's an investigation in and of itself to dig them up. It's an uncomfortable fact.

Even Erich Mielke, the Master of Fear and the head of the Ministry for State Security, wasn't convicted for any Stasi-related crime. True, he was immediately arrested to prevent his escape in January 1990, on a quick charge of using government funds to renovate his hunting estate, but he wasn't ultimately convicted of that or anything to do with his forty-year career leading the MfS. He was convicted of the murder of two Berlin police officers, and the attempted murder of a third, which took place in 1931, long before the Stasi even existed. Mielke, then a member of the German Communist Party, assassinated the officers who were deemed anticommunist. After a witness implicated him soon after, he fled to the Soviet Union and there was recruited by the NKVD. In the Moabit prison visiting room in Berlin in the mid-1990s, Mielke was overheard to boast:

'If the Party had given me the task, then there would perhaps still be a GDR today. On that you can rely.'

He served about two years for the murders before being released.

At least 400,000 people in East Germany had their lives ruined by the actions of the MfS for political reasons. Out of more than 70,000 officers operating relentlessly until the end in the most repressive secret police the twentieth century had seen, just one of them went to jail. Meanwhile, the Stasi organizations complained loudly of *victor's justice* to deflect further investigations and attempt to redefine themselves as the real victims. Then, after there could be no more prosecutions due to the statute of limitations passing, they went on the offensive.

In an ironic twist, in 1993 Berlin became the city hosting the global headquarters of a well-known watch group, Transparency International. Their stated purpose is *to work together with governments, businesses and citizens to stop the abuse of power, bribery and secret deals.* Transparency International had located itself in a place that in many ways had become one of the least transparent places in the world.

Privacy is a fundamental right, begins the purpose statement of the Berlin Commissioner for Data Protection and Freedom of Information. Yet, in a place consumed with total privacy, it's easy to hide almost anything and anyone. The perpetrators benefit the most.

———

It was April 2002 and Mario Falke stood up from the table at his Munich flat, stretched and decided to check his mailbox downstairs. It had been a long afternoon updating a website he'd started a couple of years earlier as a place to discuss Stasi issues. He had a personal interest as he still reeled from being a prisoner of the communist machine. His website helped him to communicate with other victims; it was a sort of therapy that seemed to help.

Falke had been arrested, interrogated and imprisoned as a young man by the Stasi nearly twenty years before for spray-painting a pacifist message with a fairy-tale scene in a subway tunnel in Berlin. The court told him that he was 'irresponsibly overriding his social duties', and added that it was necessary to discipline him by means of state coercion to induce a fundamental change in his attitude toward conforming to social norms.

Convicted and sentenced to fifteen months in prison, he was ultimately ransomed to the West in 1987. Falke thought it was all behind him as he struggled for years to have a normal life in Munich. Then on April 1, 2002, he opened his mailbox and found a letter from an ominous-sounding agency, the Berlin Commissioner for

Data Protection and Freedom of Information. It threatened him with imprisonment and a fine of 250,000 euros. His website, on which he shared information about his case and his life with other victims, had committed an offense, it said.

At first, he assumed the letter was an April Fools' joke in poor taste, and set it aside. But then he noticed the letter writer, 'Dr Metschke', had given him a ten-day deadline to remove material from his site, and added, 'we reserve our own further action against you'. In lawyer-style threatening language the letter told him he had 'breached rules of data protection'.

Falke, suffering even then from sleep, circulatory and concentration disorders from his Stasi imprisonment, had always wanted to be an actor. Later, he became unable to hold onto his job as a mechanic. Like so many others, he was shocked when he saw his file in the early 1990s. It was two thousand pages; he was referred to by the code name *Anarchist*. He posted the information from his file with other Stasi-related links as continued therapy, and to inform other victims. His offense this time, in 2002? Posting a link to a US website that had on it a list of former officers. The list that had been created by the Stasi itself.

Intimidated perhaps more easily as a sickly forty-year-old than he was as a twenty-year-old, Falke quickly removed the link. He no longer updates his website. He learned later that former officers routinely filed this type of complaint with the Berlin Commissioner for Data Protection as a means of protecting their identities and keeping their background secret. A traumatized victim from Munich had just met one of the big hammers used effectively by still-active former officers. Privacy for Stasi officers wins over rights of the victims.

Without a similar special exception as contained in the Stasi Records Act, following unification it quickly became difficult to obtain any information about the current activities of the former political leaders of the communist dictatorship that was the GDR.

Personal privacy became fanatically paramount to the exclusion of political transparency. It's to be expected to some degree after

experiencing little privacy in the Nazi and communist dictatorships, but the scale has tipped far in the other direction. Privacy is
paramount! But privacy doesn't mean free speech is encouraged.
Article 5 of the German Constitution clearly guarantees freedom
of expression without censorship, something that wasn't possible
in the GDR. But in what other modern Western democracy can
you be fined if you click 'Share' on a Facebook post? That's exactly
what happened to a sixty-two-year-old woman in Berlin in 2017.
She absently shared a joke post that opposed unchecked migration in
Europe and sent it along to a friend. The woman was convicted under
German criminal code section 130, 'Agitation of the People', and
fined 1,350 euros. Later, she received death threats from Germany's
Antifa groups.

In today's Germany, Stasi victims like Mario Falke have learned that
there are at least three layers of legal protection for former MfS officers
who continue to hide their backgrounds: the Berlin Commissioner
for Data Protection and Freedom of Information administers the
Berlin Data Protection Act, the Federal Data Protection Law and the
new and even more onerous EU General Data Protection Regulation
(GDPR). With the passage of the GDPR in 2016, there are even
more pillars to hide behind. That EU law, which has some laughable
side effects – such as making it impossible for a kindergarten teacher
to take a class photograph – also further protects the perpetrators of
tyranny. Currently, the Federal Commissioner for Data Protection and
Freedom of Information is targeting content placed on Facebook and
Google in a very aggressive way. Many news sites and other webpages
in the United States are now inaccessible in Germany due to these laws.

It's doubtful that any of these were intended to provide protection
for Stasi misdeeds or perpetrators, but the former officers of the MfS
have gleefully embraced them. Suddenly – nobody knows exactly
when – it became controversial to identify a former officer in society.
When it has been done, it was haphazard or accidental. Politicians at
the federal level were vetted, but it was much easier to turn a blind
eye toward everyone else. Safer, too.

What of the laws for the victims? If not for the Stasi Records Act, administered by the BStU, it now would be nearly impossible to access the 111 kilometers of secret police files in Germany. But the BStU is itself feeling the heat – access has become more problematic, delays are much longer and future funding not assured. The Act clearly provides a continued means to access MfS records. But for how long? And what will happen if the Stasi organizations succeed in their efforts to have the BStU disbanded as a stand-alone agency? No one knows, but it certainly would harm attempts at transparency.

Berlin is often called the City of Remembrance. Tourists are commonly reminded of that. As one example, they are pointed to the impressive dome of the iconic Reichstag building, home of the German Parliament. It was rebuilt after the Cold War but this time with a glass ceiling. Absolute transparency of government the glass panels represent. But there continues to be less and less transparency about the Stasi and the communist dictatorship that existed there for forty years. *Personal privacy* seems to mean privacy at all costs, even for those who ran the most repressive police state ever seen in the modern world and other remnants of their communist dictatorship. For other places in Europe and the United States, in those countries which never confronted communism or were never victimized by dictatorships, a failure to comprehend that might be expected. But in Germany it remains curious that there seems to be a rush to forget once again.

For any tourist sitting in Alexanderplatz today, under the shadow of the Fernsehturm – the tall television tower – the contrasts are obvious, if they know to look. The tower itself, nearly identical to those erected in almost every Soviet surrogate state, was not only for television and radio traffic. It was intended as a symbol of the power of the communist dictatorship. If the tourist spoke to ten random Germans passing quietly by, and selected those who were over the age of fifty-five, most of them would have a clear understanding of communist tyranny – many would have been its victims. That's the clarity that privacy for perpetrators and their machine has sacrificed.

15

SURPRISES IN THE NEW GOVERNMENT

From the very beginning, when a driven and hopeful Hubertus Knabe returned to East Berlin to make a difference, there were clear and early warning signs for all to see. Some saw them sooner than others.

The first six months after all employees of the Ministry for State Security were officially terminated was a whirlwind. One television reporter was skeptical in September 1990. Taking the same Stasi payroll list that would be sent to me years later, he started looking up names and asking uncomfortable questions. It turned out that the director of the Committee for the Dissolution of the Stasi had a personal assistant who had been an MfS officer. That director, Günter Eichhorn, was approached on camera and appeared unconcerned when asked the question. Fifty percent of his personnel were later found to have been Stasi employees. Former MfS general Edgar Braun acted as the de facto head of the Committee. Director Eichhorn, continually worried that his own secret would be discovered, was hardly in a strong position to run anything.

The reporter pushed ahead, cameramen in tow. Former Stasi officers on the list were shown to be working at the Foreign Ministry, Academy of Sciences, Ministry of Foreign Trade, Ministry of Transportation and the Ministry of Interior (Police). Incredibly, the reporter also discovered that a former officer who specialized in political investigations was the new Head of the Department for Criminal Investigation of the GDR – formed to investigate Stasi crimes. The camera next accompanied the reporter throughout the former State Security headquarters. After speaking with Committee Director Eichhorn, the reporter roamed the hallways now occupied by the Committee members and quickly bumped into a former MfS lieutenant colonel sitting calmly at his old office desk, eating an apple. For this senior officer, little had changed, except he now carried identification of a member of the West German Federal Criminal Police. He proudly produced the ID card for the reporter when asked. Yes, his name was Schulz, he confirmed, Federal Criminal Police.

Helmut Schulz, an officious-looking man with greying hair and square glasses, calmly sat back down at the desk and resumed eating the apple. At first, he denied that he had been for years a Stasi officer, but the reporter persisted. Finally, shrugging and admitting his previous employer, he leafed through his payroll book showing his salary payments. Former MfS lieutenant colonel Schulz was vague when asked what he did at the moment, murmuring 'something working for the Dissolution Committee'.

'Can you still access the files now held at the Archive?' the reporter asked.

Standing with a slight smile, Schulz took a last bite from the apple and walked to the third-floor window, tossing the remnants outside before responding.

'Yes. Full access for the past nine months.'

He had full access to all Stasi files, which were being safeguarded by Eichhorn's mandate. Nothing had changed.

The Committee for the Dissolution of the Stasi, formed by West German authorities, was littered with such former officers. And they all had new identification that gave no clue to the worried citizen activists who theoretically controlled the compound. But likely even some of them were Stasi officers, since there was no screening at all for someone to say they were an 'activist'. The newly formed Committee operated with a staff of 261, more than half of which turned out to have been Stasi employees only months earlier. Many important files went mysteriously missing well into late 1990. Destroyed or taken.

Soon, Committee director Günter Eichhorn's own secret surfaced. He was publicly identified as a longtime Stasi informant, code name *Eagle*.

Meanwhile, other officers were transferred wholesale to police and other law enforcement roles, and business units of the MfS were spun off into private enterprises. This was a nagging problem that almost nobody had the time or the will to face. Reunification was the priority and putting everything else quickly into the past the goal. The 111 kilometers of remaining files and the thousands of sacks of shredded remnants wouldn't be in any shape to tell stories for years. For many of the 91,015 just-released members of the Stasi, this was an opportunity not to be missed. And it was about to get even better for some of them. That's because those with the jobs to hand out, in business, government and international organizations, adopted the basic approach of don't ask, don't tell.

———

There was a serious problem with the police, and Hartmut wanted to explain.

Almost immediately after I made my way up four flights of creaky stairs in a section of the city that's even older than most, to the apartment of a former Berlin police director, he told me, yes, they'd had a continuing problem with the Stasi. That problem lasted for years.

A trim man with a disciplined presence answered the door on the top floor and ushered me into his small living room.

Hartmut Moldenhauer was a high-ranking member of the West Berlin Police in 1989, and in charge of Operations and Deployment. On November 9, he was sitting in a restaurant having dinner with his wife when someone told him the Wall was open. He put down his fork, but quickly dismissed such a ridiculous thought.

'I didn't believe it until I heard it on the car radio and later turned on the TV,' he said as we settled into comfortable chairs in his flat, which was filled with the usual police memorabilia of photographs, awards and symbols of rank.

'It was then I called and ordered them to send policemen immediately to our side. To keep things from getting out of hand.'

Up until that point the West Berlin Police had had few dealings with the Volkspolizei, the People's Police in the East. There was some rare interaction on specific criminal matters, but generally none at the professional level. And the two departments had far different training standards.

'Most of the Vopos the West German police ever saw were when they pulled us over on the autobahn transit corridors. They were heavy-handed and usually had a bad attitude.'

Since West Berlin was a walled-off island in the sea of East Germany, the autobahn connecting it to the rest of West Germany was all in East German territory. Western right of passage on this highway had been guaranteed since the end of the war, except when it was cut off for nearly a year in 1948 by the Soviets, who were trying to strangle West Berlin with a blockade. That caused the famous Berlin Airlift, a massive air effort by the United States and the Allies that successfully supplied the entire West Berlin population with the necessities until Stalin gave up. Hartmut understood all of this. He was born and raised in East Germany, even joining the Communist Free German Youth organization. That was a requirement if you hoped to go to the university. He passed the entrance exams, but on a whim, when he was eighteen, he decided to move to West Berlin. By luck that was in 1960, a year before the Wall was suddenly erected, sealing the border. He joined the West Berlin Police in 1962 as a constable, a street cop. He did well and worked his way up through the ranks to lieutenant colonel.

'Of course, we had no idea really what was going on when the Wall fell,' Hartmut said, pouring glasses of water. 'Would it go back up the next week? How many Stasi were coming over with the flood of East Berliners? What would happen? It was especially risky at the section of the Wall near the Brandenburg Gate; if there was to be a military crackdown it would be there. It's the most symbolic place. We held our breath and waited.'

He pointed at a train crossing sign plastered on his wall. 'I didn't steal that. You can buy them, you know. I like trains.'

A smile flickered.

'By the end of November, we started establishing direct communication. A special phone line from the West Berlin Police to the East, which had been cut forty years earlier, was reconnected. By January everyone knew that the GDR was finished for good, and a few months later we realized that the entire East German government would go away under plans for unification. What would we do? How could the West German police force handle East Berlin chaos, not to mention the similar things going on throughout East Germany?'

Shrugging, he held his water glass up to the light. 'The short answer was, we knew we couldn't.'

I nodded. The thought of unifying the two halves of Germany, one part communist and the other capitalist, and doing it in just nine months, is still unbelievable.

'What about the Stasi?' I asked him. 'What were they doing?'

'We didn't care about them at that point, as long as they didn't end up in our police department.' Hartmut stood and took a few nervous steps. 'We were too overwhelmed to care about anything else. The government informed us that as of October 1, 1990, all law enforcement responsibilities for the entirety of East Berlin would be ours!'

'So, we wanted to absorb all twelve thousand Volkspolizei immediately, but couldn't. We offered jobs to about ten thousand. The others were higher ranking and thus assured to be also working for State Security, or connected to the 1,200 charged with watching the foreign embassies in East Berlin. We knew those were all Stasi!'

Hartmut sat back down, and it was obvious the thought of these things stressed him, even after thirty years.

'The training was far different between the two departments as well. In 1990, the West Berlin Police were a well-trained European organization. Police officers were trained for three years before they were allowed on the street, and followed the legal framework in policing. The Volkspolizei, on the other hand, had typically received only four months of training, and most of that was politically oriented.'

'How long did it take you to find out who the Stasi officers or the informants were in the ten thousand?' I asked, imagining the chaos.

'About eight to ten years.'

'Years?'

'Yes, we had it pretty well cleaned up by 2000 actually. We fired them when we found out.'

So, for nearly ten years police who were either direct Stasi officers, or those who had signed a loyalty oath to the Stasi, were doing police work while wearing the uniform of the unified Berlin Police. We both sat quietly for a moment and thought about that. Hartmut poured more water from the bottle. I took a sip, and then asked the difficult question that we were both thinking:

'Did anyone go back to look at the investigative work those fired officers had been involved in since 1990? Reviewed their activities?'

He drained his glass in one gulp and stared at it gripped in his palm. The answer was a difficult one for Hartmut, and one that neither one of us wanted to hear. He finally gave it:

'No.'

Both of us knew the issue with that. I glanced over at the baton and old Prussian-style police helmet on display by the door and decided to follow up differently.

'What was the highest-ranking officer you accepted from East Berlin?'

Hartmut scratched his head, and then he chuckled softly. 'That's… a very good question.' We both looked at the model trains mounted on the wall until he spoke again.

'Generally, I decided it would be no higher than lieutenant. But the higher-ups, they decided to accept a Volkspolizei major! He was in charge of all criminal investigations in East Berlin. We took him just for political reasons, but all of us on the operational side, well, we laughed to ourselves at the time. No way he wouldn't be Stasi!'

'And...?'

A shrug. 'They found his file a year later, and he was fired.'

'What about in Brandenburg?' I asked.

'They had even more problems.'

In the German federal state of Brandenburg, which encircles Berlin, in the mid-2000s there were still nearly three thousand former Stasi officers employed, mostly in the police. More than one hundred worked in the prosecutor's office alone. In 2009, two members of the security detail for Chancellor Angela Merkel were identified as former MfS officers then attached to the Brandenburg Police Department. The two were assigned to guard her house. One of them had worked with wiretaps for the Stasi for ten years. In the ensuing investigation it was determined that fifty-eight former officers remained employed at the state prosecutor's office. At the time, even the BKA – the Federal Police – admitted they still had twenty-three such persons.

16

UNCOMFORTABLE QUESTIONS

'Why are the shredders and that big pulping machine running?' the young activist at Haus 1 of the occupied MfS headquarters repeatedly asked one Monday in April 1990 to anyone who would listen. 'Who's in charge?' The response was only a shrug.

Most of the remaining Stasi employees were officially terminated from the AfNS, the short-lived successor agency, in January and February 1990, and the MfS/AfNS itself no longer existed on paper after March 31. That's the official account. But many who were there still don't believe it.

Files and electronic media, including backup tapes of Stasi computerized files, were being destroyed throughout most of 1990, in spite of direct orders not to do so. Who was in charge? It was concluded nearly seventeen years later, after a detailed investigation, that even though the Stasi had ceased to exist in March 1990, they'd controlled the files until at least that October in 1990 and continued to selectively destroy and remove files. Exactly what they destroyed nobody knows for sure.

The Office of the Federal Commissioner, called BStU by some and the Stasi Archive by others, took over the responsibility on October 3, and was immediately faced with a huge task. Miles of files, 18,000 bags of torn or shredded documents, and the 'artifacts', as they referred to left-behind Stasi tools, objects, statues of Lenin and such. Brown-jacketed files not only filled up nearly two large buildings at the Berlin Stasi headquarters, but were also in all of the fifteen district offices around East Germany. With such a task, to deal with six million files and hundreds of millions of pieces of files, and do so together with a rush to hire hundreds of staff in a short time, it was chaotic to say the least. With chaos, of course, comes opportunity for some. Of the first fifty-two employees of the BStU, eleven were eventually found to have been former MfS members.

The first federal commissioner for the agency, Joachim Gauck, was well respected. He was a former activist who would later become the president of the unified country. A year later, when the number of BStU employees had swelled to 500, Gauck was asked if any MfS people remained. He thought about it and took what some thought at the time was a pragmatic approach:

'We need the Stasi people for a short time to show us how to find things in the records.' He assured those uncomfortable with the idea that there were 'about fourteen such people'. The fact that there were far more, and they continued to be there for a far longer time, wouldn't be admitted until years later. Some are there even now.

Many saw the problems even then, but few spoke about it. The new employees of the BStU immediately noticed it seemed odd that they were required to show ID to enter the buildings, but the Stasi workers were not. The buildings were also occupied by the watchdog Citizens' Committee, the group that originally formed loosely during the Peaceful Revolution of 1989, which anyone could easily join. Eighteen Stasi people were later identified to be among its members.

Too many empty file jackets were being found. Were they empty before or after the Records Agency assumed control? Stasi officers still had access to the files – there was no dispute about that. One who had been caught trying to sell information was fired.

An internal BStU report about the influence of officers in the Archive was finally written years later. Its 116 concise pages are marked *confidential*, and clearly show the problem. Not only had the miles of files remained under the full control of Stasi officers until October 1990, some officers had stayed on for years longer. That was a fact that few outside the agency were aware of. This confidential study, titled *Report on the Employment of Former MfS Members of the BStU*, immediately showed that the number mentioned by the first agency commissioner of 'about fourteen' was wrong at the time – there were five times as many. It contained other surprises.

In 1991 the real number of Stasi people employed by the BStU was sixty-seven full-time officers and five IMs – informers. They also identified and removed six more IMs and one more undercover Stasi officer. In addition to those, a large number of employees had previously worked for other GDR government agencies.

Fifteen years later, there were still fifty-six former Stasi employees working at the Archive; forty-two of those were former officers. Much of this had been withheld from the public and the German Parliament. The former officers had a variety of functions then, including the reconstruction of files, law enforcement and victims' issues, and even maintaining the computers. Two of them, a Stasi colonel and a lieutenant colonel, had been frequently assigned together to conduct special research with full file access. Anonymous BStU employees said the two had removed files. Once, their assignment was to prepare a special report after the September 2001 terrorist attacks. The subject was to determine the extent of MfS support for terrorist organizations. Their conclusion in March 2002 was '… there were hardly any connections or support…' That was roundly laughed at, as many other studies had confirmed the active support of the Stasi for Arab and leftist terror groups, including the RAF (Red Army Faction), who conducted attacks within German territory, and Palestinian terrorists such as Abu Nidal, only a few years before the Wall fell.

The final conclusion of the confidential report advised:

'Almost all former MfS staff in the early years of the Authority, as well as other BStU employees, had the possibility to abuse access. They were able to alter, misrepresent, or destroy files, or smuggle them out.'

Twenty-three years later, there were still thirty-seven former Ministry for State Security employees found to be working for the

Archive. Thirty years after the fall, in 2019, 'about five' former officers of the Stasi remained employed there.

The victims, and nearly everyone else, had uncomfortable questions.

What was the result of the continual employment of former MfS officers by the agency that was created to safeguard the sensitive files and deal with victims seeking truth? Nobody could say.

———

Hubertus Knabe worked hard at the Records Agency those first years. He kept late hours and buried himself in the issues even later, but Annette seemed to understand. Diving eagerly into research projects and other assignments, he was seeking answers, not only historical facts and figures. Some there grumbled that he was a bit too persistent in dealing with obstacles and never hesitated to unmask members of the new government who had been secret police informers. The agency quickly ballooned to over five hundred employees, and then more than one thousand as many more requests were received for file access. Those numbers helped hide the hundreds of former Stasi employees who remained working there.

There were a billion pieces of paper in the brown-jacketed folders. Who would know if some important pages went missing?

Hubertus was of the generation of Germans who in their youth had watched people in government continually surface who had connections to the Nazi regime. They were able once again to hold high office despite the crimes of National Socialism. With the collapse of yet another German dictatorship that also claimed socialist ideals, this one on the left of the political spectrum, he sensed nearly immediately that the same thing was happening. The methods of the Nazis – harsh repression, control and belittlement – were the same tools wielded by the Stasi. The obvious difference was that the Nazis only lasted twelve years; the communist dictatorship was in place for forty.

Hubertus began to realize that people of the communist government were being treated much differently in unified Germany than

the Nazis ever were. There were no foreign powers holding trials for
the most serious offenders; in fact, as the mid-1990s passed it became
apparent that few MfS officers or their leaders would be convicted
of any crimes at all. Hubertus wrote passionate warnings that if the
same standard had been applied to the Nazis, perhaps the Waffen-SS
and their superiors would have been deemed innocent also? There
were no pensions for the Gestapo, but the Stasi officers insisted they
were just deserving government workers who had earned lifetime
public support.

His writings and speeches began to distinguish him as an advocate
for the rights of the hundreds of thousands of silent victims of the
communist state. Papers he wrote, such as *Overcoming the Past by Law?*
and *Opposition in Half a Country*, started appearing in the first part of
the 1990s. Unlike the more typical historians in Germany, who even
today carefully limit their writing to academic topics, Hubertus Knabe
was always also speaking of current matters. He was asking, why are
the rights of informers and perpetrators more important than those
of the victims? He asked that question again and again. Some people
didn't like it.

As he saw all of this unfold, he sensed that there would be no
accounting of any substance in the unified Federal Republic of
Germany. Hubertus later called the early 1990s 'dark times'.

The newly unified Germany hadn't had such a chance since the
1930s. All of these questions deserved to be asked – they demanded
attention – shouted the press and public opinion at first. Still working
at the BStU, but becoming increasingly frustrated in the confines of
the rigid hierarchy of a now massive Records Agency, he was targeted
by a whispering campaign. Many continually thought he was over-
stepping his bounds as a researcher, even as lead researcher. He was
acting as an investigator, a Stasi hunter, a prosecutor, they whispered.
Who does he think he is?

Thankfully, in late 1999 a solution presented itself for everyone.

It had been finally decided that the languishing and infamous
Stasi Berlin prison for special political prisoners, called simply

Hohenschönhausen because of the neighborhood it secretly dominated, would become an official foundation with social funding. That
foundation needed a director to make it into something. Hubertus
Knabe would be perfect for the position, some thought. Others
expressed relief that at least he would be kept busy there and away
from the issues of the Records Agency. A safe place, with no records.
Only empty cells. A nice museum maybe.

Hubertus jumped at the opportunity. He had his own ideas of
how Hohenschönhausen must live in the public memory – it must
be a powerful place of clarity and focus. If anything, he now would
write even more about the dangers of the remnants of the communist
state, and make the tired Nazi and Stasi prison something that people
would visit in the process.

So, one morning after New Year's Day 2000, Hubertus Knabe
walked down Genslerstrasse in the Hohenschönhausen district, past the
neat and tidy homes of MfS officers in the area, and through the barred
gates into the tired former Nazi, Soviet and Stasi prison. He carried
a small box of personal items and a few files under his arm and got to
work at once with a tiny staff. The longtime commandant of this place
and head of MfS detention apparatus, Colonel Siegfried Rataizick,
lived even now nearby, one of the few staff members told him.

Hubertus had a plan to craft Hohenschönhausen into something
more than the quiet museum that most expected. He wouldn't create
a museum after all, but a *memorial*. It had been the main and largest
of the seventeen Stasi-run prisons. From 1990 it had at first served
as a normal prison again, briefly and symbolically holding Minister
Erich Mielke. In 1994 it was first opened as a museum but only seven
thousand people came the entire year. It stood in a remote location
and wasn't yet developed for visitors. Hubertus saw the potential
for the place, as somewhere to make sure people didn't forget. He
immediately got busy restoring the prison to be as it was when the
Stasi operated it. The 120 interrogation rooms, the hundreds of
austere cells, even the 'submarine', a cold, dark place in the basement
also called the 'U-boat', having special sensory-deprivation cells that

had been used to break the unbreakable prisoners. Next, he secured funding to hire actual victims, former prisoners who could find some personal solace in giving tours and reflecting the true human suffering that had happened here. He would pay them for their time; it was the right thing to do, although many would have done it for free. For those who didn't wish to, or couldn't relive it face-to-face, he arranged for trained historians to compile audio, video and written victims' statements. Their stories of imprisonment, interrogation and mental anguish must not be lost to time. The excesses of the communist dictatorship must be remembered. They would be real, and shocking.

A professional website was developed and outreach to schools and victims' groups was started. He himself spoke at many events and hosted victims' meetings at the Memorial.

Things rapidly started to pay off. Hohenschönhausen, long a place of quiet torment and despair, quickly began to be a major destination for groups of visitors wishing to see the true face of the Stasi and the dictatorship it protected.

The first activity report, written two years later by Director Knabe, showed the results:

Over 100,000 visitors.

———

It was late in the day that the phone rang on Director Knabe's desk at the Memorial. It was someone at the BStU. They were investigating the Stasi employees at the Records Authority and planned to write an internal report. About time, he thought. He wanted those answers himself.

What was his feeling about the fact that even now there were still fifty-six former Stasi members at the Records Authority, they asked. Fifty-six?? Even now, years later? He answered directly, as he usually did.

'These persons must be removed. They could deal directly with victims!'

He went back to expanding the reach of the Memorial, and writing about not just history, but the remnants of the GDR in unified Germany. It was a dangerous thing, he knew. Soon, the problems started. Hubertus had expected it – lots of MfS officers lived around the prison. Many sometimes privately referred to the area still as 'Stasi-town'. Once, in 2006, he hosted a panel discussion at the Memorial and 200 former Stasi officers showed up. When anyone who was remotely critical of the communist regime spoke up publicly, they rose up loudly and violently.

Some of these men had worked interrogating and playing the psychological games they were so well trained to do. He suspected the four or five associations of former officers were behind things, and knew they were watching him.

As executive director of the Memorial, Hubertus was criticized for allowing former inmates to give the tours; it was offensive to those in the neighborhood, some said. One of the former inmate tour guides, Mario Röllig, responded that he wasn't a historian but was necessary to be 'a needle in the red flesh'.

The cornerstone Hubertus dedicated at the restored Memorial following the completion of the restoration reads:

To the Victims of the Communist Dictatorship

The neighbors complained again. Who was Director Knabe anyway, someone who grew up in West Germany, to use this place to condemn communism? The Stasi organizations were now focusing on him. They began to criticize him by name on their websites and through some sympathetic media outlets.

Hubertus was under siege, and knew it. He decided to fight back any way he could.

The time of the revisionists was starting. 'Be careful!' colleagues and family cautioned him.

His response was to take steps to again double the number of visitors who would see the truth at the Hohenschönhausen Memorial.

By 2008, a quarter of a million visitors a year would pass through the gates, many of them student groups. The Memorial had become one of the most successful places of remembrance in Germany.

At night and on weekends Hubertus shut himself in his small study, and with thanks and apologies to an understanding spouse, he continued to write. He was determined to expose connections of the Stasi and the other communists to the current German state. The GDR-ruling SED Communist Party had legally changed its name in 1990 to the Party of Democratic Socialism (PDS), and then merged into a new political party called The Left, which was gathering influence. He was also writing about that. Wait, what happens in the present isn't history, some told him. He should be a *historian* not a prosecutor, others said among themselves. Others who had power in today's Germany were angered.

But he had decided something long ago. Perhaps it happened when he was that frightened young man standing at Friedrichstrasse checkpoint being refused entry to East Berlin, or maybe later when he saw how lightly the Stasi and the communist regime was being treated. Whenever the exact moment was, Hubertus was clear now on what he must do. Some things are more important than academics, some things must be said directly and openly, and must not be allowed to be hidden away in silence. He was convinced that was bigger than the country, even larger than Europe.

17

THE LAST OFFICIAL MEETINGS OF THE FIRM

It was an operation that was shrouded in secrecy in the expected Stasi tradition. They were meeting with the Master of Fear.

On a warm June afternoon in 2000, more than a decade after the MfS was officially disbanded, dozens of the former senior-ranking officers made their way quietly to a location only a short distance from their former headquarters in Berlin. In charge of the clandestine event that day was Stasi officer Hubert Hunold. He had been careful to invite only the most trusted ones, and to tactically leak the possibility of the meeting to the press via back channels, but with the wrong date mentioned. Those invited were only informed by telephone at the last minute of the actual time and place of the meeting. Hunold had kept previous meetings secret in similar ways. Today, it very nearly worked once more. They were here this time because of a man named Müller.

Over one hundred, mostly men, arriving from different directions, made their way down a carefully tended but damp path, occasionally nodding at each other. It was familiar territory, here in the Lichtenberg borough that contained Hohenschönhausen, the Berlin district heavily populated by former Stasi officers and still referred to by some as the neighborhood of the colonels.

June 10, the terse final call had told them. The selected people arrived promptly and filtered in without speaking. They stood loosely under the trees at a place first created by the Soviets in 1945 and called proudly the Memorial to the Socialists. The heavy tree cover blocked most of the sun, and the foliage and damp silence added an air of heavy shadow and privacy.

Minister Erich Mielke, who always preferred to be called 'Comrade Army General Mielke', had done his part for today as well. He had died two weeks earlier, on May 21, but even that had been kept secret until four days after. Mielke lived his final days and passed on living under the alias of Herr Müller. The Master of Fear, the longest-serving State Security chief of the Eastern Bloc, responsible for the imprisonment of 200,000, the death of thousands, the destruction of hundreds of thousands of lives in other ways and the failure of countless dreams, died in bed alone in an old-age home.

The group of grim Stasi men stood now in what's also called Friedrichsfelde Socialist Cemetery. They spoke in hushed tones under the fir and linden trees, as they searched the crowd carefully for any unknown face. A red flag fluttered in the breeze on the outdoor table as the dapper grey-haired General Willi Opitz, former head of the MfS training school, stepped up to speak. As he did, an uninvited and overlooked man standing near the back of the crowd casually slipped his hand into his jacket pocket and flipped on a small recorder.

'The life of Erich Mielke has been completed. But in the hearts of his family members, in the memories and thoughts of his comrades and friends, Erich Mielke, our minister, lives on.'

It was a long speech in the communist way, incredibly crediting Mielke as the architect of today's free and united Germany. It was Minister Mielke, Opitz claimed, who suggested the lifting of travel restrictions in 1989 and who later issued the order in the end not to shoot the demonstrators. The audience murmured and nodded.

Opitz continued, describing how Mielke was a great defender of socialism, and quoting the founder of the Cheka, Felix Dzerzhinsky, who was the special favorite of Mielke and the foundation for the KGB.

'As he repeatedly told us, a Chekist can only be a man with a cool head, a warm heart and clean hands. He must be clear as a crystal!'

He paused to allow more approving comments from the crowd and then continued, mentioning Karl Marx and Lenin along the way.

General Opitz finished with a solemn promise:

'I assure you in the name of yours, the faithful to our cause, that we always honor your life and your struggle. We vow to faithfully continue to work for social justice and peace, to face up to lies, and to persist in our convictions. To serve the truth. I say this in full agreement with all those people who, with their heads up and not their hands, face the demands of the present convinced of a socialist and peaceful future.'

Former lieutenant general Gerhard Neiber, who had been in charge of the core eight Main Departments of the Stasi until 1989, stepped up next. He silently snapped a slow, smart salute to the container on the table in front of him. The bronze urn had no inscription.

The group stood together talking for some time as the urn was buried discreetly without any marker. Then they disappeared in different directions through the trees and between the other more traditionally marked headstones of well-known communists.

The person in the back followed for a short distance. Then, he returned on the path past the grave and stopped. The man had turned off his recorder now and hesitated when he noticed that an expensive floral wreath had appeared at the grave. The straggler bent down and searched for something.

Ah, there.

The card read simply:

From the friends and veterans of the KGB.

The site, near the Memorial to Immortal Fighters for Socialism and the gravesites for the founders of the German Communist Party, Karl Liebknecht and Rosa Luxemburg, was vandalized later that night.

Today, the Memorial to the Socialists remains a heavily shaded and eerily damp place of whispers. Everyone knows it's where the communists are buried, and it's popular as more of the older guard fade away and are placed with their comrades. It's the welcoming soil of the former East Germany.

The gravesite of Stasi minister Erich Mielke is still unmarked, and the flowers remain fresh.

Seven years later, in mid-November 2007, they gathered once more. It was their chance to change history.

More than ninety former MfS officers and supporters stepped on specially chartered buses in Berlin and headed north. The buses were supplied quietly by a successful retired East German turned Berlin transportation company tycoon operating as Dr Hermann Travel, who started in 1990 with a single bus which was previously owned by the MfS.

Perhaps two-thirds of the men who stepped onto the buses that morning had been key members of the Stasi foreign spy apparatus, the HV A. The others were high-level officers from other departments. The MfS prison chief Colonel Siegfried Rataizick took his place and chatted animatedly with the others. The generals and colonels were afforded proper deference. Three revisionist Stasi groups were well represented. There had to be two buses to carry them all.

Both buses merged smartly together onto the autobahn and accelerated en route to Odense, Denmark. It would be a little more than a six-hour drive, north toward Hamburg before crossing the Danish border near the small German town of Flensburg. It wasn't a holiday. They all intended to set the record straight.

Everyone on the buses would naturally have preferred to do this in Germany and planned to do so, but there were problems. Attempts to hold such an event, billed as a historical conference, in Berlin the previous summer had failed, as none of the usual German institutions would agree to participate, following a public outcry. And the date that they'd selected turned out to be June 17, the anniversary of the brutal crushing of an uprising in the GDR in 1953, during which fifty-five people were killed and 10,000 were arrested.

Seventeen years after the most feared secret police of the twentieth century dissolved, Germans were not quite yet in the mood to hear excuses and serious attempts at revisionism.

So, with funding and an offer from the University of Southern Denmark, the Stasi officers traveled. One German historian also went, to be present as an observer. He traveled separately.

As the buses rolled into Odense, the group took charge in true Stasi fashion. They carefully ensured that all members of the Firm were comfortable together in one hotel, while other attendees – especially the press – were sent to another. As the meeting began on Friday, November 16, the hope of the Danish historians that it would be some sort of reckoning for the ruthless tactics of the MfS, such as the use of the Romeos, and involvement with terrorist organizations like the PLO, RAF and Red Brigade, faded fast.

The senior officer present, Ralf-Peter Devaux, strode briskly to the podium and read a statement from General Werner Grossmann, who had been in charge of all Stasi spies during the 1980s.

'We didn't carry out *coups d'état*, murders or kidnappings as other secret services did. We didn't work with terrorists.'

The statement continued, '… We were peace scouts!'

The assembled Stasi men, many in coat and tie, clapped.

Even though the bulk of the HV A files were shredded in December 1989, by 2007 the actual history of the MfS's role in foreign operations was pieced back together and well enough known. They had fostered a close relationship with both Iran and Iraq, the RAF, Red Brigade and Venezuelan turned Palestinian terrorist Ilich Ramírez Sánchez. Sánchez, or Carlos the Jackal, remains one of the most prolific terrorists of the 1970s. Sánchez, who is now serving three life sentences in France, was a frequent guest of the Stasi in East Berlin in the 1980s.

The Romeo project was one of which the leader of the HV A, Markus Wolf, had always been proudest. Recruiting young and good-looking East German men, they targeted lonely secretaries in the West. After a whirlwind romance, the women would be asked for information. At least fifty women in Western government service were compromised in that way. Sometimes they used homosexual Romeos in the same fashion, but with a simpler goal of photographing and later blackmailing the hapless victims. The project was a specialty of the Stasi.

The assembled group of former officers, including eleven generals and colonels, took the opportunity of the conference, and the passive audience who didn't challenge them, to claim that the Ministry for State Security had done nothing wrong at all. They set the agenda and decided who would speak, even who could ask a question. They dominated the event, quickly shoving aside any member of the press who asked an uncomfortable question.

'You have no idea what you're talking about!'

A press representative called the men 'self-confident and aggressive'.

Ralf-Peter Devaux told anyone who would listen that weekend that he was 'proud of his service, and the outstanding results'.

The guilt of the 'imperialist West in the Cold War' was then enthusiastically discussed.

In their eyes they were representing the GDR and all of Germany at that event. With no participation from any current German government or intelligence agencies, there was no one to challenge that view. It was the opportunity they had been waiting for. The deputy mayor of Odense even hosted a formal dinner for the group, just like the old days. The Stasi was once again in all its glory, and Germany was silent. The ranking men made a long statement of thanks to the deputy mayor, in the style of communist diplomacy.

One of the outsiders who was there described the scene as having little to do with the hoped-for historical research at all; instead there was only self-justification. Ninety men who put on a coat and tie, once again intent on justifying their Stasi careers, and renewing their old contacts. It was observed by another that few historians were present, and those there were forced into the background by the self-confident and aggressive Stasi men. The sole German historian at the conference didn't participate. He represented only himself he was careful to say, before afterwards commenting privately: 'Our fears that this is not a suitable forum have more than been confirmed.'

A spokesman for the Stasi Archive who was contacted later was more direct:

'These old Stasi generals have no idea of what they have done. For them it is about acquitting themselves and fighting over who was at fault.'

When Hubertus Knabe's phone rang at the Hohenschönhausen Memorial and he was asked for a comment, he was incredulous and the most direct of all:

'It would be like inviting Osama bin Laden and his followers to a conference on terrorism,' he said.

For the ninety Stasi men, satisfied as they climbed into the two sleek and modern buses for the trip back to Berlin, their mission was once again accomplished. Network together and plan like before. All without being confronted with the hard questions.

There has never since been a similar event held publicly – the Stasi officers were satisfied. They had done what was needed.

Curiously, the University of Southern Denmark, a public university and the event host, keeps quiet. More than ten years later they declined to provide the recordings made of the public presentations at the meetings, photos taken or even a meeting agenda. They cited privacy that the Stasi officers are entitled to under the recent European General Data Protection Regulation (GDPR), and said they feared a large fine.

18

POLITICIANS

Many remember it as the day Wikipedia was turned off.

If you were among the millions of users of Wikipedia in Germany on November 13, 2008, you were in for a surprise. A member of parliament and former Stasi officer had it shut off. Instead of the familiar welcome page, this note appeared:

> By means of a provisional injunction of the regional court Lübeck on the 13th November 2008, brought by Lutz Heilmann, MdB (Left Party), the registered association Wikimedia Germany is forbidden to forward the website Wikipedia.de to the website de.wikipedia.org, as long as the website de.wikipedia.org reproaches Lutz Heilmann of certain statements. Until further notice, the offer on Wikipedia.de in its previous form must, therefore, be stopped.

Lutz Heilmann, a member of the Bundestag from the newly named Left Party, accomplished that by filing a lawsuit in accordance with onerous privacy laws, saying there was a threat to his personal privacy. He objected to certain information about him on the site, namely that he had served as an officer of the MfS. Unfortunately for Heilmann, when Wikipedia users visited the site they were instead directed to the message that the entire site was offline due to the lawsuit filed by him.

Those who had no idea who he was the day before quickly learned the truth.

The issue had come up in 2005, after Heilmann had been first elected to the Bundestag, representing what was then called the PDS Party, the legal successor to the East German communist SED. When the facts came to light, his supporters claimed that no, he had not lied about working for the Stasi by claiming years of 'military service' in his webpage and election information, but had only 'concealed a part of his biography not mentioned publicly'. His official biography on the party site read '1985–1990: Military service'.

Hubertus Knabe paused at his desk at the Memorial one day shortly after, when he received a call from the press asking for a comment about Bundestag member Heilmann. He sat and thought for a moment carefully before answering.

'If a former full-time Stasi employee sits in Parliament, it would play down the participation of an instrument of internal oppression to a minor offense.' He added, 'For victims of the GDR regime it is an unbearable idea that a man with this past sits in Parliament.'

The PDS voted to keep Heilmann in office anyway, in spite of the public outcry and false statements he had made. Three years later he pursued those who had leaked the information. Then came 2008, and his aggressive campaign backfired. Because of the extra attention when Wikipedia was taken down in Germany in 2008, Heilmann quickly withdrew his privacy complaint and the site returned several days later. It turned out that Heilmann's Wikipedia page had been mysteriously edited to include his true background from an IP address located within the German Parliament building.

Records of the MfS show Lutz Heilmann was accepted as a Stasi officer and took the lifetime oath on October 1, 1985. He was assigned to Main Department PS in Berlin, the MfS section that was entrusted with personal security for MfS leaders and senior Communist Party officials. That included those occupying the luxurious housing development in Wandlitz, north of Berlin. Only twenty-three homes occupy two square kilometers there; they were then reserved for senior Politburo members only. Some former members live there still. But Main Department PS was far more than that. Having more than three thousand members, it also took direct action against real or alleged opposition to the GDR regime. By May 1989, the last entry in his personnel file shows his salary had increased by 50 percent and he had become a sergeant. He had been preparing for success, having been a member of the Free German Youth (FDJ) and the Society for German–Soviet Friendship.

Heilmann continued to serve as a member of the German Parliament with the Left Party until 2009, usually espousing his favorite two issues of fixing climate change while lowering the city bus fares. He hasn't run again, and currently works at an old job at the district court in Lübeck. It's the same place where he filed his privacy complaint against Wikipedia. His telephone there was picked up by someone late one Friday afternoon in 2019 who advised that Herr Heilmann would be back on the following Monday. Monday afternoon that number was instead disconnected.

———

Andrej Holm, a chubby-faced man with a perennial condescending smile and thick, black-framed glasses, appeared disarmingly surprised when he was asked the question. It was 2017 and he was being quizzed about his previously hidden Stasi past by the media. He'd been nominated by the Left Party to a high position in government, to be the Berlin housing secretary. Unknown to him, that triggered a routine inquiry with the Archive. The response that came back was: *We have a file.*

Holm had been working as a successful professor at Humboldt University for the past twelve years and many of the students loved him. He called himself an urban sociologist and talked a great deal about the need for cheap rents and for government control of housing so as to avoid the gentrification of neighborhoods. Who wouldn't be popular on a college campus with that platform? Now, as housing secretary, he would be in a position to implement his ideas about restrictions on property investors and landlords. Those ideas sounded a great deal like old textbook socialism and GDR communism.

Holm was asked the standard questions on his Humboldt University application form in 2005. The same things they asked everyone:

Did you work for the Ministry for State Security? Did you receive payments from them? Did you sign a letter of obligation? Holm answered 'No' to each.

But when he was appointed to a high position in the local government, somebody wondered again and submitted the inquiry to the Archive nonetheless. The truth surfaced; he appeared on the ranks of the Ministry for State Security. He seemed amused at the inquiry and responded in a way that he thought was sure to easily take care of it.

Oh, the Stasi stuff? Not serious – I was young, it was military service and I only wrote a couple of reports.

His 200-page MfS personnel file told a different story. His personal oath to the Ministry for State Security was a three-page handwritten signed commitment. Part of his statement reads:

I oblige to:

Use all of my strength and skills to fulfill the honorable duties and tasks of a member of the Ministry for State Security…

… to strengthen the union with the members of the committee of state security of the Soviet Union and the members of the security organs of the socialist states community yet further and to always act in the spirit of the socialist internationalism;

… to strengthen the socialist relations of the members of the Ministry for State Security to one another incessantly, to be a role model while on and off duty as well as to always protect the honor and dignity of the Ministry for State Security;

… even after my dismissal, act in such a way that a security hazard for the work of the Ministry for State Security and myself cannot arise.

Holm actually grew up in a Stasi family. His father was a longtime officer in Berlin, and Andrej volunteered to join the ranks at the age of fourteen. When he was eighteen he wrote and signed the obligatory oath of allegiance, and penned his personal oath. He wouldn't travel outside the GDR and would report any family members who did. The oath of allegiance was intended to continue for the rest of his life.

The Left Party chairman vigorously defended him, and their appointment. 'He only wrote reports for a month before the GDR ended. We have always supported Andrej!'

The truth came out slowly, and only after a newspaper found his file. By then he had already been confirmed as state secretary.

Holm was recommended for officers' training in July 1989 by the district office in Berlin, which also confirmed his membership in the SED Communist Party. He entered officers' training on September 1, 1989, as events with protestors began to spiral out of control. The file reflects he did very well there, including with his use of the pistol, submachine gun and RGD-5 Soviet antipersonnel fragmentation grenade. Holm was assigned to the information and control group (ZAIG), the focal point for all information about the citizens' resistance movement.

It didn't end in 1990. Holm also had connections to leftist movements in the new Germany. In 2007, the Federal Police arrested him early one morning on terrorism charges for his connection to a radical leftist militant group, including meetings apparently arranged to avoid surveillance. He spent a month in Moabit prison before being released on bail. The charges were dismissed a year later for lack of evidence.

By 2017, it couldn't be ignored further. The mayor of Berlin removed him from his position due to the now undeniable revelations that he was a Stasi officer and had lied about it, saying that Holm 'had not faced up to his past'. Humboldt University also suspended him, due to the obvious lies on his application to be a professor. 'I wrote things as I remembered them at the time,' he said. There were some protests in his support, organized by students who understood the term 'low rent' more than what Stasi, secret police and truthfulness stood for.

After Holm eventually admitted to making 'objectively false statements', the university let him off with a warning. In 2019 he planned to be back teaching students his message of government control of property and low-priced apartments. Others refer to that platform in a different way.

They say it's part of a GDR 2.0.

The Party had thought about its future, and took action as the GDR crumbled around them. *Being a Chekist is having a cool head, a warm heart and clean hands* went Erich Mielke's oft-repeated statement that was drilled into every MfS officer. A cool head also means that one must have a *plan*.

The telephone rang at a West German equipment wholesaler on Saturday morning, March 24, 1990. The sales manager gripped the phone and reached for a notepad; he recognized the sound of a sale when he heard the very direct request. The voice on the phone needed to make a fast deal. A special order was placed within minutes for the largest paper shredder then available in Europe, along with plastic bags to handle 350,000 pounds of shredded paper. Not a problem. The deal was completed and a happy sales manager hung up the phone. A cash payment of 800,000 DM, equivalent to $500,000, was made days later out of a suitcase carried in by a person who appeared at the office and didn't identify himself. The machine was to be quickly delivered to a motor vehicle maintenance company in East Berlin on a certain day – April 6. The job wasn't the destruction of Stasi files. That was being handled another way. This was destined for something that the citizen activists hadn't even thought about. It was destined to secure the future of GDR communist politicians.

Sometime in April, all the personnel files of thousands of key members of the SED Communist Party, called *cadre files*, were shredded. The files had compromising and embarrassing details on how they had worked for years to support the communist dictatorship, and with whom. All those secret backroom deals that formed and supported a forty-year dictatorship. Too many uncomfortable facts recorded in there for the leaders who planned to survive and prosper in the new system. The Stasi only succeeded in destroying 10 to 20 percent of their own files; the SED Party officials, with the help of the MfS, destroyed all of their own.

The past of the SED speaks loudly for itself. It was formed after the war to be the governing Marxist-Leninist party of the GDR, a one-party state. Holding the hard-left line, in the 1980s they rejected the easing of restrictions proposed by Soviet president Mikhail Gorbachev, and held out until the bitter end. They were able to do that for forty years only because the Ministry for State Security made it possible, and because of the harsh actions and laws that the Party members had consistently put in place.

While the anger of the population was focused on the Stasi, all of whom were also SED members, more quiet plans could be made by the political elite. First, they needed a fresh new name. They had already thought of that too.

––––––

Five days before the fall, a new political career was already being launched.

It was November 4, 1989, and a cold wind was swirling around the huge radio tower and through Alexanderplatz, the central square of East Berlin. The gathering that day was approved by the state, the first-ever such gathering not also totally sponsored and controlled by the government. It was a last-ditch effort by the gasping dictatorship to survive. More than a half million people turned up, mostly to drive a nail into the coffin of communism.

On the impressive list of Party cadres who were determined to settle people down was someone who had no interest at all in that goal. He was focused on his own future. The man who liked to be described as the East German Mikhail Gorbachev saw a chance and seized it. Gregor Gysi stood and spoke to the huge and restless crowd at Alexanderplatz that afternoon, denouncing the mistakes of the regime, of which he was part, and demanding reforms. At the same gathering, Markus Wolf, the legendary mysterious spymaster and head of the HV A, with a previously unknown public face, was brought in by Erich Mielke to defend the Stasi. Wolf was roundly booed, shouted down and laughed at and ridiculed by thousands. His hands were seen trembling at the podium.

Less than a month later forty-one-year-old Gregor Florian Gysi, already sporting the Gorbachev receding hairline, wire glasses and gentle smile, became the new head of the GDR Communist Party. He was a longtime party functionary. In true Soviet style, and as the GDR crumbled, he repudiated the leaders before him and announced he would lead the country with a new form of socialism. Everything in the past was a mistake, he said. He was a lawyer and had represented activists charged in the GDR for political crimes, he emphasized. A charismatic speaker, he told the people what they wanted to hear. Occasionally, he would mention his distant relationship to the popular British Nobel laureate Doris Lessing.

The real plan unrolled in the months that followed.

February 4, 1990, was when they made the next move. The SED Communist Party was officially renamed on that day the Party of Democratic Socialism (PDS), to be led by Gysi. Instantly the PDS became the richest political party in Europe, with assets equivalent to nine billion euros. They were caught almost immediately trying to make a huge cash transfer from Germany to a Moscow bank. Those funds were seized.

Less than two years later, the German Gorbachev had a problem. Gysi had been connected to Stasi files that said he had for years provided the MfS with inside information about the dissident clients he was representing in court, reporting as an IM to the Stasi under the code name *Notar*. Over the years, Gysi waved off and denied the claims, saying that he was never an informant and that 'Notar' must be someone else. Nonetheless, the parliamentary committee that investigated and reviewed the files found in the Archive voted to accept the conclusion that Gysi was indeed 'Notar'. He still denies it.

For this, and other reasons, the PDS languished early on. It was also perceived as too East-focused. That wouldn't do. So, in 2007 the PDS and a West German left-leaning party, Laboure and Social Justice, merged and became The Left, and they quickly allied themselves with the European-wide left movement. Their influence has been increasing ever since on a platform of the elimination of NATO and a closer relationship with Russia. They promise wide-ranging socialist carrots of lower rents, free healthcare and other enticements designed to attract the youth.

The Left remains legally the same party as the East German SED Communist Party, and they still occupy Karl-Liebknecht-Haus in Berlin-Mitte, conveniently the original headquarters of the German Communist Party. The unanswered question that some continue to echo in frustration remains: where did the SED's ill-gotten billions go?

By agreement at unification, all SED assets were required to be surrendered. All that had been done at the time, they said. Inconveniently, in 2006 yet another SED/PDS/Left Party account was found in Liechtenstein containing 2.7 million euros. And what of the Party secretary who reportedly showed up at a bank in Luxembourg in 1990 with large plastic bags filled with Deutschmarks? Or the documents that surfaced about the son of a former Stasi general who sent funds to Chile? The official search for the untold missing billions ceased in 2006 anyway.

The PDS/Left Party has continually been found to have Stasi connections. A chairman of the PDS, and later co-chairman of The Left, Lothar Bisky, was discovered in 1995 to have been an informant for the MfS for years. The Stasi called him 'a reliable comrade'. Normally, SED members were secure in the knowledge that their cadre files had been destroyed as the shredding continued well into 1990. They could safely deny all and build a new history. But sometimes that proved to be less than perfect. In the case of PDS chairman Bisky, and unfortunately for him, his wife had a Stasi file that survived and documents in there quickly confirmed his Stasi connections.

Without the Firm, the SED could not have accumulated billions, enabling its survival for four decades, and until today under a new name. The Stasi organizations have continued to be involved in many activities of the Left Party as it increases its power. A number of former officers were among the top PDS/Left Party officials. Due to the nature of the German coalition-type government, The Left can and does appoint members today to key positions within the German government.

Meanwhile, required formal screening with the BStU archives for public office holders and other government agencies, other than those in executive and parliamentary positions, ended in 2006. Private employers have never had the right to consult the Archive to determine if an executive was a former Stasi officer, and most don't want to know anyway. European and American companies and agencies dealing with someone whom they may suspect of being a Stasi officer have no way of asking for the records to be searched, giving them easy deniability.

Any information that surfaces about surprising new careers of the Stasi Grey Men is most often haphazard, or the one-off result of a dogged reporter still focused even after the passage of time. But these have increasingly been few and far between. Outing a former MfS officer who is now in a key position in business or government has become risky.

And since the SED cadre files were all intentionally destroyed, there are simply no records that can be searched to reveal the past official actions of a Communist Party official who may now work with the Left Party or have been appointed by them to a key political office. There aren't any Communist Party official personnel files like the Stasi Archive that can be checked to see who the members of the Left Party actually were until 1990. They have long been free to create their own new backgrounds.

Gregor Gysi never shook off the common belief that he informed on his activist clients. But he did well anyway, and spent years in Parliament, finally surrendering leadership of the reinvented SED Party in 2015. The Party needed a new face, one without controversy, they said. So Gysi nodded and stepped aside.

———

In Brussels, Belgium, on a quiet Saturday morning in December 2016, a man carrying a briefcase walked with a spring in his step as he made his way down Rue du Luxembourg before turning left.

He stopped at one of the low-profile buildings at Square de Meeûs and stared at the simple gold address plate to the right of several security cameras. *Number 25*. Checking his watch, he noted with satisfaction that the place was a comfortably short walk to the EU Parliament.

Passing through the building's dark wooden doors and a few steps up, he was inside the offices of the EL, the European Left political organization. A rising force in the EU, it serves as the official European-wide association linking and influencing twenty-five member organizations, including the German Left, and other observer socialist and communist parties.

Adjusting his wire glasses and smoothing his now nearly bald head, Gregor Gysi smiled slightly and was ready. Today was a good day to start his next job – president of the European Left. His first call would certainly be to Berlin.

19

KINGS OF THE RUSSIAN MACHINE

St Petersburg, Russia
April 2014

It was a busy evening in the city known as Leningrad during communist times, and a big celebration was in the making. Everything had been prepared hours before, and they all waited for this moment. The stretch black Mercedes sedan turned right along the Moyka River around 10:30pm and slowly approached the massive gold stone building that is the Yusupov Palace.

One of the most well-known buildings in St Petersburg, the palace stands both as a symbol for glamour and wealth, as well as for communist victory. Originally built on land owned by the niece of Peter the Great, it served proudly as the palatial home to a Russian aristocratic family, the Yusupovs, until it was seized in 1917 during the purges of the Russian Revolution. But its lasting fame today, at least until this damp April evening, was as the place where Prince Felix Yusupov murdered Grigori Rasputin, the close confidant of the last Russian tsar. The murder of this shaggy, bearded former peasant turned influencer and spiritual healer to the tsar by a jealous, rich aristocrat was another violent act that helped launch Vladimir Lenin and the Communist Revolution. As far as anyone knows today, Rasputin actually died in the river, just a few steps from the front door. A ruthless man in the old Russian fashion with a reputation for survival, he was said to have been first poisoned inside the palace, and then shot eleven times, including at least once in the head. When he was found to still be alive anyway, he was dragged a few paces outside and drowned in the river after being thrown through a hole in the ice.

The Yusupov Palace, with all its glitter, today speaks of old and new wealth, intrigue, despair and victory, and the violent birth of the communist state.

The heavy black sedan slid to a stop in front of the twin white pillars and huge doors of the palace, and a small group rushed down the steps to greet it. The passenger door was opened and a man of slight stature with thinning hair stepped out and clasped the hand of a tall, dark-haired German. The other backseat passenger bent over, revealing a black pistol strapped to his waist. At that moment, a camera with a telephoto lens, well positioned across the Moyka River, clicked softly. Even from the back, Vladimir Putin was recognizable, but the other man hugging him and smiling broadly, Gerhard Schröder, former chancellor of Germany, was less so in Russia. Few if any that night knew who the stocky, well-dressed man to Schröder's right was. Even the next day, when Germany was incensed by Putin attending the birthday party for Schröder at the palace that night, not many likely recognized Matthias Warnig. Fifty-nine-year-old Warnig, standing with Schröder and Putin, is a very low-profile former Stasi officer who knew Putin long before even the former German chancellor.

The group moved inside the palace for the sumptuous event sponsored by Nord Stream, the gas pipeline company. Warnig is the CEO of the company, and without the assistance of Chancellor Schröder just before he left office, the pipeline, which has ensured Central Europe's dependence on Russian energy for the future, would never have been built on German soil. It also would never have been approved if not for a trip former officer Warnig took to Washington DC in June 2009.

The MfS personnel file for Matthias Warnig was opened in September 1974 when he began his career as a member of the military arm of the Stasi, the Felix Dzerzhinsky Guards Regiment. Within a year he was recruited to the HV A. As he said he spoke both conversational Russian and French and wanted to study economics, it seemed a good place for such an ambitious officer. It was decided he would be placed undercover with the GDR Trade Ministry.

After receiving a degree in 'national economy' from a school that later closed when the GDR collapsed, Warnig was sent to Düsseldorf in West Germany under cover of the Trade Mission. He was assigned to steal technology from the West, an important Stasi function. He wrote reports about espionage and the West German energy industry.

He rose quickly, which maybe had something to do with his assignments, or maybe it was because of the close relationship he developed with a KGB officer in Dresden, Lieutenant Colonel Vladimir Putin. Some say they worked together to recruit West Germans to spy, something Warnig has since denied. After returning to East Berlin and Stasi headquarters in the middle of 1989, he was already focused on his own future. That future, he decided, was called *capitalism*.

With perfect timing, Captain Warnig received nine medals for unclear reasons from Minister Mielke on October 7, 1989, the fortieth anniversary of the GDR. The next day, Minister Mielke would start preparations for mass arrests throughout East Germany as the regime crumbled.

As the GDR and the Stasi came apart over the next six months, Warnig, who was then believed by West German intelligence to be mainly an East German trade official, met an old contact from Düsseldorf, the CEO of Dresdner Bank, who asked him, 'What do you want to do if the GDR no longer exists?'

Warnig took a job with Dresdner in May 1990, less than two months after the Stasi was dissolved. The bank amazingly loaned him to Treuhand, the agency tasked with finding the missing GDR assets. They sent him to London, to learn more about the banking business. Not bad for a thirty-five-year-old whose last employer had just ceased paying him.

By the middle of 1991, the CEO of Dresdner already had another job for him. The bank wanted to expand into Russia and Warnig's CV said he spoke Russian. 'Go look around that country, and let me know what you think.' Warnig went, and promptly returned to Berlin with an interesting suggestion. Shall we open a representative office for the bank in St Petersburg? The CEO liked the idea and named him to start it. By October, Warnig was already calling on his old colleague Vladimir Putin. Putin was by then a rising member of the St Petersburg city administration. Putin quickly approved the open-ing of the bank office, after the two had a meeting speaking solely in German. That was a relief, as Warnig really didn't speak Russian at any passable level. But just as the Dresdner Bank saw some potential in Warnig without asking too many questions, so did Putin.

They both once again started spending time together, as did their families. When Putin's first wife, Lyudmila, was seriously injured in a car accident in 1993 and needed treatment in Germany, it was Warnig who provided needed assistance.

His credo became 'Friendships do not hurt.'

In 2005, Warnig was publicly identified in Germany as a former Stasi officer. But it didn't matter. By that time Putin had been Russian president for five years and was forming a company that would build a gas pipeline to Europe. To the former KGB officer that was useful for all sorts of reasons. The company, called at first North European Gas Pipeline Company, but shortened to Nord Stream AG, was incorporated in 2005 in Switzerland. Warnig would be perfect as CEO, everyone who mattered decided. The major shareholder was the other Russian energy giant, Gazprom.

As always, the now-stocky Matthias Warnig got to work with his contacts. The fact that most now knew he had been a successful MfS officer, and was a close friend of the Russian president, only made things easier. But he knew he also had a problem. Not surprisingly, intelligence agencies in Germany, most of Europe and the United States were all convinced it would be a security disaster if Russia had its hand on the valve that delivered energy to NATO countries. Practically, there were only two ways to run the pipeline to Europe. The first was down the center of the Baltic Sea, and turn west toward the German coast. The other was to run it through Ukraine. Putin didn't like sending it through Ukraine for some reason. That meant Warnig had to make some new friends.

The outgoing German chancellor, Gerhard Schröder, surprisingly approved the project to transit that country on his way out of office in 2005. He then surfaced with a new job with Nord Stream as chairman of the shareholders' committee. America was left to Warnig. In 2009, he made two visits to the United States. The first was to attend a public relations event organized by a Washington DC law firm hired by the company. The second was to attend a German Embassy-hosted event, hoping to convince policymakers that the Russian gas pipeline supplying Europe was somehow in the national security interests of the United States.

Ultimately, as Germany was intent on pushing forward, even over the objections of their own intelligence community, there was little the United States could do, other than strongly oppose the project.

The pipeline was opened amid great fanfare in 2011, leaving the owner of the gas – Gazprom – with its 400,000 employees and 17 percent of world gas reserves – firmly in control of Europe's future. It would be most unfortunate now if energy-poor Europe offended the Russian state.

In 2012, President Putin awarded Matthias Warnig the Order of Honor of the Russian Federation.

Warnig has since gone on to hold positions with Russian state-owned oil company Rosneft, and also board positions with VTB Group and Bank Rossiya. Both were heavily sanctioned by the United States and the EU following the Russian invasion of Ukraine in 2014. In 2015, a former Hillary Clinton fundraiser, Emanuel 'Mike' Manatos, filed a disclosure that his lobbying firm would advocate for VTB Group in the United States.

Today, the former officer remains the German with the closest relationship to Vladimir Putin. In a 2007 interview on the Nord Stream Russian site, he described his prior career with the GDR as 'an employee of the main Intelligence Department'. By 2019, the Nord Stream AG biography of Matthias Warnig made no mention of his

Stasi past. Instead it said: *'Previously, Mr Warnig had several functions in the German Democratic Republic's government from 1981 to 1990, including roles in the foreign trade ministry and the Cabinet.'*

———

Another now-wealthy man sat in his office only months after Matthias Warnig had been unmasked as a former Stasi officer and paused to stare out the window at the Berlin skyline. He had heard those rumors and more. The chattering of those warning of continued Stasi influences within the Russian energy industry. But he was lucky; his position as chief financial officer didn't require him to pay much attention to such things. His company was an astounding success also, having been formed in Germany only in December 1990. Could it really already have been sixteen years? Sure, he knew of MfS officers who had leveraged their contacts into positions with his industry and prospered. Lost in the chaos and apathy, things like that had been protected by staying silently out of public view. It was all working out well in the company with the cheerful blue logo, Gazprom Germania, the 100 percent German subsidiary of the Russian energy giant Gazprom.

The circle wasn't yet complete, but it soon would be.

In the waning days of 1990, there was another young and eager man who walked confidently into the Berlin offices of Dresdner Bank, ready and willing to go to work. It was odd enough that this bank, well known years before as the financiers of the Nazi regime and especially the SS, would so easily find persons such as this one. But business is business. Times change, sometimes rather quickly. *Long live capitalism!*

The man who rushed through the heavy doors of the Dresdner Bank headquarters that day had something else to offer. He had banking and foreign exchange experience with a large firm after all, and a degree in finance from East Berlin's Humboldt University. So, why not?

As Felix Strehober sat down at his desk that first day as an official capitalist, he was listed on the roster as just another bank trainee. That changed with amazing speed. Within two years he was corporate accounts manager, and two years after that, in 1994, he sat in the new Dresdner Bank representative office in St Petersburg with Matthias Warnig. He was now head of corporate banking for the bank in Russia. An amazing leap for a man with an odd background.

Strehober certainly had foreign exchange experience in the GDR. It was with a company called Intrac, the largest of the shell companies set up under the Commercial Coordination Unit (KoKo) by Stasi officer Alexander Schalck-Golodkowski. That helped. What also helped were his four years of school in Moscow, and his knowledge of Russian. True, he himself had been a Stasi officer since 1985, and had sworn the oath in a handwritten statement to the MfS as was usual. But there was no need to talk about that. And Strehober didn't talk about it at all, or list it on his CV, and still doesn't. That worked, or at least it did for the next decade and a half.

The other reality that stayed hidden was that Felix Strehober had prospered also in the Stasi. First in the Dzerzhinsky Guards Regiment, where he received sixteen commendations in just two years.

'Comrade Strehober has always identified himself with the requirements of an employee of the Ministry for State Security.'

Next as a Stasi officer in Special Employment, undercover for the Foreign Intelligence Department. As an Officer in Special Employment (OibE) he was one of the elite within the HV A. Placed in key jobs within their own society, they worked quietly but never forgot to whom they had sworn the lifetime oath.

Perhaps he had even convinced himself over the years that nobody would really know the difference. They wouldn't guess his role in the KoKo machine that was 50 percent MfS officers and concerned with getting hard foreign currency to prop up the SED by any means possible. That could mean stealing art, selling blood or trafficking in arms to both sides in the Iran–Iraq war.

Intrac, I worked for Intrac.

The transition was painless, he thought.

I'm now a banker. Simple!

By 1998 he was on the move again and eagerly accepted the offer of a job back in Berlin. He would be the chief financial officer for Gazprom Germania. At that time the company was small and operating under a different name. Formed in December 1990, two months to the day after German unification, it was to be the umbrella company for many others to be opened throughout Europe to facilitate the sale of Russian natural gas and move the resulting billions of profits. And there was also talk of a new pipeline, and more.

How did the trainee at Dresdner Bank become so successful so quickly and now land this job with the soon-to-be-named, wholly owned subsidiary of Gazprom, the Russian state-controlled energy giant? Maybe it had something to do with its director of personnel, Hans-Uve Kreher. Kreher, who by his own later admission had been an informant for the Stasi for many years.

As CFO, Felix Strehober, an intensely private man with the smooth look of an executive, was once again in charge of foreign currency and money flows, and of building the financial structure of a rapidly growing international company. Gazprom Germania, a German-registered company, was founded by the former deputy chief of the GDR state-owned oil and gas industry. It got busy setting up affiliates and subsidiaries throughout Europe at a brisk pace, especially once the large pipeline in the Baltic was assured. By 2007, CFO Felix Strehober was responsible for dealing with over eight billion euros that the company was earning.

He was comfortable, making very good money and being nearly anonymous.

But then, on an otherwise normal business day in September 2007, the mild-manner accountant type with amazing influence made a serious mistake.

His glass-enclosed office at the Gazprom Germania headquarters, Markgrafenstrasse 23, was quite near the former death strip between East and West Berlin. He sat every day barely in the West. It was hard now to see any remnants. Nearly impossible for the casual visitor. But if he had ridden the elevator down to the street, stepped out to the sidewalk and walked twenty paces to his left, one was still clearly visible from the corner. A circular, smooth basalt stone column embedded in the sidewalk, usually even now always with fresh flowers placed carefully at its base. People who worked near there rushed by on their way to and from coffee or lunch. The stone marks the place where eighteen-year-old Peter Fechter died. Fechter was one of the first and one of the youngest to be shot trying to get over the Wall. He was desperate at the time for something more than his assigned lifetime job as a bricklayer in the GDR. He was shot through the pelvis while trying to escape, and lay not ten feet from freedom. His screams were heard by all on both sides for nearly an hour, as he slowly bled to death.

But on that day in September, CFO Strehober was holding a document in front of him. It was a routine court affidavit needed for his latest attempt to stop the press from implying that he had troubling connections in the former GDR. There had been occasional references in the newspapers over the past couple of years, but he had privacy rights under new German laws, and he intended to insist on them.

He looked at the signature page.

'[I certify that] I have never been an [official] employee or any other full-time employee of the Ministry for State Security.'

The court must handle thousands of civil matters every year. He picked up his pen and signed it and put it aside. Routine. The affidavit was filed within days with the regional court in Cologne.

The problem was, somebody noticed.

It was a reporter from the newspaper *Die Welt* who called first. Did you ever work for the Stasi, Mr Strehober? Of course not, he replied.

The newspaper next published his statement alongside part of his Stasi personnel file they found at the Archive, the part with his handwritten oath. A Cologne prosecutor took notice of his false affidavit and opened a criminal case. Lying to the court was a crime, not something to be ignored. The case was ultimately settled swiftly with a fine being assessed, and without any criminal blemish. Discreetly.

Strehober then spent the next five years filing lawsuits trying to eradicate the news reports, and even trying to purge from Google references to the truth that he had in fact been a Stasi officer. His personal privacy was paramount, he argued. Incredibly, one court agreed with him, but it was a short-lived victory. Ultimately, a higher German court rejected his appeal, saying that in this particular case the public had a higher right to know the truth.

Strangely, the incident didn't seem to affect his standing with Gazprom Germania. No criminal conviction resulted. For a Russian conglomerate, having worked for the East German secret police was an asset anyway. After all, the parent company was routinely reported in the news as employing former Russian intelligence officers. By the time former Stasi officer Felix Strehober left Gazprom Germania in September 2014, he was managing the finances for a company with annual revenue of twelve billion euros flowing among forty subsidiaries in twenty countries, including the United States.

Under his watch as CFO, the company had diversified into a major German sports club, and ownership of many subsidiaries, including one in Houston, Texas. It became the main gateway to European influence for its Russian parent, and Putin's government. Testimony provided to the US Senate Foreign Relations Committee in a 2008 hearing about energy and Russian oligarchs, summarized the company's role:

> *Gazprom, with the silent support of the Kremlin, has set up fifty or so middlemen companies, silently linked to Gazprom and scattered throughout Europe – such as the Centrex group of companies and the Gazprom Germania network – which do not add any value to the price of Russian gas being sold on European markets; yet they earn enormous sums of money which appears to simply vanish through shell companies in Cyprus and in Liechtenstein.*

The former Stasi officer, and now the former Gazprom Germania CFO, currently advertises his services as an independent financial advisor. The glasses have gone but the cold stare remains on the online CV. Once again it says that in 1989 he was really an import-export businessman for Intrac Corporation.

————

Family influences can run deep.

Franz Thomas Alexander Wolf, son of legendary Stasi spymaster Markus Wolf, is by all accounts now operating in an even more mysterious fashion than his famous 'man-without-a-face' father. Franz Wolf was thirty-six when the Wall fell. He has since become a director of a major Russian energy enterprise in Gibraltar, CTF Holdings, where he currently manages $60 billion globally for Russian oligarchs and the well-known Alfa Group. He never worked as a Stasi officer, though he had no real need to. His father was perhaps the most infamous and mysterious network-builder within the MfS.

Markus Wolf, head of the HV A, fled to Moscow one month before German unification and requested political asylum. That was eventually denied as the Soviet Union was fragmenting too and briefly courting the West, so he was sent back to Germany. He died in his sleep in Berlin on November 9, 2006, strangely enough on the seventeenth anniversary of when the Wall fell.

Franz Wolf first surfaced in public view during 2013 in a massive leak of information concerning offshore tax accounts that was anonymously sent to tax authorities around the world. The database, which is available from the International Consortium of Investigative Journalists (ICIJ), has connected Wolf to a half-dozen companies that operate quietly in Gibraltar, Liechtenstein and the British Virgin Islands. He never grants interviews.

Having been a Stasi officer, or being closely related to a senior Stasi officer, certainly seems to be an asset in today's Russian energy machine.

Former Stasi officer Matthias Warnig (far left) arrives with President Putin at a party for former German chancellor Gerhard Schröder in St Petersburg, April 2014.

Former Stasi captain Matthias Warnig, current CEO of Russian pipeline company Nord Stream (center), former German chancellor Gerhard Schröder (center left), and then Russian prime minister Dmitry Medvedev at Putin's 2018 inauguration, Moscow.

Stasi Central Card File for officer Matthias Warnig.

Stasi Central Card File for officer Felix Strehober –
recent photo overlay added from another source.

20

PROFESSOR MURDER

The man known to many as simply 'the Professor' preferred to think of himself as exactly that. Later he became better known as something slightly different, *Professor Murder*. But for now, he was a respected member of the faculty of Humboldt University, and an expert in forensic sciences.

He was a lanky, square-jawed man with a dark receding hairline who favored the sturdy plastic-framed glasses of a scientist. It was just past 8am on a sunny winter morning in 1988 as fifty-five-year-old Hans-Ehrenfried Stelzer strolled briskly to work. It was a twelve-minute pleasant walk at his usual brisk pace from his flat at 18 Neue Grünstrasse. Today, he increased his stride as he turned right along the Spree Canal and over Bebelplatz, the plaza best known as the site of the mass Nazi book burnings of 1933. Holding impatiently for morning traffic, he weaved his way across the bustling boulevard Unter den Linden and rushed up the stairs into a soaring grand façade that loomed as a crown jewel for East Berlin and the communist state. Humboldt University, founded in 1810 in the grand Prussian style, was the oldest university in Germany, and certainly the most prestigious. It still is. He hurried up the marble and granite stairs most likely lost in thought, making his way through the halls to the Criminalistics Section. The placard on his office door read *Direktor*. It would be a busy week. He was supervising a special project of great importance for his real employer.

Stelzer was a Stasi colonel in Special Employment at the time, an OibE. Humboldt University deans would officially claim surprise and shock when this was revealed less than two years later. Since he had many MfS officers parading in and out of the department all day long, it's unlikely that there was really much surprise.

Stelzer first swore the oath and joined the MfS on New Year's Day 1962, fresh law degree in hand. Even before that, in his position in the Criminalistics Section, which was then contained within the Humboldt law school, he was already training MfS officers in forensic techniques. He was very valuable to the Stasi. Personnel records show his entry was coded 99 00, meaning he reported directly to the minister's level. And he didn't need to worry about surviving only on the paltry salary of a university professor. His second paycheck of 42,000 DM a year made him one of the highest paid colonels in the Firm.

Professor Stelzer was fifty-five and soaring along at the peak of his career. He had taught many Stasi officers how to locate criminal elements who sprayed graffiti, by analyzing the paint and writing styles, and how to find and arrest others who tried to conceal their critical writings behind a typewriter keyboard. He had recently returned from visits to Hanoi and Havana – sharing his techniques. The professor took pride in all that, and the fact that he was known in government circles as the first forensic scientist of the GDR. His personnel file reflects twenty-one medals and cash awards. Even elsewhere in Europe he was known and well respected in criminal justice circles by those who didn't yet know his first loyalty was to the Stasi.

Secure now in his office on this winter day in 1988, he plunged into work with his usual fervor. The project on his mind, and what he had been working on for years, was in essence a database. Now it was time for the finishing touches.

He called it TOXDAT, and was nearly done. When giving updates to the impatient but always interested deputy minister at Haus 1 at headquarters, he usually kept it simple.

TOXDAT is a detailed report and database outlining all the different ways to kill a person with science and poison. A death database. Ways that could avoid detection, so that even the victim would have no idea they were being murdered. How to use 200 toxic or radioactive elements in such a way that they were easy to conceal and administer. Useful information, as critics of the Stasi sometimes met untimely and unusual ends. We will use it only to deal with terrorists, Deputy Minister Neiber assured him. No matter. He was a scientist; those other considerations were for someone else, the professor told himself.

Stelzer and his deputy triumphantly put the last entries in TOXDAT later that year and delivered it complete to Lieutenant General Neiber. It was 911 pages.

Like his other undertakings in the Criminalistics Section, this one also shaped up to be precise, detailed and accurate. So accurate in fact that even thirty years later the database would be marked *confidential* by the German government. A copy is kept in the Stasi Archive, but they refuse to talk about it.

Stelzer was excited again about his next idea that he presented to the deputy minister. How to use science to focus more on the fascists. That was always a popular topic.

Then came the end of 1989, and everything in his orderly world fell apart. Soon, the Stasi Officers in Special Employment, hidden in plain sight within many German institutions, would be exposed. Stelzer was one, and in the best tradition of the communist university that Humboldt had become over the past forty years, officials feigned outrage that a Stasi officer was in their midst. He was abruptly terminated. It wasn't long after unification that many of the professors and administrators of the university were also fired. It was revealed that most had been placed in their positions as rewards by communist cadres for reasons unrelated to competence.

Stelzer's staff, in a final act of attempted self-preservation, gave away the secret of TOXDAT, and the new government seized the database of death. But what it was and what it was intended for leaked to the press, and he became *Professor Murder*.

Like many well-educated and driven Stasi officers, Colonel Hans-Ehrenfried Stelzer used some time after the fall to think. It was the end of March, and both his Humboldt University salary and his State

Security income had been cut off. On his CV he would call the nine months after being fired his 'voluntary research year'. As the ink dried on the signatures on the Germany Unification Treaty, he already had a new plan. In many ways it was far more astounding and even bolder than when he created the murder database. That's because he had a very unusual secret friend.

Stelzer yawned after his research year and shrugged at it all. He put aside his books and all thoughts of criminalistics research, which was now impossible to continue due to his new reputation, dredged up his law school papers from thirty years earlier and went to work in Berlin as an attorney. He became one of the thousands of former officers who used the same carefully crafted loophole in the treaty. He might have been fired from Humboldt University, but he was a Stasi officer until March 31, and thus could transfer his degree. He didn't remember much about being a lawyer, but it didn't matter. He soon had a better idea.

Even in Berlin at that time, when the odd and the bizarre were happening every day of the week, nobody could understand how the connection had developed between Professor Murder and the head of the BfV, the West German internal intelligence agency. Or when it had started. Neither Stelzer nor Heribert Hellenbroich ever spoke about it. Stelzer hadn't quite yet been given his new nickname in 1990, as TOXDAT hadn't been publicly disclosed. But Hellenbroich, who had also served as the head of the Federal Intelligence Service, the BND – Germany's equivalent of the CIA – would be expected to know better. He had only lasted less than a month in that job, due to a high-level BND deputy under his supervision abruptly defecting to the GDR in 1985.

Curiously, when asked about why he would form a company with a now well-known Stasi officer not even a year after the Wall fell, Hellenbroich gave a mysterious answer:

'His past is of no interest to me.'

They both had a plan for a business in financial services of some sort. The company registration was filed late in 1990. It was named the International Institute for Economic Security (IIES), and its stated purpose seemed noble, even if a bit cumbersome when translated into English: *Trouble-free East and West economic relations, benefiting entrepreneurs, fending off white-collar crime, informing about bank and data security.*

Professor Murder, a member of the Communist Party since June 1958, with no financial background, bounced back quickly and rushed out immediately to become a capitalist protector. Nobody was more surprised than his old colleagues at Humboldt University in the Criminalistics Section. There he'd been known as a Party hardliner who liked to heap praise on the head of the GDR. They remembered him by one of his trademark phrases he would cheerfully repeat as he walked through the office:

Nothing beats the beloved Comrade Erich Honecker!

As years passed after the fall, Stelzer became dissatisfied. His company was too centered on Europe, and in Berlin everyone still knew who he was. Especially the press – they wouldn't let him move on. More privacy was required.

On July 18, 2000, a new company appeared in New York, with the prestigious address of 575 Madison Avenue, 10th Floor. Goldman, Morgenstern & Partners, LLC, GoMoPa. Its business, it said, was financial intelligence, investor protection, combatting fraud through active education and permanent transparency. It sounded vaguely familiar, maybe connected to another famous New York giant – Goldman Sachs? In truth, it had no relationship to any New York company, the address on Madison Avenue was a business mail center and nobody named Goldman or Morgenstern was ever connected with the company. It was a New York shell with all business to be conducted in Germany. The identity of its founding members is hard to confirm. The State of New York doesn't require members to be listed when filing the registration for any limited liability company.

GoMoPa actually operated out of a small office in central Berlin. Years later, a company official would comment that it was set up as a US company in New York City for reasons of 'press privacy'. From the beginning, the clients were those who subscribed to its financial protection service.

In 2004, another strangely similar-sounding organization, the German Institute for Investor Protection (DIAS), was formed in Berlin. Its mission: investigation of unfair financial transactions. Stelzer became managing director of DIAS in 2009, and immediately fired the other board members. Even those in Berlin, by now long accustomed to astounding revelations related to actions of former Stasi officers, found this hard to swallow. Some claimed that DIAS, billing itself as an independent and nonprofit protector of fleeced investors, was a great way to troll for possible clients for GoMoPa.

Professor Murder, unable to make much of a life from his reduced Stasi pension, made a better living being a financial protector. GoMoPa meanwhile developed a curious business strategy, as a financial information service for the risks of the 'grey market'. Sometimes, GoMoPa would write and publish an unflattering article about a company only to offer to remove the article from its site later, for a consulting fee.

Colonel Hans-Ehrenfried Stelzer, square-jawed Professor Murder turned dubious international grey-market financial protector and profiteer, was ultimately proud of all of this. Being the managing director of DIAS in 2009 gave him the new credibility he was desperate for.

Less than nine months later Stelzer collapsed and died at a Berlin hospital. He nearly made it to seventy-eight. The circumstances of his death were never disclosed, and all of his mysterious connections to 'financial protection' died with him. Nobody seems to know where he's buried. His only family member was a long-estranged daughter said to be living out a bad marriage in Britain.

To those in Germany, Hans-Ehrenfried Stelzer will always be Professor Murder. TOXDAT remains locked safely away in the Stasi Archive, marked *confidential*, one of the few records out of the 111 kilometers of files that's permanently barred from release. Maybe part of the reason for that is the section on the use of radioactive elements for killing someone would seem oddly familiar to anyone who reads the news.

Goldman, Morgenstern & Partners, GoMoPa, has survived to the present day, with its small but unidentified membership base who pay for tidbits of financial information and those other companies that pay consulting fees. The company maintains its prestigious Madison Avenue mailbox and answering service in New York City. Its website was recently registered in Phoenix. GoMoPa GmbH, the wholly owned subsidiary of the empty New York LLC, actually operates from a much less impressive and lower-rent second-floor Berlin office, using outside 'contractors'. In that office recently hung an impressive picture of the New York City skyline.

21

GOVERNMENT CONSULTANTS

NSA – Fort Meade, Maryland
Sensitive Compartmented Information Facility (SCIF)

The only sound one could hear was the hushed tapping of a computer keyboard. It was the middle of an April week at the highly secure headquarters complex of the National Security Agency. A cryptography specialist sat at his desk, which was in a large SCIF, completing a quarterly report of major events including a report of a trip to Europe. *Done.* With a click the specialist added the following classification marking before sending it into the mainframe and up the chain:

NSA – Top Secret
This Document Contains Codeword Material
Classified by NSA/CSSM
13 April 1994
National Security Agency
Top Secret – UMBRA

The document with the included high-level warnings was declassified by the NSA in 2012, eighteen years later. The markings above were then carefully lined out in the usual fashion. Afterward, the report was lost in the shuffle. Even with certain passages still withheld and some names blacked out, it clearly describes a gathering of experts in encryption who met in Balatonfüred, Hungary, for four days in May 1993. The Stasi was in attendance, but now represented a unified Germany. So was the NSA.

The meeting was called *Eurocrypt* and sponsored by the International Association for Cryptologic Research. It was organized for the elite in encryption and network protection. Twenty-nine countries attended; the United States sent a delegation of thirty experts. That was overshadowed by Germany with forty-two, including three or more of those who had until recently been employed as officers of the MfS. The People's Republic of China was also an interested participant.

The NSA report details the meeting of cryptologists that took place that week, at the exclusive setting in Balatonfüred, an idyllic spa and yachting retreat on the shore of the Hungarian resort destination of Lake Balaton. One of the Germans, Ralph Wernsdorf, of the company Gesellschaft für Systeme der Informationstechnik, Society for Information Technology (SIT), was scheduled to make a presentation. The report writer had received some interesting information about that company from a German source. According to the NSA, SIT was a company now composed of ex-Stasi people. Two other names identified in this NSA report as part of the NATO-German delegation had both also been Stasi officers. One of these, whose background is not well known to the public, is currently an honorary professor at a Munich university.

As Wernsdorf took to the podium and cleared his throat to present his paper, titled *The One-Round Functions of the DES Generate the Alternating Group,* he couldn't help but look nervous. After all, most of the people in the crowd had been the enemy, until a very short time ago.

The MfS file for Ralph Wernsdorf, born in Potsdam in 1953, tells the story. Wernsdorf joined the Ministry for State Security in Berlin on September 1, 1982, but by then had already been a loyal member of the SED Communist Party for years. They liked that he spoke Russian, and after taking the Stasi oath and getting on the payroll, he returned to Humboldt University to finish a PhD in mathematics. His assignments included Main Departments VIII (Observation/ Investigations), IX (Investigations) and X (International Contacts). Almost immediately after the MfS was dissolved in March 1990, Wernsdorf went to work for Rohde & Schwarz, and their IT security encryption subsidiary, SIT. The company's two most important customers were then and now the German government and NATO. SIT is the subsidiary concerned with global communication networks, computer abuse and espionage.

It's not known how many multiples of Wernsdorf's State Security salary he was awarded when he transitioned from Stasi captain in 1989, earning 1,050 DM per month, to cryptospecialist for NATO and the German government. However, it certainly was a winner for him, and the other officers like him who made this move. The Stasi codebreakers did well.

After a Berlin newspaper published his work location in 2010, Wernsdorf switched to another company, Secunet Security, located in an even more affluent area of Berlin-Charlottenburg. Just meters from the River Spree, along the former impassable barrier to freedom for countless East Berliners, his office was in Alt-Moabit, in a high-security building that the Stasi would certainly have been proud of. It stands now not surprisingly in a new place of gleaming tech offices and a high-end business hotel. A plush neighborhood that in 1989 was barely but comfortably on the Western side, and thus out of reach to his desperate countrymen in the GDR. For most of them, who weren't studying for their PhD while earning a comfortable State Security salary like Wernsdorf, it still is.

Secunet Security Networks AG, the small gold sign reads, another specialist in data encryption. The company had a new role in 2019 – partnering with the controversial Chinese company Huawei for the rollout of Huawei's 5G network throughout the EU.

————

Germany has long been determined to do something about all those inflammatory Facebook comments posted on private accounts. According to their own study in 2011, one in six of all global Facebook moderators worked in Germany. And there were laws passed requiring 'hate speech' to be taken down in twenty-four hours. But it wasn't enough.

So, in 2015 Justice Minister Heiko Maas created a task force to police speech. One of the first things he did was to partner with an organization called Network Against Nazis (NAN) for help. NAN was part of the Amadeu Antonio Foundation (AAF) in Berlin. The chairperson of the AAF, Anetta Kahane, was very enthusiastic about the opportunity they were given.

Anetta Kahane was not a former officer of the Firm, but she had been a very active Stasi informant. The left-wing activist, and former member of the Communist Party, by her own somewhat reluctant later admission, also worked for the Ministry for State Security for eight years as IM V 55/74 under the code name *Victoria*.

Right-wing speech and Nazis, those are the real problems, the foundation loudly advocates. The same rationale was used by the Stasi to crack down on most anything in the GDR. There was no problem with left-wing speech and there were no political prosecutions in the GDR, Kahane and the former Stasi officers even now continue to insist. The 280,000 prisoners, and the 33,000 that were ransomed to the West, would disagree.

Kahane didn't admit to working for the MfS until after she was nominated to a position with the Berlin Senate in 2002 by the PDS, successor party to the SED Communist Party. That nomination triggered a routine inquiry with the Stasi Archive. Their official initial reply came through quickly. *Her file was 800 pages*. Although only 400 of the 800 pages were released, it was apparent that 'Victoria' had been quite active, providing useful information about others at least seventy times. Reporting on students, writers, journalists and foreigners, 'Victoria' had been given cash and gifts by the Stasi over the years for her loyalty.

By 2007, in the increasing and never-ending attempt to focus conversation on one end of the extremism spectrum, Kahane nearly succeeded in appearing on a serious panel discussion sponsored by the Stasi Archive. But some others objected. How appropriate was it to have someone who worked for years for the Stasi, reporting on many who would become victims, involved now in discussions with those victims? She decided to go anyway, before the controversy caused the invitation to be withdrawn.

By 2015, all of that about IM Victoria had seemingly been forgotten and the mission to police speech gained speed. Kahane and her foundation had developed a name ostensibly opposing racism and right-wing groups and their speech on the internet. Following the creation of the task force by Justice Minister Maas, Kahane was pictured smiling proudly as a newly selected speech monitor. On her site and in the related newsletter, the *Belltower News*, not only is the need to aggressively delete content deemed 'right-wing' from Facebook, Google and YouTube advocated, but also familiar revisionist topics about the GDR are repeated. Those bold attempts at reinterpretation include such things as arguing that the communist GDR state wasn't a dictatorship like the Nazis at all, and decrying how the Stasi is portrayed unfairly, and especially claiming that the Hohenschönhausen prison memorial is wrong since it's presented from the victims' perspective.

Opposing fascism – who can argue with that? Certainly not the German politicians, or groups identifying as antifascist in Europe or the United States, who zealously use the same methods to argue for suppression of only one kind of extremism. Meanwhile, Germany is filled with victims of the East German left-wing communist state, and the Soviet left-wing communist state before that. But they are aging, and poorly organized, and don't have slick websites like the Amadeu Antonio Foundation. Nevertheless, they remember the forty years of the GDR well. Memory of the victims remains a stumbling block to those who long to control speech. But a stumbling block that is now dangerously weakening as the victim-witnesses start to fade away.

IM Victoria, the official consultant and member of the free speech task force, working hard to monitor everything for the unified German government.

22

THE QUIET NETWORK

East Berlin
Ten years after the fall

He said what? The man at the tidy desk repeated to himself slowly.

He called it… the voice on the telephone repeated.

Hold on! The man searched for a pen. The phones were constantly ringing more than usual in the reception room in an office building that bore the name in huge letters of the GDR Communist Party newspaper, *Neues Deutschland*. But it wasn't in the second-floor offices of the newspaper that the telephones were ringing that morning, it was the floor above, in the GDR-style linoleum-covered corridors where the Stasi still lived.

Okay. Now, he called our place what?

The year 2000 had nearly passed, and most prosecutions of former officers were now barred by law. They had thousands in their networks they could call upon to pressure politicians about pensions, and fading attempts to out their well-placed friends.

The phone slammed down, and the man made a careful note with his pen. This was serious and would be discussed at their weekly meeting, and he knew many members would be calling before that to demand a response. There would be one.

Ten years after everyone was assured they no longer existed, the tightly organized Stasi organizations in Berlin had a clear new number one enemy. The enemy was a threat to their efforts to 'correct' the misguided views of the actions and role of the Ministry for State Security. Even worse, the enemy had a platform that attracted attention, and that didn't work with the operational plans for quiet revisionism that they were unrolling. Hubertus Knabe wasn't being a good *quiet historian*, like so many of the others who sat safely in their offices typing away and analyzing convoluted issues and producing technical papers with charts and footnotes that most people wouldn't read. Those papers were usually tucked away far from the eyes of the young people who would ultimately decide the future of Germany and Europe. Those who would write the history for the generations after. But Knabe also knew how to attract the young to that place, and maybe also how to keep the light shining on what had happened there not so long ago.

Warnings about Knabe started almost immediately after he took over as director of the Memorial at Hohenschönhausen. The comments in the Stasi circles and those of their supporters, usually former Communist Party loyalists now in the PDS/Left Party, grew also. The names they called him reflected their disdain:

Stasi hunter!

The commander!

The prosecutor!

The enemy was identified shortly after he stopped being a historian and became director of something now referred to as a *memorial*.

The term 'memorial' alone angered them. *Those people we put there were criminals!*

During Knabe's first interviews with the press as director, he challenged them by the way he spoke. He was direct in a clear way that people could immediately understand. There, in his office in the center of their Lichtenberg district and in their prison, Knabe turned to face a visiting reporter and went to the point:

'Hohenschönhausen was really the Dachau of communism.'

Comparing communism to the Nazis? That can't be tolerated. He was a threat. And threats require action. Steps would need to be taken. First though, for the men of the Stasi and their political partners at the renamed SED Party, it would get much worse.

———

Hubertus sat at his desk at home late one Sunday evening in 2007. Wearily he stared at the cursor blinking on the screen in front of him. He'd finished it. But would anyone in Germany publish what he'd written? Turning off the lights in his study, he wasn't so sure. It was passionate, whereas a historian is expected to be almost clinical, removed and distant from the events. It wasn't about facts long ago, not at all safe to discuss. It made no effort to not offend, or not to expose. He warned clearly about the dangers of whitewashing the past. He named names.

He decided that clarity of the title of his work was essential. It would be called *The Perpetrators Are Among Us*. In it he clearly illustrated how being anti-totalitarian has recently been replaced by the more comfortable term of being antifascist. It's the old tool being used by those trying to rehabilitate the leftist communist dictatorship and socialist state.

Hubertus included information about the founders behind each of the Stasi organizations, and how they and their politician allies have since attempted to minimize what was done to the people of East Germany for forty years. He named former secret police informants appointed to positions in state parliaments by The Left – IMs, some of whom had been previously identified but that fact later tactfully ignored. He didn't hesitate to highlight attempts by former Stasi colonels to attack him and the victims and oppose memorials. He didn't pull punches; what had taken place in the past twenty years wasn't the reckoning that Germany and the world needed, and that he and so many others had expected. People must know.

Pausing to look out the window to the quiet, dark street, he shook his head, surprised at himself. He thought that finishing this work would give him some peace, some assurance that once published he would start a desperately needed conversation. He did what he had to do, but at the end of days like this one he had no illusions about what he faced. He drew the curtains shut in the small living room and decided to schedule more public speaking appearances. It would

be good for the Memorial. It was already on the way to becoming
the most visited communist memorial by the youth in Germany and
much of Europe. *Leave it alone*, some said to him. *Act like a historian!
Think of your family!*

True, it had been seventeen years now since the fall. He'd been
director of the Memorial for seven of those, and they were now a
blur. A reporter asked him expectantly not long ago, 'When will you
leave this position, Dr Knabe?' He hadn't thought about it before,
and replied simply:

'I'll leave when someone else comes.'

Tossing and turning into the early Monday morning hours, he
finally gave up and prepared for work. There was something else to
do. The writing he had just finished was only part of the conversation.
The other part was to shine a light on the survival of the East German
Communist Party. What had happened in Germany was unlike anywhere else in Eastern Europe when freedom was reclaimed. The
Baltic states, the Czech Republic and all the others had made a fresh
start. They banned the Communist Party, even declared it a criminal
organization, and kept the old comrades away from government. But
not in Germany. There, the SED first legally changed its name – twice.
Now they called themselves the Left Party. But the money and the
old cadres were the same. Communism wasn't dead in Germany, even
after forty years of a communist dictatorship, hundreds of thousands
of victims, the Peaceful Revolution and unification. And many worried that Germany could export their troubled creation once again to
Europe and the rest of the world.

By the time Director Knabe sat down at his desk at the
Hohenschönhausen Memorial that Monday morning, he had already
decided how he would spend his evenings and weekends for the next
year. He would ignore the warnings from his friends, and veiled threats
from others, and write what should be written next. He would write
the truth about The Left.

The man at the other end of the phone wasn't so cooperative. 'Yes, yes, this is Klaus Eichner.'

I had been given his telephone number, but warned that he might not care to talk. His last media interview had been three years before. He didn't like the way he'd been portrayed, they cautioned.

'I said everything I said before, I don't want to say more about these matters!' He had a cordial, but firm, gravelly voice, like a man accustomed to being in control.

I had part of Eichner's Stasi personnel file in front of me and looked at the picture. An intense man wearing a stylish jacket and necktie stared back at me. He was one of the old guard – those who had been in the Ministry for State Security for more than thirty years. When the picture in his file was taken, he was a recruit, identification number 424967. The man I was speaking to was the same one who had received over twenty medals and cash awards from Minister Erich Mielke. He had been a full colonel and a department head of counterintelligence with the elite HV A, until he suddenly lost his job in March 1990 with the others.

Eichner became one of the founding members of the first association of former officers, *The Insider Committee for Critical Analysis of the History of the MfS*. Formed in May 1992, after a meeting of twenty former officers that took place in Berlin, it was seen as an early example of the continuation of the tightly organized structure of the Ministry for State Security. Their attempts to be involved in deciding what information should be released to the public was one of the first projects. That was quickly rebuffed in those early days.

Former colonel Eichner briefly and incredibly tried a job as an 'environmental consultant', as he was also a Stasi-trained lawyer. Next, he discovered a better route. He quickly reinvented himself as an unapologetic revisionist author and 'expert' about the NSA with the international news media.

Along the way, as he maintained the website for The Insider Committee, he also published books with titles such as *Espionage for*

Peace, which fit neatly with their new definition of the Stasi as brave guardians focused on preventing war. The spies, including Americans, whom the Stasi recruited to be traitors to their own countries, were called *peace scouts*. Eichner wrote or contributed to eight to ten other books that in general had a small circulation in Germany, but were promoted heavily to the 91,000 former officers. Written in German, his other non-MfS countrymen were not yet so accepting of Stasi revisionism. Some copies can be found in used bookshops in Berlin. But it was his last book about what the GDR knew about the NSA that launched his next identity. Coincidentally, it was published in 2014, the year after NSA contractor Edward Snowden published classified American secrets before taking up his current residence in Moscow. Timing is everything.

Since current German intelligence agencies weren't talking to anyone about such things, former Stasi colonel Eichner became the go-to person for the foreign press. Some wanted a German comment about a diplomatic row that ensued when it was revealed by Snowden that the German chancellor's mobile phone was being monitored during the Obama administration. At the same time, the CIA station chief in Berlin was ejected over a different spy scandal.

All in all, it was the perfect opportunity for Eichner to once again position the Stasi and its 250,000 officers working over the years as really just another acceptable and normal intelligence agency. That's been the favored spin of many of the old guard, while many of the younger former officers instead depend on privacy and careful silence as they pursue new successes.

Eichner was asked by *Spiegel*, a major German news magazine, how he would advise Snowden. He responded, not surprisingly, with something to be expected from a Stasi officer: 'Tell the Russians everything you know.' The reporter followed up by asking, 'Wouldn't that subject him to the death penalty in the US?'

'Of course,' he replied.

It probably wasn't the fact that *Spiegel* reported his comment that soured Eichner on talking. Maybe it was what he told another German reporter working for *Stern* magazine during October 2015 that finally did that. They used that remark as their article title:

'Moral Issues Do Not Matter.'

The once Stasi colonel, pictured in the plaid jacket in his file, whose entire life was defending the Ministry for State Security both before and after 1989, didn't wish to talk further in 2019 and hung up the phone. In his eyes, he likely thought he had already done well at both tasks.

———

The major general in charge of Main Department VIII managed all investigative and surveillance activities of the MfS from his third-floor office in Haus 1 of the sprawling Berlin headquarters sometimes just called Normannenstrasse by the officers. That senior employee, holding personal identification number 430018, had gone hand in hand with Minister Mielke throughout nearly the entire history of the MfS. The two of them shaped, directed and were responsible for crafting and expanding methods and systems of abuse and repression over four decades.

The personnel file reflects a notation he should be called *Dr General* due to the PhD he was awarded at JHS – Potsdam, the Stasi University. His dissertation was co-authored with two other people, which was strange enough in academic circles. Its title reads:

Enforcement by the Ministry for State Security of Criminal Responsibility on Citizens on Non-Socialist States.

He alone managed the three core investigative parts of the massive organization – Investigations, Arrests and Surveillance. As head of Main Department VIII, tasked with arresting thousands more in 1989, when the final Day X code word order was given, he was ready and willing to aggressively implement the plan.

It was mid-1989, well before Stasi head Erich Mielke thought it necessary to consider issuing the order for Day X. At the moment, Major General Karli Coburger sat in his office at Normannenstrasse and worked on his draft report for the minister. In it, with his hand-written line corrections, Coburger detailed just how the GDR, already Europe's largest prison camp, would be further locked down. It was called the *Defense State*, and outlined his careful planning for standing orders for the '*...Operational investigations in residential areas... Arrest, preliminary arrest and search... Securing transit routes... Monitoring the driving and deterring of the activities of the three Western MVM (governments).*'

And he continued, adding much more about how to '*Combat the enemy underground, criminal gangs, liquidate enemy commando companies, fight against sabotage, terror, espionage and diversion as well as for safeguarding vital and defense-important objects.*'

Coburger carefully jotted in the margins last-minute corrections to his seven-page plan, which promised additional updates in the last quarter of the year, and handed it to his secretary. He wouldn't have believed that he would never finish and present his report, or that it would become useless anyway in a few short months.

He had seen the Firm through from almost the very beginning, since swearing the oath in 1952 in Leipzig. It was a time when most of his comrades barely had a high school education, but he studied at night. Years later he was awarded a law degree at the Stasi University. In operational work for his entire career he was the image of the ruthless secret police organization that terrorized its own citizens for forty years.

The task of implementing Day X would largely be his – his career accomplishment. But the final order was never given. Instead, things came to an abrupt halt and he was let go from the MfS in March 1990. *Released* the file says, just like all the others. Months before he could settle into the very comfortable retirement of a senior State Security leader on his own terms and with the prestige he felt he deserved.

It wasn't Coburger's role in the unfulfilled Day X that was of immediate interest to prosecutors sifting through recovered files in 1992, but rather another operation outlined in plans with handwritten notations. Operation Prince, the planned assassination of a thirty-three-year-old dissident named Siegfried Schulze in 1975. Schulze was struck on the head twice before a pistol was jammed into his mouth and the trigger pulled. The gun failed to fire. In the unplanned violent scuffle, the pistol's magazine had ejected. Schulze escaped by sheer luck, and lived to talk about it.

In August 1992 Major General Coburger and several others were arrested. He avoided prosecution for the attempted murder of Schulze, but was almost immediately charged with the death of another well-known dissident, Robert Havemann. Havemann, a chemist, had escaped a Nazi death sentence in 1942 only to die in Stasi custody forty years later under suspicious circumstances. In the early 1980s the MfS saw him as their number one dissident target. Coburger seized the stage of the trial as an early opportunity for the revisionist message, and was aggressive, argumentative and unrepentant. He was convicted, one of the few to be. That surprised some, but what followed didn't:

Sentence: One year's imprisonment – suspended.

Meanwhile, Coburger became a founding member of the first revisionist Stasi organization. With what many say was an insult and a defiant gesture to those who started the Peaceful Revolution in St Nicholas Church in Leipzig, the first of the revisionist organizations, called The Insider Committee, or MfS-Insider, was formed by Coburger and a core group of former officers who met at Berlin's Church of the Redeemer in 1991.

Coburger later co-wrote *Victors' Justice?*. It was a book that complained that officers were now victims of political persecution in the unified Germany. It was a bold argument from the man who ran all surveillance, arrest and decomposition of lives by other means for years from the favored safety and privilege of a communist dictatorship. The Stasi are the real victims, his story goes, which by then was already a familiar theme to anyone who noticed the strategy. The book received scant attention outside the former cadres, but the tone and the direction were set.

Major General Coburger was busy while fighting pending prosecution. He was also a founding member of another Stasi organization begun in 1993, following the 1992 formation of The Insider

Committee. It would be named much more benignly, The Society of Legal and Humanitarian Support (GRH). Following the end of this court case, Coburger continued to be active with the GRH and in 2002 appeared in a film with several other former Stasi officers and even Minister Mielke in perhaps the first professional attempt at mass revisionism. The movie was called a documentary and titled *The Ministry for State Security – Everyday Life of an Authority*. The intent was to show how the Stasi was only following the laws of the GDR and really was protecting the people. It failed miserably in spite of, or maybe because of, Coburger announcing on camera, 'You have to respect the person!' Or maybe it failed because it also starred Erich Mielke repeating his favorite quote:

'A warm heart and clean hands!'

Karli Coburger, the senior founding member of the unapologetic Stasi revisionist movement, collects his monthly pension from the German government and continues to live in Berlin.

———

Like some others, Wolfgang Schmidt remained hard at work in the early twenty-first century, crafting his own legacy as a reformed Stasi officer who wished to wisely counsel Germany and America about abuses of authority.

Since joining the Communist Party at twenty-two, and State Security a month after that, he had a varied career through a half-dozen departments. He just made it past his twentieth MfS anniversary when he was released in 1990 while still a young man. Schmidt went from the privileged life of a lieutenant colonel in the prestigious Main Department XVIII, responsible for monitoring threats to the national economy, while earning a high salary of 34,000 DM per year, to being suddenly unemployed.

Schmidt was seated in front of the camera carefully choosing his words during the filming of the documentary with Karli Coburger and Erich Mielke. Dapper and relaxed in a polo shirt with his hair slicked back, he was speaking of the development of the Stasi over his twenty years.

'It can best be described as the relationship maybe like a father to his children. You can see the children grow and make their mistakes; you can't correct them.'

When the film was met with derision in Germany, he went back to his work at the Stasi organization GRH. Those at the GRH like Schmidt and the other active former officers were turning their attention to the director of their prison at Hohenschönhausen. They refused to refer to the place as a *memorial*. They insisted it was only a prison for criminals, like the others. And some were angered by what it had become, here in their special neighborhood, not far from where many, including Schmidt, lived.

They complained that Hubertus was mischaracterizing their work. *Dr Knabe*, they called him with distaste.

One day in late 2005, Schmidt penned an open letter about Hubertus Knabe that they would publish on the website. In the piece, he angrily called Knabe 'an inciter of the people', a term with especially harsh connotations in Germany even now, since it harks back to the Nazi times and to the stirring up of hatred against the Jews. He received positive comments from the cadres about the letter.

In March 2006, Schmidt received a complaint for libel, filed in a Berlin court by Knabe. Schmidt could be fined almost 3,000 euros. Worse, the newspapers were calling it the first time ever that a Stasi officer had been sued for libel!

It was soon after that a small group of former Stasi men, led by a former lieutenant general, were briefed in detail and told where to meet on a Monday morning. They would be using the cover of a group of historians from the Saxony region to gain access.

Monday, a handful of men walked through the barred gates of the Hohenschönhausen Memorial, and checked in for the tour. Yes, we are the group, the historians from Saxony who called and booked, they told the scheduler.

It was a large tour group, as was now normal at the prison, and the men from Saxony were silent as the tour progressed through the intake garage with its covert prison transport truck, up the stairs to the intake areas, past rows of cells and the wing of interrogation rooms. They were waiting for the right moment. As the former inmate guide took the group into the basement cells, which were used to break the difficult prisoners, Lieutenant General Wolfgang Schwanitz glanced at the other men, who were ready. He stepped close to the guide and raised his voice so that everyone on the tour could hear in the confined basement:

'What! Torture in a Stasi prison?? Do you have any proof?!'

On cue, the other 'historians' scattered throughout the group grunted in agreement.

'Fakes of history!' one shouted.

'Lies!' said another, while nodding as if agreeing with a stranger. The guide was speechless, and intimidated.

The former officers filtered back out of the prison, walked past the cherry trees that would soon bloom again, and returned to their neatly kept homes close by. Homes that had been originally issued to many of them by the Stasi. It wasn't the first time variations of this strategy would be used, and wouldn't be the last either. Next, they planned a letter-writing campaign to schools throughout Germany, and then some other direct operations.

Schmidt would later comment to the media, 'We made mistakes like everyone else, but our conscience is clear. We worked within the law.'

Six months later, more than two hundred former Stasi men would show up again near the Memorial to oppose the plans to place plaques to commemorate the former restricted neighborhood. In Parliament a week later, a member of the Social Democratic Party stood poised to give a speech about the old cadres who opposed the commemoration at the Memorial. The day before, she had received an anonymous call. 'Be careful what you say,' the man on the phone warned.

By 2013, Wolfgang Schmidt had become the most senior former officer spokesman, as some of those who outranked him had aged badly. American Edward Snowden had just published via WikiLeaks information about the NSA intercepting Chancellor Merkel's mobile phone. That was sure to generate press interest in German intelligence.

Today he was on his way to meet with an American reporter. He held the meeting this time in the restaurant at the top of the television tower at Alexanderplatz, a symbol of the GDR. More impressive than a café somewhere, and more dramatic – reporters liked that sort of thing.

An hour later Schmidt looked across the table at the reporter, who was seeking a quote about NSA spying under the Obama administration. He decided to cut to the chase. A smile spread across his face.

'You know, for us, this would have been a dream come true,' he said, referring to the scope of the capabilities of the NSA. 'So much information on so many people.'

Finishing an expensive lunch at the top of the television tower at Alexanderplatz, he was just a few blocks from the agency charged with making sense of the more than 100 kilometers of files that he had helped to collect for twenty years – at least those files that remained and were not destroyed. He nodded at the reporter and, seemingly ignoring his previous 'dream come true' comment, he professed to be appalled at the NSA activity.

'The only way to protect the people's privacy is not to allow the government to collect their information in the first place,' he advised wisely.

––––––

There are few things that unite people like sports. In the United States it's baseball and football, and in Europe it's what Americans call soccer. In Europe and in most of the rest of the world, football is a huge industry and an easy way to transcend national boundaries while instilling national pride. That's one reason why the Stasi ran a football club and sports network for thirty-five years.

Sportvereinigung Dynamo, or SV Dynamo, was the official sports organization for East Germany. It participated in the European Championships, the World Cup and the Olympics. At its peak it had 280,000 members, more than 200 teams, sports stadiums and even hotels. All of it was owned by the Firm and run by a major general listed on a special section of the MfS organization chart as reporting directly to the minister. The major general presided over the club winning 215 Olympic medals, assisted by the state-sponsored doping of athletes, which was common. Naturally, no one with Dynamo ever *officially* failed a state drug test.

Having a prestigious sports club was always an important part of the façade of a successful communist dictatorship. The side benefits for the Stasi were numerous; for intelligence collection, identifying foreign athletes who could be blackmailed, obtaining hard currency and so on. It was essential for the state to be in tight control of the East German players, to ensure they didn't defect and cause embarrassment. Everyone in German and European sports knew all about SV Dynamo and who was behind it. It was just another abnormal, yet common, fact of life during a Cold War filled with strange circumstances and odd bedfellows.

As the club was integrated into the Stasi, it was dissolved with the MfS almost immediately after the Wall fell. It was about time anyway for Germany to have sports teams that were independent from the communist state, it was decided.

That's why it was so curious when it was discovered nearly twenty years later that a present-day German football team, FC Union Berlin, had a mysterious major sponsor.

It was June 2009 and Dirk Zingler, the president of FC Union football club, had some truly exciting news for the board. An international sporting association had offered to invest ten million euros in them over the next five years! The club buzzed with excitement. So much could be done with that sort of investment. Although they were only second tier in German football, they had been well known as a cult club all over Europe for their enthusiastic fan base. The team could be traced back to 1906, but during the Cold War years they were loved by fans as the East Berlin underdogs who frequently faced down Dynamo, the Stasi team. Their slogan was 'better to be a loser than a Stasi pig!' The fans' songs were thinly veiled criticisms of the GDR. FC Union maintained a rabid wild fan base because of this, although the club never finished higher than seventh place. That mattered little; supporting the renegade team was an important act of defiance to supporters.

But who would invest that kind of money in them? Ten million euros? And who would invest it in a team with such a dismal record? Zingler asked few questions when contacted by a voice on the end of a telephone call who described himself as the CEO of International Sports Promotion (ISP). He said his name was Jürgen Czilinsky, and something about the money being from international investors. No matter. Good news was good news and the club started to put together the paperwork and make plans for the money.

Over the next couple of months, the uneasiness continued to linger with club officials who were otherwise happily making plans for expansion. Word of the deal had leaked to the press and some wondered, who was ISP, and who was Jürgen Czilinsky? Reporters started to make calls and ask pointed questions. It was soon learned that International Sports Promotion was a company based in the UAE whose principals had taken significant steps not to be identified. That piqued even more interest. An intrepid reporter contacted Chairman Czilinsky and asked him directly about his background. Czilinsky said calmly that he was German, had worked in 'GDR foreign trade', was trained as a paratrooper and today specialized in the 'networking of networks'.

Even to a young reporter in 2009, that simply had *Stasi* written all over it.

More mysteriously, the Archive said yes indeed they had records about a former MfS officer under the name of Jürgen Czilinsky. Once identified as the same person as ISP chairman Czilinsky, the reporter was unable to find him again. When numerous calls were finally returned, Czilinsky said he was in West Africa, in the Democratic Republic of Congo (DRC). He wouldn't say why. The DRC is a huge, constantly war-torn country, most of which even now isn't controlled by the government, but it's also one of the richest in terms of natural resources to be exploited. The Congo had been the site of a great many Cold War intrigues. When confronted with the results of his file found in the Archive, Czilinsky calmly admitted to having been a Stasi officer, but said he 'doesn't deal with those questions after 1990'.

That wasn't good enough, and the FC Union fans erupted in outrage at the Stasi connection. After discussion the club turned down the ISP initial payment plan of five million euros, even after they had already received the first million. They decided it just wasn't worth ruining their reputation, the club's main and arguably only asset. Nobody knows the real reason ISP wanted to invest ten million euros in a second-tier club. Some speculate money laundering was involved. Perhaps it was also a chance to influence the club from the inside.

Two years later in 2011, things became even worse for the cash-starved football club. Club president Dirk Zingler was revealed to have his own Stasi past. Zingler had served three years in the military arm of the MfS, the Felix Dzerzhinsky Guards Regiment, in the 1980s. Zingler brushed off the questions. He was only doing 'military service', he said and incredibly claimed that he had no idea that the Dzerzhinsky Regiment (named after the founder of the Soviet secret police) had anything to do with the Stasi.

Former Stasi captain Jürgen Czilinsky remains connected to several other Berlin companies. He's not talking about who ISP really is, or what business he had in the DRC. He's once again dropped from public view, but is shown as vice-president and member of the board of directors for Sowareen Solutions, a company based in Zurich. That company describes its business as 'other freelance work'.

23

NEW ORGANIZATIONS

Standing on a winter's day next to a bronze bust of Franz Mehring, which is carefully kept clean of the city's otherwise constant graffiti, I stare up at what every East Berliner over forty would recognize instantly. The building is impressive if a bit worn, as it stands at the exclusive address of Franz-Mehring-Platz 1 in central Berlin. The former home of the SED. Mehring was one of three founders of the Communist Party in Germany. The statue seems to scrutinize approaching visitors, as it looks on facing the street.

Ancient old-growth trees frame the building's entrance, and the hand at the bottom of the Mehring statue clutches a copy of what appears to be *The Communist Manifesto*, written by another German named Karl Marx. The eight-floor building proudly bears the name *Neues Deutschland*, or New Germany, the name of the longtime SED Communist Party newspaper. It's located a few blocks from Ostbahnhof, former main showpiece railway station for East Berlin. This was the home of the headquarters of the East German Communist Party and rulers of the state.

It's a comfortable location for the Grey Men, friendly territory. Only a few miles away is the Lichtenberg district, even now called Little GDR by some German politicians, and referred to as the neighborhood of the colonels by others because of the density of occupants with Stasi pasts.

Within months of the unification of Germany in October 1990 the first of the four organizations designed to carry on the interests of the Stasi was formed. In those early and mostly pre-internet days that organization was named The Insider Committee for Critical Analysis of the History of the MfS. It was followed quickly by The Society of Legal and Humanitarian Support (GRH). Both were started by former officers, with the support of East German politicians. Then there is the ISOR Social Club, and the rather innocent-sounding Society for the Protection of Civil Rights and Human Dignity (GBM). The website of The Insider Committee (MfS-Insider) was until recently maintained by HV A officer and self-proclaimed NSA expert Colonel Klaus Eichner. That website proudly claimed more than 125,000 visitors in 2018.

These organizations had several immediate goals. The first was to maintain a Stasi-like tight organizational structure and chain of command that would carry forward and enable the comrades to maintain contact and share successes and frustrations. The second was to advocate for higher pensions from the new German government. Since officers had routinely been paid many times the salary of the average East German, they would argue for a pension based on those salaries. Third was the direct action and revisionist element. For years these groups would dispatch members to attend public tours at Stasi prisons and the Stasi Museum to argue anonymously with the tour guides in front of guests about one issue or another. It was also the political advocacy and legal action of these groups that prevented the posting of lists of Stasi officers in public or on the internet, and that sued German publications that spoke ill of the Ministry for State Security. They had some notable successes. It's impossible to find the list of Stasi officers or a separate list of the Officers in Special Employment, the OibEs, on any publicly available site in today's Germany.

The groups have even provided technical advice to movie producers to ensure that the Firm is not, in their view, defamed. Most notably, the popular movie *The Lives of Others*, which was a hit in Europe and the United States in 2006, consulted heavily with the GRH and Insider Committee for the techniques used by Stasi officers. The film, which won awards elsewhere, was controversial in Germany as it contained a key bit of misinformation, and some other mistakes. It portrayed the mental struggle of a Stasi captain in charge of developing information to be used against a writer. In the movie, the Stasi officer ends up taking the side of the dissident writer and protecting him from arrest. In reality, that was something that had never been known to happen in the Stasi's four decades. The revisionist, favorable and sympathetic portrayal of a ranking Stasi officer in the script resulted in the producers being denied permission to film at the prison memorial.

The organizations also maintain connections with their American comrades.

The February 2019 newsletter published by the Society for the Protection of Civil Rights and Human Dignity (GBM) features Angela Davis, the aging but well-known American communist and member of the 1960s leftist domestic terrorist group the Black Panthers. Featured in their newsletters today and still proudly referenced on their websites, Davis remains useful to former Stasi officers.

Few over the age of forty have forgotten who she is, especially those of us working for the FBI. Davis visited East Germany many times and later received a PhD from Humboldt University, which she attended at the height of the Cold War. She was also briefly on the FBI's Ten Most Wanted list after being charged with conspiracy, aggravated kidnapping and first-degree murder in connection with the execution of a Superior Court judge and the killing of three others, taken hostage by a member of the Black Panthers in a California courtroom in 1970. Davis had bought two of the guns, including the shotgun that was used to murder the judge. After being acquitted of all charges while being defended by a lawyer paid for by the Communist Party USA (CPUSA), she was hosted often in the GDR as well as in Moscow and given awards relating to her communist activism. Several times a candidate for vice-president of the CPUSA, Davis consistently defended repressive Soviet governments. For this she was given the Lenin Peace Prize during a ceremony in Moscow in 1979, referring to the audience there as 'comrades'. More recently she found a niche as a college professor at the University of California, Santa Cruz. A 2019 GBM newsletter celebrates her 'scientific career' and also at the same time the seventieth anniversary of the founding of the GDR.

I had phoned the main number for the GRH about a week earlier, asking for some general information. The man who answered provided his name only when I asked. 'Stiebert.' He suggested I send an email so a committee meeting that afternoon could discuss my request. After a week with no response, I phoned again. This time I was put through to the GRH's chairman, Hans Bauer. Bauer said unfortunately his schedule was too full with travel to speak about current issues. He was leaving at once. Nobody else was available in his absence. He had sent me an email response, he said, which was never received. Perhaps in a month he would have time. I knew that Dieter Stiebert, who had answered the telephone, was a former Stasi officer, and that Bauer was the former deputy attorney general of the GDR.

Hanging up the phone and noticing that office hours were posted on the GRH website, it was a few days later that I decided to stop by.

Walking into the lobby, I looked at the directory. The third floor was occupied by what's now called the Communist Party of Germany, the KPD, in suite 323. But there are other interesting tenants sharing the same floor. Conveniently, on two floors are grouped Stasi-related organizations. The building directory describes them as *Industry Associations*. The elevators with no doors, common in communist state buildings in the 1980s, hummed busily.

The hallway on the third floor appeared sterile, floors covered with the usual GDR linoleum, and lined with tightly closed doors bearing frosted glass. With two Stasi organizations and the German Communist Party in residence within a hundred feet, I supposed this was as anti-capitalist a place as there could be. I tapped on the door of the GRH office, The Society of Legal and Humanitarian Support, it said, and opened it. Inside sat a man at a desk next to a freshly opened box from Amazon. He looked up, surprised.

'Herr Stiebert?' Nodding, the man, wearing gold-framed glasses and a sleeveless cardigan along with police-type thick black shoes, stood as I introduced myself. I explained that I had called before and was stopping by to pick up some literature.

'Perhaps you have a minute also for a couple of questions about GRH?' He paused, but waved me over to a chair at a small table. The shelves were lined with books and newsletters. A large metal safe stood in the back, key stuck in the lock. To the right were outgoing mailboxes labeled ISOR and GBM, the other Stasi support groups, and KPD. The door to a large conference room was slightly ajar, and I noted movement inside.

'Could you tell me what the general purpose of your organization is?'

'We work for our members to ensure the proper understanding of history.'

'And who are your members? Where do they come from?'

'They worked in the GDR as lawyers, NVA and border guards.'

'Anyone else…?'

'… And… there… are… a few… MfS.'

I asked him about some of the literature and books on the office shelves and he warmed up and began to talk.

Stiebert's last rank in 1989 was lieutenant colonel. He had been in the MfS for thirty-three years, nearly all of that in Berlin. He received a degree at the JHS in Potsdam and preferred to call himself 'a lawyer'. In fact, after the Wall fell he said he had no problem finding work in a law firm and practicing law in unified Germany for the next eighteen years.

GRH has about eight hundred active members as of 2019, most of them former Stasi officers. It handles what he described as 'issues other than the pension project'. Attempts to get legislation to increase pensions are handled by ISOR. 'They're in the same building,' he said. 'Just down the hall.'

'So other than ISOR, I noticed another group – GBM?'

He nodded. 'Yes, yes, and two others also, OKV and MfS-Insider. That last one is really just a website at the moment though.' OKV is the abbreviation for another innocuous-sounding group, East German Board of Associations.

I looked up from my notes, noticing activity as the door to the conference room swung open slowly, carried by a draft from the hallway. On the far wall hung a huge painting of Lenin, staring down at two men who were hard at work with documents and binders. They looked up at me, and the larger of the two moved to close the door. I stood, stepped into the doorway and introduced myself.

The bigger one spoke first. 'I'm Vandamme,' he said.

'Eichhorn,' the other nodded to me. They appeared somehow satisfied and returned to their work at the large conference table, now ignoring me.

'We keep all our records here,' Stiebert mentioned, sweeping his hand at the neatly cataloged file folders that filled the wall of bookcases. 'But we will talk out here.' He closed the conference room door behind us.

'There's some interest now that it is the thirtieth anniversary of the end of the GDR and next year being the thirty-year mark of the ending of the MfS…' I began.

'No,' he said. 'No.' He shook his head. 'It's the *seventieth* year of the *formation* of the MfS actually. We celebrate it every year.'

'An official event?'

'Yes, of course. These days we have a harder time attracting the younger people. But we're working on that,' he added softly.

I get the sense he's recruiting for an organization that ceased to exist twenty-nine years earlier.

'And many of the East German states are still having problems with integration.'

There was a 'bong' from his mobile phone and he quickly jumped up to answer. After some discussion about the week's planned events, he returned to the small table where we sat and slowly smoothed his cardigan.

I continued. 'Thirty-three years you were working for MfS – you were there for most of its time, and you've since had some years to reflect. Do you have regrets?'

He stiffened immediately.

'None. We were just an agency in a government, a normal government operation like any other.'

I put down my notebook and looked closely at him. He continued quickly.

'Our government just had different laws, that's all.'

In all the conversations I'd had with Stasi officers, I had never found any who expressed regrets for the victims, for the excesses of the police state, or for any of the more than 200,000 people jailed for political reasons. Many were like the two in the back room, not interested in talking much.

I'd heard astounding rationalizations from many people I'd interviewed in my years as an FBI agent. For the moment, I decided to let him keep this one.

'Tell me about November 1989. When the Wall came down. What did you do?'

'We all knew something was coming, but not that. It was... extraordinary. Nobody saw it coming. Not even your Western services, by the way.'

I nodded and continued to jot some notes.

'I was in Berlin at Normannenstrasse, and decided it was best to go visit the district offices.'

'Because of the chaos?'

'No, no. I wanted to make sure that there was no violence there from our end.'

'Things ended quickly after that, didn't they?'

Stiebert looked out the window but didn't immediately respond.

'We could have handled it... handled everything. But, *they* lost the political will.'

In that office, it seemed that the last twenty-nine years hadn't passed at all.

Several more calls came in, resulting in more rapid conversations. He was a busy man.

I asked about the current projects, what were they planning now, but Stiebert remained vague. 'You must talk with Chairman Bauer about that.'

What about the recent visit of MfS officers to the federal commissioner of the Archives a few months ago?

Stiebert reached over to a box and pulled out a slick green booklet, which he handed it to me. 'This was our list of... questions that we posed to him.'

'And what was the result?'

He smiled. 'We accomplished our goal.'

I thought of the green booklet, and wondered how many of those had been distributed. I had seen it myself before, in the office of a top German Stasi expert only weeks before. The organization appeared well funded, even after nearly three decades.

Soon it became apparent he wasn't inclined to talk further about what they were planning at the moment, so I changed the subject.

'How do you think the MfS would have done in the information age, if the Wall never came down back then? With the social media we have and technology.'

He sat back in his chair, and carefully adjusted his gold sweater. 'It wouldn't have been a problem at all – we were very advanced. You know we had Department III, with General Männchen. His people were very good at electronic interceptions. By the late 1980s that department was already hacking into computers and places also.' He continued to speak proudly of their abilities.

'So... what would you have done in the time of Facebook and Google?'

'We would have... adapted. Quite easily, I expect.'

'Do you have many members now outside Germany?'

'Yes, some. And we stay in touch with the three Americans also. They're out of prison now.'

'Oh? You mean the two men and the woman who were convicted of espionage?'

Stiebert smiled broadly and nodded. 'Espionage,' he repeated.

It was unexpected that they even now maintained contact with those he called 'the three'.

Kurt Alan Stand, Theresa Marie Squillacote and James Michael Clark. All were arrested in the United States in 1997 and served long prison sentences for spying for East Germany, including passing along classified information. Squillacote, who had worked for a defense contractor and took documents from the Pentagon, wasn't released until 2015, after serving eighteen years in federal prison.

I recalled something on the website for MfS-Insider. It had described the three as 'peace scouts' in 'political detention' and lamented that they would have been much more usable in 1995 due to their positions then, but unfortunately the GDR was dissolved. To the Stasi, spies in Europe and America were there to 'work for peace' and nobody in East Germany was ever arrested for political reasons at all. At least, that's the version when they speak to outsiders.

As Stiebert took another call, I looked up at the wall behind the door where a framed photo of Rosa Luxemburg, another founding member of the Communist Party in Germany, was affixed. It included one of her quotes:

'Joy in spite of everything. To cry is a business of weakness.'

He handed me some other materials and I stepped out the door, leaving him sorting through papers and speaking loudly into the phone as I continued down the hall.

The Initiative Community for the Protection of the Social Rights of Former Members of Armed Bodies and the Customs Administration of the GDR, more commonly referred to as the ISOR Social Club, which is what it said on the door. The office looked darkened and closed, but I saw a shadow moving inside and knocked and then tried the door, which opened.

This office was even more organized than GRH, and had one occupant, another former Stasi colonel named Peter Ott. Ott admitted that to me when I introduced myself, and when I asked him. Yes, he was a former MfS officer.

'You just missed them,' he said. 'The chiefs just left an hour ago.'

'Do you mean Wolfgang Schmidt?'

'Yes, and the others.'

I was aware previously from the ISOR website that Schmidt, the most active senior Stasi officer in Germany at present, was the managing director of ISOR. Bauer had told me on the phone that Schmidt was also unavailable.

I spoke with Ott, who said he just volunteered to help out in the office. ISOR was mainly focused on increasing the pensions of Stasi officers, and other 'armed organs' of the GDR. He said that at the moment ISOR had about ten thousand members, with about two-thirds of those coming from MfS ranks.

Ott called himself a 'lawyer' and said he attended the JHS University in Potsdam for his training. He'd been working for a Berlin law firm until he retired just last year. He added that he worked more as a type of legal assistant, as his particular 'legal experience' didn't technically qualify him to directly transfer and practice as a full-fledged lawyer in unified Germany, unlike most of his other colleagues.

While we spoke, two other former Stasi officers arrived. Eyeing me, they spoke guardedly with Ott about an upcoming event by the Left Party that they were headed to. They animatedly displayed a splashy flyer from a young member of the Left Party running for office in the Bundestag. I casually chatted with them. Ott opened the adjoining door to reveal a well-organized file room with a large conference table. He grabbed a couple of large boxes of documents from the shelf and handed them over. The others were assigned to attend the event and distribute the materials.

Three flights up, at the office of the Society for the Protection of Civil Rights and Human Dignity (GBM), I surprised an office assistant sitting in front of a computer busily typing a report. I introduced myself as usual. The woman appeared uncomfortable. She gave her name as Ms Franz, and added that she couldn't comment on what the GBM does or how many members they have, but yes, they represent former MfS officers as well as others. They have fewer members than the ten thousand who belong to ISOR, but more than the GRH.

'There's a big difference between the organizations,' she said. 'But I really can't say what it is. Maybe you can make an appointment for later.'

I mentioned that I had seen on their webpage a statement of partnership between GBM, ISOR and GRH dated January 2019.

'I can't talk about that either,' she said. 'Please contact the chairperson of GBM, Helga Hörning.'

The GBM website contains the usual language of 'imperialist aggression' and being against 'distortions of GDR history'. It was now a familiar theme. Hörning was most recently mentioned on RT, formerly called Russia Today, an international television network funded by the Russian government, when she gave a human rights award in 2018 to Hans Morrow, the last head of the SED. Also, she appears active in pro-Russia issues shared with the Left Party.

'Take a newsletter.' Ms Franz gestured, pulling one off the shelf. I pointed to another. 'Do you mind if I take a copy of that one also? She's an American.'

'Ah yes, Angela Davis.' Franz retrieved the newsletter. 'Certainly. That's last month's.' I thought of staying for a longer talk with Ms Franz, but from the tension that filled the air it was obvious that she was worried about somebody returning and catching her talking.

Instead, I thanked her and put my hand on the door. She looked instantly relieved. I walked down the linoleum hallways. It was a place that seemed to be on the move, far from being a monument to history. The building itself seemed to be in waiting.

Once again I found myself passing through the garden, and being scrutinized by the stare of Mehring, the bearded, stern-faced statue that commemorates one of the German founders of global communism.

24

REVISIONISTS

'Who controls the past controls the future'

GEORGE ORWELL, *1984*

Most efforts to revise history are usually slow and easy to overlook, but sometimes they rush up and hit you in the face.

It was late on a weeknight evening. I stood in a hotel bar with a handful of others in a former communist state, a freed former servant of the Soviet Union. I was there to meet with a group of Western police and intelligence attachés assigned to the region. We waited for our host, a member the intelligence service of that country, which was now a proud NATO member. We'd all been invited to see yet another remnant of Soviet KGB repression.

I glanced at my watch. He was late.

I turned to a UK associate from the Secret Intelligence Service (SIS), better known as MI6. 'Is he still coming?'

He checked his phone. 'Yes. Five minutes,' he said. 'Parking now.'

As our host joined us, the bar was slowly emptying as some businessmen and a couple of happy tourists filtered out. The hotel was large and modern; foreign travelers even now preferred it.

Marco burst in with a wave. He was somewhere in his late fifties, a slightly overweight man with a tired smile who spoke English, Russian and his own country's language. Sometimes he spoke them all in the same sentence. In his generation he would have been forced to study Russian, but he only spoke it now if he had to.

He clutched a mobile phone in each hand this evening, as he did every time I ever saw him. Tonight was an impromptu meeting with the invitation extended only to this select group.

'So sorry, sorry! Everything is arranged. Up we go!'

We all crowded into the elevator and he jabbed the button for the seventh floor.

'I arranged also for a few refreshments, the traditional kind. You'll see.' One of his mobile phones rang again and he stared at the screen before pressing it to his ear and speaking rapidly.

We all filed off into the seventh-floor hallway, which was empty save for a casually dressed younger man who was staring out the hallway window. Marco caught the man's eye and nodded.

With a gentle motion the younger man touched the mirrored panel next to the row of elevators and it slid open, revealing a spacious room. We all stepped in and the panel slid closed. We were instantly transported back to the technology of 1980. Banks of recording equipment filled one wall, as well as a couple of well-worn cots and several typewriters. Ashtrays overflowed with Russian cigarette butts.

'We kept it exactly as we found it in 1994,' Marco explained. 'From here every room on the seventh and sixth floors could be easily monitored. They were the floors all foreigners were sent to. All rooms were wired from the beginning, phones and microphones.' He gestured to the panel on his left. 'Just flip a switch.'

Some of the equipment had been hastily smashed, but there was still torn and burned paper in the trash and one sheet rolled halfway through one of the Russian typewriters. In the corner was a coat rack with a faded KGB colonel's overcoat hanging.

'They left in a hurry,' Marco said. 'We didn't know about this place until a month later when we got a call from an old handyman who had worked in the hotel for years.' He checked both his mobile phones again before sliding them into different coat pockets and waving his hand at the door behind us.

'He told us that something odd was going on up on seven. I guess he was searching for an electrical fault one day in the mid-1980s and came across this door, which had been left open a crack. He thought it was a utility closet. He pushed it, and was immediately threatened by a man who looked to him to be KGB.'

'Forget about this, if you know what's best,' the man whispered to him before slamming the door.

'He was an old man, and old men here and then knew what that meant all too well. So, he forgot about it. For a little while, anyway. Some years.'

We looked over the recorders, mid-1980s electronics of the Russian kind, which I had seen before. Not cutting edge even then, but serviceable and sturdy. A phone was mounted on the wall, wires cut and dangling. These places in hotels in communist Eastern Europe were common, but seeing it as if the KGB was here minutes ago wasn't. They had left after 1991 in a hurry. For some reason, they just didn't wish to be around once the Russian military pulled out.

'All the papers they left here were useless of course, and we almost threw everything out, until we had an idea,' Marco said to me, smiling. 'We would use it as part of the training program for our recruits and to show foreign… partners.' The management was happy to agree for now. Just no tourists or any media, they pleaded. 'Please! Our hotel is popular!'

'We'll keep it like this for a bit longer,' Marco announced. 'But we don't show it to many foreigners these days. It's a good way to remind our younger recruits that it wasn't so long ago. The hotel swears they didn't know anything about it during all that time…'

The younger man from the hallway reappeared with a tray bearing the traditional small glasses of vodka and a plate of pickles, which he slid on the table before saying something to Marco and leaving again.

Minutes later, there was tap at the door and an older man was let in. Marco immediately whispered in my ear, 'He's KGB.' I recognized the face – he was one of the officers at the nearby Russian Embassy. Old-school KGB. Since the Soviet Union came apart, the KGB was reincarnated into two agencies, the SVR RF (Sluzhba vneshney razvedki Rossiyskoy Federatsii) and the internal Federal Security Service,

the FSB (Federal'naya sluzhba bezopasnosti Rossiyskoy Federatsii).
The SVR simply took over foreign intelligence from the KGB First
Chief Directorate in 1991. So, Vassily was called an SVR officer now.
Meaning he did the same job as he'd done somewhere else before. He
was always invited to events by the local service here, but never came.
This evening, he did, but he looked upset.

Vassily glanced around and ignored the group.

'That's all wrong,' he declared to nobody in particular, pointing
at the KGB colonel's overcoat hanging on the rack.

'So is this.' He waved at the wrecked equipment. 'It wouldn't have
been this way!'

Marco said nothing but merely offered the tray of vodka. Vassily
brushed it away.

'None of this is right!'

The room quieted for a moment, as others stopped talking and
waited to see how things played out.

The silence was awkward, even though most of the people in the
crowd were accustomed to such odd things while serving in Eastern
Europe. After a brief pause, the conversations continued, with everyone politely ignoring him. All people in the room knew what had
happened here, and in this country. They weren't buying Vassily's
bluster and denials. They didn't need to think twice about it. With
the passing of another generation, some might.

I eventually nodded my thanks to Marco and headed for the elevator, leaving Vassily and the others. He was still pointing at things
and shaking his head vigorously.

That evening reminded me again just how fragile historical clarity
is, even when it stares right at you.

————

It was a sunny morning in June 2014 when Hubertus Knabe left his
Berlin office located above the prison cellblock at the Hohenschönhausen
Memorial, and climbed into his car. He was satisfied and frustrated at

once. Maybe the drive would clear his head. He passed through the prison gates and into the quiet Lichtenberg district, the neighborhood of the colonels, where many times it seemed that people continued to watch. In fact, there was no doubt that they did.

Just last week he had filed his most recent two-year activity report with the Berlin Senate, as was the routine. Report number seven, he knew it was a good one. In the last two years more than 800,000 people had visited the Memorial, at least 200,000 of those from school visits. In the almost fifteen years that he had been director, he and his many staff, and now nearly fifty former inmate guides, had turned this former warehouse of hopeless despair into what had become the most successful and prominent testimony to communist repression in Europe. There could be even more people squeezed in, but it wasn't a museum, and wouldn't be as long as he was here. He kept the prison original, which meant it wasn't suitable or safe for visitors to roam unescorted. It could still be a dangerous place, like many old buildings with dark histories. But no matter – accompanied tours are best. The human face of the repression that went on in these cells and 120 interrogation rooms must never be allowed to waver. Never.

Since the guided tours were often overbooked, they had also created an informative permanent exhibit of communist repression in the waiting area. A place to find many small books with a limited general circulation but nonetheless bearing powerful voices and writings by victims that might not be found so easily these days.

He had ensured the Memorial stayed focused far beyond the iron gates. In the past two years he had also sent the inmate eyewitnesses to give more than three thousand seminars and personal presentations at schools. No other institution in Germany highlighting political repression had reached as many young people to teach them about the communist regime of East Germany. There had been over 1,700 media reports throughout the world in the past two years in which the Memorial had been profiled. And the visitors recently included German president Joachim Gauck, the president of Hungary, the Tunisian prime minister, and even some celebrities like Tom Hanks.

Various foreign delegations from former communist states visited as well, looking for suggestions on how to deal with and confront their own pasts. The Memorial was doing tours in English, French, Spanish, German, Italian, Norwegian, Danish and Dutch. Hubertus planned to expand that, too. He had himself given many speeches throughout Europe, and in the United States. Speeches of warning, with personal stories instead of history lectures.

By any standard, the Hohenschönhausen Memorial was an astounding success. It was the eyewitnesses, the victims, who made the difference, he told anyone who asked. Many of them had thanked him for the opportunity. They were paid a small amount, but mostly they did it as a sort of therapy. He made sure that their eyewitness statements were also recorded in a permanent digital archive. People must remember. Generations of the future must not forget.

As he recalled last week's report, he thought of the quote he'd included in the introduction. Just before he passed it on to the Berlin Senate, Hubertus typed in one of his favorite remarks made by former president Gauck:

'We learn from the past, because the future is not indifferent to us.'

His thoughts were jarred back by a distinctive clang known to Berliners, and he twisted the wheel to avoid a fast-moving yellow electric tram. As he turned off Freienwalder Strasse toward Alexanderplatz, he shook his head as he tried to dispel that familiar nagging feeling that had returned again. The shiver he felt when he worried that maybe he wasn't doing enough – that Germany and the world were blindly making the same mistakes again.

It had been about five years since he had written about the perpetrators of the communist dictatorship who were still active in German society. Some people didn't like what he said. It was uncomfortable to be sure, but necessary to be clear, especially since few others were talking about it. It had become like a hushed family secret.

The Stasi, and those who depended on them to keep a dictatorship afloat for so long, continued to be proudly unashamed and active, and were gaining influence yet again in politics. He wrote the truth about how the SED elite still lived, in the nice gated community where they were living before the fall. How the money that went missing was never found, and how the two name changes of the party to the PDS and recently to the Left Party changed little. How the Stasi remained scattered in the neighborhoods of Lichtenberg and the neat little houses on the streets that surrounded the Memorial. Some of the inmate eyewitnesses sometimes encountered them while walking down the street nearby. They especially remembered Colonel Siegfried Rataizick, longtime head of the prisons and in direct charge of Hohenschönhausen until it was taken away from him in 1990. Rataizick was said by more than one eyewitness to turn silently and spit on the sidewalk whenever he recognized a former inmate walking by.

Ex-Stasi officers would even sometimes attend the tours at the Memorial to argue with the former inmate guides. 'That's nonsense! You're wrong! This place wasn't like that! You only tell one side.'

He thought of one of the eyewitnesses, Mario Röllig, who once stopped his tour when confronted by a former officer loudly protesting: 'This is wrong, it wasn't like that! Who told you it was?'

Röllig turned and pointed.

'I don't claim to be an unbiased historian, but over there was my cell. I was nineteen.'

It seemed that no matter how much Hubertus warned about the Left Party, the inheritors of the SED communists and perhaps also their money – which was never accounted for – they still became increasingly powerful in Parliament and in Berlin.

The worst was the silence of almost everyone else. The uncomfortable chilling stillness in the air. The German media had tired of reporting about the GDR and rarely challenged the twisted version of history that many on the left now liked to present. The historians at the Archive, and those who worked with them frequently, were being careful. Too careful, he thought. Most historians in Germany were consumed with narrow topics that the average person had no interest in and wouldn't even notice. They all knew where the minefields lay, what line they shouldn't cross. But it's safer that way, some would say. *The job of a historian is to address those things that happened more than thirty years ago,* others cautioned him. *We are not politicians or prosecutors,* others said as they wagged their fingers at him in private.

To Hubertus, it mattered. *Yes, I'm a historian! But that doesn't mean I must be a spectator, as the truth is twisted, lied about and the victims are attacked or marginalized! I cannot!*

His family and friends told him constantly that he must be more careful. The more international exposure the Memorial received, the more often the foreign press contacted him for visits or quotes, the personal risk increased. He was honest with the press who were looking for a quote. That was a problem, he knew; it disturbed the deafening silence that everybody had come to expect. That same silence is what many now count on in their new careers working to reinvent communist ideals.

Hubertus found himself parking his car and reached over to shut off the engine. He sat with his hands gripping the wheel. Stasi officers and SED officials shouldn't have a place in Europe's democratic governments! Even now, twenty-five years after the Wall came down. Maybe even more so now, as memories faded.

He gathered his notes from the seat and shoved them into his briefcase. Today he was speaking to a group of university students about the MfS and the communist state. It was to be streamed afterward to reach many more people. That thought brought a momentary satisfied smile as he checked his watch and rushed inside.

————

Two hours later, Hubertus was back sitting in the car and feeling queasy. The speech went well, he thought. But he felt obligated once again to explain the GDR and Stasi from scratch, and received few questions. It was hard to tell if they were interested at all. Most of them registered disconnection, as if it were just another stale history lecture. More than a few were staring at their mobile phones. A different time, and a different generation, he supposed. But not so different. Many of them were about the same age as him when he was banned from entering East Berlin, and kept from Annette.

He closed his eyes and still saw the look on the border guard's face that day in the wooden booth at the Friedrichstrasse checkpoint as he was sent away. It was the face of a dictatorship in which they controlled you. The look of someone who had unchecked power and knew it. That S-Bahn station – Tränenpalast – the Palace of Tears.

Hubertus jarred himself back to the present. Maybe he should have mentioned his own story in the talk today? No, no, that would have been too personal and out of character. Germans are usually private people. The audience would have thought it odd and uncomfortable too.

He switched on the ignition, shifted the gear and started to back up. Then he remembered it – the one good thing that had come out of the trip. He had a new idea, moments after stepping off the stage. Tossing it over in his head as he somewhat impatiently shook hands with the event host and a few others. He would apply for additional funding from Parliament. A new proposal. He could use some of the many vacant offices at the Hohenschönhausen Memorial for the added staff. For now, he would call it the Center for Left-Wing Extremism.

It would be much more broadly oriented than the prison memorial. He might incorporate some of his findings about the Left Party and their roots. It could be a way of further engaging the thousands of young visitors who were coming. Show them the true face of left-wing extremism, something they certainly weren't shown anywhere else.

The ideas were swirling madly in his mind as he stomped on the gas and rushed back to the Memorial to get to work. There was so much to do.

———

Two men stood proudly in snappy business attire at the front of the conference room at an undeniable bastion of capitalism, the Berlin

Ramada Hotel, each holding their own. They looked harmless, as many former Stasi officers do. One of them even flashed a slight smile as he held up a book. It was sixteen years after the fall.

Gotthold Schramm and Peter Pfütze had been colonels in the MfS HV A, until released in 1990. Today would be a book reading from each of their recently completed works of revisionism.

It had been hoped that the former head of their department, Markus Wolf, would attend to give the books a boost, but that wasn't to be. He was ailing and would be dead in six months. But the number two, Werner Grossmann, and many of their former comrades were present. So too were a few from the press, and some other unknown faces sitting alone and silently in the crowd.

Pfütze stepped forward first, and opened his paperback, which sported a glossy cover: *Visiting Time – Western Diplomats on a Special Mission*. He was, he explained, responsible for contact with more than 3,400 Western diplomats who came to visit prisoners in Hohenschönhausen. Pausing, he looked out at the crowd and turned the page to start reading.

'Not one of them ever complained!'

The room immediately erupted with derisive laughter from the non-Stasi audience members. Turns out there were more of those present than had been expected.

He pretended not to hear them, and continued reading: '… the prisoners were treated correctly!'

The mocking laughter now sounded angry.

When former colonel Gotthold Schramm began with his book, titled *The Embassy Refugee, and Other Agent Stories*, he didn't get much past the foreword. Werner Grossmann, who was sitting in the front row in the room at the time, had written that part. In it, he complained of those trying to defame the honorable MfS. The officers were the real victims, he said.

The crowd erupted. A restless woman hesitated but then stood up and yelled: 'I was drugged and imprisoned by the Stasi!' And another man: 'I was in prison for seven years and never confessed!' Moments later the same man jumped to his feet, pointed at the two of them and shouted: 'A bunch of red-painted fascists!'

Grossmann, then the most senior former MfS officer, rose and turned to stare at the man.

'Give me your name so we can report you!' he demanded angrily. The crowd instantly hushed, if only for a moment.

Another former prisoner present, Hans-Eberhard Zahn, who spent years as a political prisoner and is now a psychologist, commented afterward that the writings and actions of the Stasi officers toward the victims that day were similar to the old methods – fear and decomposition.

Schramm wrote a number of other revisionist books, including one that belittled those who believe what they see within MfS records and memorials. Later, the Stasi man denounced the Hohenschönhausen Memorial as a false 'chamber of horrors'. Schramm also co-authored books with Stasi colonel and self-proclaimed NSA expert Klaus Eichner.

———

No one visits the *Victims of Communism Memorial* or the *Memorial to the Known and Unknown Stasi Victims* in Berlin. That's because they don't exist. And, every time there is a movement to create places like that, there's highly organized opposition. Having memorials like those seem all too official, and make it much harder to shade and revise history for the next generation. Similar memorials are common in other former communist countries, and even in Washington DC, where a Victims of Communism Memorial has stood since 2007. But not in Germany, the birthplace of global communism.

There were 400,000 victims of the Ministry for State Security, and many more victims of the larger communist dictatorship. One would think it would go without saying that something would stand in Berlin, the City of Remembrance. But in Germany, even twenty-seven years later, where the government spent 350 million euros in

2017 sending monthly pension checks to 66,077 former members of
the Stasi, living all over the world, it's not so easy. Stasi victims are
entitled to compensation of only about 300 euros a month if they
were unjustly convicted during the communist regime, but only if
they are also financially destitute and were imprisoned for longer than
three months. The average MfS pension is many times that amount,
and without any restrictions.

Victims remain firmly stuck in their own internal prisons, frequently unable to hold jobs due to physical issues, or have menial
work limiting them to low wages. The effects of them being barred
from higher education in the GDR also restricted their later work
choices in free Germany. Getting rid of their criminal record was
another harsh journey. It took years for thousands of political prisoners to navigate the long process to have their GDR arrests and
summary convictions wiped clean, a frustrating process called *reha-
bilitation*. But even that did little to solve their real problems. Those
were the things that continued to wake many of them in the middle
of the night.

In the early 1990s a former prisoner named Andreas Möller visited a therapist who specialized in Stasi-related trauma. He had been
arrested at age nineteen and spent years in prison when his plan to
help a pregnant woman escape to the West was discovered. While the
nineteen-year-old was being interrogated at Hohenschönhausen, the
Stasi officer told him repeatedly:

*'If I want you to, you'll get out of here. But aggravate me, this will be the
end of the road for you. You will evaporate like water in the sun.'*

The therapist listened politely to his story, which was like so many
of the others, and finally put down her pen:

'Mr Möller, you were barely twenty years old when you were
thrown in jail. You have to accept that you may never really get out.'

For the victims, no matter how far away they move – elsewhere in
Europe or to the United States or further – it doesn't end. And now,
the embarrassed silence strongly encourages aging victims to keep it
all to themselves. They suspect they all too soon are becoming faded

memories, destined to be confined to a paragraph in a school history book that precious few will read.

This method is the latest and boldest of all the ex-Stasi's operations. Reinventing themselves and the communist dictatorship in a favorable light, while working to silence and belittle victims, has to a large degree worked. It's another form of decomposition. They never allow others in a public setting to refer to the GDR as a 'dictatorship' without challenge, even though it most certainly was. Recent polls in Germany show that a majority of students now think there were democratic elections in the GDR.

I asked a young woman in Berlin what she had learned in school about the dictatorship next door.

'Well, we watched a movie…'

Asking the same question in London, Paris or Los Angeles would result in an even more startling response.

It's become politically correct to discuss the threat of right-wing extremism but not the victims of the left-wing dictatorship that existed just across the street. The remnants of the East German SED are active today in politics and continue to downplay forty years of the communist dictatorship. Denying that the Nazi Holocaust happened is ridiculous and widely offensive. In Germany it's also illegal to do so. But not so for those who deny and minimize the trauma of the hundreds of thousands of victims of the forty years of German communism. Those who do so are usually not confronted in the press, and only silence is seen in public speech. This dangerous stillness enables similar revisionist efforts in Europe and the United States.

Just as in Europe and America, those now protesting while wearing masks or burning cars usually call themselves antifascists, or Antifa, and little mention is made of their ideological partner, communism. Both fascism and communism have only existed as tightly controlled dictatorships. Each relies on the same oppressive central government that serves the elite, while suppressing free speech. The tactics of today's Antifa, mob violence and shutdown of speech, seem oddly familiar. When the SED was established, as a twelve-year German

Nazi dictatorship ended with the Second World War, they called it the 'anti-fascist democratic revolution'. Then they named their communist dictatorship the German *Democratic* Republic, with the government constantly referring to it as a 'socialist paradise'. In reality, one totalitarian state was quite easily replaced by another.

The communism created by Marx, most often called socialism, has been responsible for nearly one hundred million deaths globally in the past one hundred years. And that number continues to grow.

PART III

25

DESPERATE SECRETS OF THE PUZZLE KEEPERS

The helpful man jangled his ring of keys as he unlocked the double door and fumbled for the switches, flipping on long rows of lights. As the fluorescent light bars flickered on, off, and finally on again, some of what was in the darkened room could now be seen. 'Come, this way.' He stood aside and pointed. 'There.'

We stood on an upper floor of the building called Runde Ecke in Leipzig, an hour from Berlin. There they have thirty-year-old secrets. Lots of them. The city that was center stage for the beginning of the fall of the communist dictatorship is one place where the secrets remain secrets even now. Row after row of guarded and unknown mysteries lay waiting.

They sit neatly at Runde Ecke – the feared former district office of the Gestapo and the Stasi – where only blocks away the Peaceful Revolution began in 1989 with quiet conversations in the pews and the prayers for peace at St Nicholas Church. There, in Runde Ecke, I was first shown one of the large, dark and musty-smelling rooms years later. When the clerk who followed me in flipped the switches, I was looking at endless rows of grey metal shelves filled neatly with huge, bulging paper and canvas sacks.

The fact that they have the shelves of untold secrets there is no particular surprise. The same can be found at many of the fifteen district offices for the Stasi and at the Berlin building now called the Archive. In that building, called Haus 7 by the members of the Firm until 1990, and still called that by those that have reason to visit now, the files are there too. It's long been known that at least 20 percent of the brown-jacketed files of the Ministry for State Security were torn, shredded, turned to soggy pulp or burned. Only the remnants of those were found when the citizen groups descended upon the Stasi offices.

It was only after the first inventory following unification that everyone learned the sheer volume of the 18,000 bags filled with shredded and torn file remnants. Files that the secret police thought most sensitive and were desperate to destroy. An estimated 600 million pieces of paper. A public outcry demanded immediate action. The excesses of the Stasi were fresh in everyone's mind, and the files not shredded were already turning out to be explosive enough. It could only be imagined what the files considered so sensitive they were marked for destruction would contain. People wanted to know. Yet most of the 600 million secrets haven't been disturbed at all since 1990, and likely never will be.

The undiscussed fact is that in spite of thirty years of painstaking recovery efforts, the Grey Men will soon have succeeded in hiding what those sacks contain.

The new allies of the Stasi have become time, apathy, the few staff assigned to the task, outdated technology and limited funding for an otherwise insurmountable task. Restrictions were imposed by a political decision years before, driven maybe by national pride, to keep the puzzles in the bags firmly in German hands. Now the problem is worsening as the urgency to expose the perpetrators or provide closure to victims fades with each passing year. For thirty years every- one knew that the contents of those 18,000 brown paper and canvas sacks were likely to be explosive not only for Germany, but also for other places around the world. Perhaps that's been the real problem.

For political reasons they couldn't be easily ignored. As with the clamoring of Germans to see their files, suspicion was intense about what was hidden in the thousands of sacks. So, a plan was approved and money was spent. The people would accept nothing less.

Mistakes were made, not unexpected at a time when Germany and most of the West was reeling from the heady events of the unraveling communist dictatorships. But most who have ever conducted a major criminal, terrorism or intelligence investigation will confirm that merely waiting for technology to catch up has ultimately solved many difficult cases.

Of the 18,000 bags of partially destroyed Stasi files, it was quickly learned that about 3,000 had been machine-shredded and a fateful decision made at once that they could *never* be recovered. And so, in 1991 those were simply burned. That act would make any investigator wince, since with the rapid advances of technology and forensic science there really is never a *never*. So, what of the 15,000 remaining bags, containing more than 600 million pieces of paper fragments? Less than 5 percent have been reassembled in the nearly thirty years since, and most of those were processed painstakingly, solely by hand and eye.

For the first twenty-five years the task was run out of the small village of Zirndorf in Bavaria. Coincidentally, it's only a fifteen-minute train ride from Nuremberg, best known as the site of the Nazi war crimes trials. In 1995, the Federal Refugee Agency was headquartered in Nuremberg and handed the task. They had available workers for a tedious job. They had some success, primarily with the contents of those bags the Stasi had rushed through and failed to rip the pages effectively. But the employees assigned to the job by the refugee agency, who were mainly women and sometimes referred to as the *puzzle keepers*, quickly discovered the limitations of the human brain. They learned that if a document was ripped into more than nine pieces it became an issue for the eye and brain to mentally put it back together. Some progress was made anyway, enough to tantalize, but it was slow work. Over the years 1.5 million pages were put together this way. At that rate, completion would take another 300 years.

A prestigious research group in Germany, the Fraunhofer Institute, was contracted seventeen years later to write software from scratch to solve the problem. Since nobody knew what explosive things might be found, the government insisted that none of the materials must be allowed to leave German control. The use of a good German company would ensure that. Technicians at Fraunhofer got busy writing special software and hooking up scanners. They gave the project a not-so-creative name, Automated Virtual Reconstruction of the Pre-Destroyed Files of the State Security Service of the Former GDR. The name given to the software written was the E-Puzzler.

Seven years later, the project ended. It didn't work. Only twenty-three bags of documents had been successfully virtually reconstructed by the E-Puzzler software. Fraunhofer hastily pointed out that it wasn't the software's fault – the scanners just weren't good enough.

Even with the few pieces of the puzzle put together, new and sensitive facts quickly emerged. Explosive records about those spying on prominent activists in the GDR, and about how those activists were persecuted. Details of yet unknown informants, and insights into the state-sponsored doping practice of GDR athletes. Most significantly, finds included reconstructed documents about GDR State Security assistance to the terrorist group the RAF, Red Army Faction, who committed a string of attacks over twenty years, including assaulting a US military base and conducting the sniper strike on the American Embassy in Bonn.

In 2015, the Records Authority ended the contract with the refugee agency in Bavaria. Now it was up to workers at the Stasi Archive in Berlin to come up with a plan.

Twenty-nine years after the files had been shredded or torn to pieces, I climbed up a dozen stairs and walked into Haus 7 at the former Stasi headquarters in Berlin and stepped into the elevator. I was there to see the current status of reconstruction efforts of the remaining 14,000 bags. A smiling minder ushered me into a room in which a solitary man sat at a small table in front of a huge brown paper bag. The bag had been split open down the middle and torn paper was spilling out. He demonstrated how he would spend all day removing fragments and trying to piece them together into a document. 'When I maybe finish a page, I pass it there,' he motioned to the only other person sitting in the office, a woman poised in front of what looked like a normal desktop computer and scanner. Her job was to tape the fragments to a sheet of paper so she could scan it. The man had no idea how long it would take to finish the one bag in front of him. He seemed surprised that I asked.

'How many others are doing this?'

'We are nine.'

It was hopeless. The urgency, if it had ever been present, had faded. Those who had demanded the government find out what was in the thousands of bags are also fading. Justice for the victims is gone. Criminal prosecutions haven't been possible since 2000, except in cases of murder. But some people remain worried. Many others want to know the truth, but fewer now raise their voices. A reckoning need not involve a prosecution, the fading voices say, just an awareness, an acknowledgment and public discussion would be in some ways acceptable to many. For many victims, the only remaining answers may be in the paper fragments. The sense that hangs heavy in the air is that the project continues to exist only since it's politically uncomfortable to announce that the failed efforts have ceased.

The Fraunhofer Institute is negotiating with the Records Authority about a new contract, and two million euros more was allocated by Parliament in 2016. Maybe with some new scanners our software can do its job, they promise.

One more question was needed to disturb the uncomfortable silence of Haus 7. I turned back to the man as he reached for another small fragment from the paper bag. 'Couldn't a technology giant such as Google, who would employ today's technology with a team of hundreds, be given a chance? Even shredded paper can be treated today – torn pieces are far easier.' The man looked down as he neatly adjusted a tiny new fragment of paper on his desk, while his eyes flicked to my minder. She put her hand on the door. 'This way...'

Everyone knows the questions that remain. Is it essential to complete the project while those who were victimized and their perpetrators are still alive? How long will the remaining political will last? Or, with a quiet nod, will the Stasi and others with desperate secrets to keep hidden in 600 million pieces be allowed to finally win?

Stasi lieutenant general Alexander Schalck-Golodkowski,
head of the Commercial Coordination Unit, KoKo.

Stasi file extract with photo of Colonel Hans-Ehrenfried Stelzer, known as Professor Murder.

The 381 CDs containing the Stasi foreign agent files returned to Germany in 2003.
Non-German names were removed. The mystery of who sold them to the CIA remains.

One of the *Rosenholz* CDs returned by the CIA, years after the
foreign agent files disappeared from East Berlin.

Building from where Stasi organizations operate from in Berlin, 2019.
It also houses the German Communist Party, and the former GDR state
newspaper operating now with backing from the Left Party.

Two former Stasi officers at their book launch in 2006 — former Stasi colonel
Peter Pfütze (right) and former Stasi colonel Gotthold Schramm (left).

Poster promoting upcoming socialist/Antifa/Left Party event in Berlin, 2019. Former Stasi officer Andrej Holm is pictured.

26

THE GREY MEN PERSIST

The paper that lay by itself and almost unnoticed on a table in the Archive contained an excerpt from the Stasi oath of lifetime allegiance:

I swear:

To fight along with the national people's army and the other armed forces of the German Democratic Republic, the military, the defense and security forces of the Soviet Union and allied socialist countries as a member of the Ministry for State Security against the enemies of socialism, even risking my life, and to fulfill any assigned order to guarantee state security.

Should I ever violate this, my solemn oath of allegiance, the severe punishment of the laws of our republic and the scorn of the working people shall come upon me.

Even after my dismissal, to act in such a way that a security hazard for the work of the Ministry for State Security and myself cannot arise.

Time had passed so that those who should ask, and even the media, had long ago turned to different things. The quiet network had made it uncomfortable for many by using the courts when a former officer or IM was exposed. But it was hard to get to everybody.

––––––

Vilnius, Lithuania
April 2015

He had come to the grand hall in the center of the city of cobblestones to speak of heroes. The city of Vilnius is many things. Well known now as a charming tourist destination, it's often visited by the movie industry for spy films, and even is a place favored by Russian computer hackers. It possesses an edge of intrigue and sadness at the same time. If one pauses to look beneath the surface, it's much more than that. It's a capital city that understands the meaning both of freedom and senseless death.

Not long before, a construction crew was digging close to the town center and stumbled upon yet another mass grave containing thousands of bodies. It hardly raised eyebrows. Jews executed by the Nazis, or Lithuanians or Poles murdered by the Soviet communist state, everyone assumed. Strangely, not this time. A button off a uniform told the story. The 3,269 corpses that were all packed seven to the square meter were Napoleon's soldiers, and they had lain there since being tossed aside during the Russian campaign of 1812.

Vilnius is now once again an achingly beautiful town, but it's also known as the City of Strangers due to the repeated genocide of its inhabitants. It somehow bears the incredible burden with grace, and so do its residents. In that way, it was an obvious place for the serious man with greying hair to step forward and to speak of heroes, dictatorships and mass trauma.

A few minutes' walk from where he rushed up the stone steps that morning, wearing a dark jacket and striped dress shirt, is likely the most somber place in the city. Sitting just blocks from where the Neris River finds its way idyllically through town is a stark white building that stretches a long city block. It's old, but possesses a special and much more recent feature. From a distance, it's easy to notice the white pillars of a turn-of-the-century government structure, but as it comes into better focus the thick band of dark stone encircling its pale base also stands out. When you get much closer, you see the names. Simple names of men and women inscribed carefully along the darker stone, along with a date. It's impossible to walk by without pausing. Until 1991 the building housed the KGB, and its predecessor agency, the NKVD. The 195 names chiseled along the stone base are among the first of those Lithuanians who were murdered in the building by the secret police of the communist dictatorship. Once the KGB left town for good in 1991, the people came out again and the dark panels went up. In Vilnius, there's no nostalgia for communism and no appetite for historical revisionism.

Hubertus Knabe took the stage that day in 2015, coughed and stared out at the crowd.

'I would like to speak about heroes,' he began.

It was something that both Lithuania and Germany knew about only too well.

As was his custom, he began speaking with a passion that's rare in a historian. He's lived it himself in many ways, but he never mentions that. What he described in detail are the victims of the GDR dictatorship, and the price they paid. It's become his trademark, his personal way of chiseling their names into the stone.

Hubertus went on to speak of the unsung heroes who were locked up at the Berlin prison. Eleven thousand inmates were jailed there, most of them for political reasons, he passionately communicated to the crowd. One of more than a dozen he spoke of that day was Vera Lengsfeld. She was arrested by the Stasi as a young woman late in the 1980s, and is still sometimes seen guiding groups of students through the Memorial. A hero for surviving what many would consider not survivable.

Hubertus concluded his remarks to the Lithuanian audience after challenging them to be unsung heroes in the future. It's likely that some of them or their parents already fit that definition. He gathered his few notes and stepped down from the stage, hoping that the video link had reached others in Germany and throughout Europe. Maybe even in America.

If someone in the crowd in that room, or elsewhere viewing on the video simulcast, looked up the name Vera Lengsfeld that he mentioned, they would soon have understood two important things. One was the uniquely evil nature of the Stasi, and the other was the startling inspiration of a victim who refuses to give in.

Vera Wollenberger, as she called herself in the early 1980s, started off in a life of guaranteed privilege in the GDR. She was the daughter of an MfS major, and was herself headed for membership in the SED Party and a good education and successful career. But by the age of seventeen she instead began to question the system. The dinner table became a conflict zone as her father called her a 'Trotskyist', a traitor to socialist ideals, for doubting the state. Nevertheless, she obediently joined the Communist Party, graduated from university and secured a good job with the Academy of Sciences. Her future was assured. But then the questions in her mind surfaced again even more strongly and she could tolerate it no more. Vera began to take part in public protests when the Soviets placed nuclear missiles in East Germany. By 1983 she had lost her job, been ejected from the SED and been banned from working or traveling. That didn't stop her. What happened next was the last straw for the Stasi. It was in 1988, when she made a handwritten sign, bearing a single quote from the GDR constitution:

'Every citizen has a right to express his opinion freely.'

She displayed the sign at a protest gathering and was summarily arrested by the Stasi for 'hooliganism'. Dragged off to Hohenschönhausen for interrogation, and later convicted, her world could get no worse, or so she thought. Released after the fall, it was soon after 1990 that she applied to see her file, determined to find out who had been reporting on her activities all those years. Buried in the hundreds of pages she found a reference to the informant, an IM code-named *Donald*. But IM Donald's file had been one of those shredded, or maybe was just missing, she was told at first. Then, in a quirk of fate that was either lucky or unlucky, a second copy was found. IM Donald, the person diligently reporting on her for years, was Knud, her husband and the father of her two young sons. Devastated, she divorced him immediately and took back her maiden name. After some time, she pulled herself together and went on to success serving in the German Parliament. Even recently she maintained the attitude of a survivor. Asked not long ago if she thought she could ever trust again, Vera Lengsfeld replied immediately:

'Of course, because otherwise the Stasi would have won.'

Another East German dissident, Jürgen Fuchs, mentioned by Hubertus Knabe that day, once described the collection of miles of Stasi files and their contents as 'the Auschwitz of souls', for reasons like this. The row upon row of brown files, where many fear to go, are that and more. Miles of now-musty testaments to how easily a ruthless dictatorship turns one against another and in the process strips away all humanity from a society.

————

Almost at the same moment as Hubertus Knabe rushed up the stone steps in Vilnius, years of smug celebration and sweet victories at a villa along the shores of Lake Tegernsee in Bavaria were taking a fatal turn for the man called *Snow White*.

Three years before, the celebration had begun. The man who procured billions in hard currency for the GDR communist state, by stealing art and trafficking in blood, trading in weapons and selling 33,000 imprisoned and traumatized young East Germans, had seemingly won. Former Stasi lieutenant general Alexander Schalck-Golodkowski had carefully selected his trademark Cohiba cigar, the long ones of the type originally hand-rolled for Fidel Castro, and stepped out into the cool Bavarian air to savor it. It was done. He had beaten them.

After 191 witnesses, 500 hours of interviews, little money found and a silly minor conviction for violating embargo regulations – but no jail time – Volker Neumann and the KoKo Investigation Committee had come up short. Oh sure, they'd identified boatloads of cutout companies, and Neumann had a huge chart spread over his entire desk that he liked to show the press to prove he had tried. But most of them were pass-through entities, which led nowhere. Now, there was nothing more they could do. Even amusing foreign attempts to find the billions had ended. Schalck continued to live well, taking his walks along the lake with plenty of money in his personal accounts. Even the Federal Intelligence Service, the BND, had stopped caring what he did. He had only told them what they already knew, and after twenty years it didn't matter anymore to them either. He had many more favors he could call in to ensure a steady supply of cash 'loaned' to him from those who owed him. Money no one expected to be paid back. His villa was a rental, he constantly reminded others; he barely got by, he told them with a wink. People in the West knew that he was a person best to have on their side – he had secrets. Lots of them.

He had held steadfastly to the same story in his television interviews and in a book that he had written ten years earlier. He stopped giving interviews after that. What purpose would they serve? Many of his old connections, including the politicians, worried so much about what he might say in that book. In the end, no surprises. Not yet.

'Truth, I tell you, truth and always truth – of course: my truth; because otherwise I do not know it.' Schalck used a clever quote from Johann Wolfgang von Goethe, the famous writer and statesman, to commence his account about how he had been an unknown lowly bureaucrat, singled out in 1989 to be a fall guy, forcing him to defect.

He was just a cog in the machine of the GDR, he didn't hide any money and had acted in the best interests of all Germans. That was his story. Few believed it. He cared little what they thought. In private conversations he was known to enjoy his reputation as the only man who knew where all the money went, and he did nothing to discourage that image. Useful, it kept people afraid. People like Marc Rich, the American fugitive financier, pardoned by President Clinton in the final hours of his presidency. Rich had taken refuge in Switzerland in the 1980s and had been a very good partner of KoKo in many deals.

And what of those who literally paid with all they had, their freedom, their well-being and even their blood? With a wave of his hand he would dismiss such questions. KoKo was a big organization – how could he know about everything? Privately, he summed it up:

'My power was the money.'

Some of that money was also still finding its way to immediately enrich the successor to the SED Communist Party. The PDS inherited much with the name change, plus sometimes there were anonymous contributions of large amounts. He couldn't claim all the credit for that, but he did his part.

He beat it all, beat them all. There was suffering of many along the way, but was it his doing? Taking a long, satisfied draw from the cigar that victorious evening, he watched the smoke swirl up toward the lake. He'd won. But he wished he felt a bit better lately. No matter. Tomorrow he would see that Swiss doctor once again. He took one last pull from the fading Cohiba, and smiled.

There was nothing anyone could do now.

He was a scapegoat and had no money hidden. He had only concerned himself with foreign exchange and was now a simple pensioner. He had repeated that so many times that even he started to believe it. The silliness of the prosecutors and the Western press annoyed him the most. At one time there were maybe fifty investigations. True, he was convicted finally of a single charge of arms trafficking and import violations. An 'administrative violation' was how he brushed it aside if anyone asked. A short period of probation only. He had very good lawyers, who were well paid. All of that was over, and not a day in jail except for when he surrendered himself in 1989!

Where are the billions from all those deals? Where's the money from the stolen art? What do you say to the victims? His response to such demands was always a dismissive look. *Insolence!* The truth was, he never thought much about them at all.

The statute of limitations had tolled, and his life was starting anew. It helped that people in politics would continue to be afraid of him, and that his old comrades from the SED had reinvented themselves. It was hard not to smile when he thought of the money freely flowing into the coffers of whatever the SED called themselves these days.

Schalck had operated at his best for decades under the radar, anonymous as a figure who handled foreign exchange and procured unusual things in unusual ways, but never was publicly identified, especially not as a State Security officer. That only came out at the turn, when the Wall fell. When that happened, his name surfaced and his response was to run. Flee to the West and save himself.

He had won it all, and in the process had kept his lakeside villa, his comrades and his friends in business in the West. He had been careful not to out those useful people when he wrote his autobiography. Many of them would be happy to give him more unsecured 'loans' in the future. If not, there could be another book or another interview – they all knew that too well. Tapping out the cigar, he switched off the light and headed to a warm bed. He had his status and a very comfortable life to enjoy.

Judgment may have been delayed, but it nonetheless came swiftly to Alexander Schalck-Golodkowski. In fact, by 2012, while he stood in the cool Bavarian air smoking his Cohiba and congratulating himself, his fate had already been sealed. He was dying but didn't yet know it. Death pronounced its own victory nonetheless soon after in his villa late one Sunday night in June 2015. It came without care of whom he knew or what he had, without pausing to be swayed by smooth denials. And it came with a vengeance. The tall, heavy-set man had won the battle, but something else intended to win the war.

The progression of the cancer from his prostate began slowly, but by 2015 Schalck had become a gaunt shadow. It was a painful way for him to ultimately lose, especially as he finally also lost his most valuable asset and source of financial support: his memory of people and numbers. Memory of where the money was, and how to get it. But before that happened, in one final glimmer of his last public statement even before he knew his fate, he was heard to say in his distinctive Berlin dialect:

'I've fought for the GDR, and in the end, we lost.'

Alexander Schalck-Golodkowski, a Stasi officer for more than twenty years, as well as the elusive hard-currency procurer who kept communism afloat no matter who paid the price, died in his well-appointed villa that June night. Germany had moved on and there were few who paid any attention to the news.

Meanwhile, 5,000 miles away in the United States the sad drama he took so much pride in creating continued. Some of KoKo's stolen artworks from one victim had mysteriously shown up at a Florida art auction. The son of another victim also had little time to celebrate. He had just returned to his home in Boston from Germany after a failed attempt to reclaim art taken from his father in the 1970s. His claim was denied by courts, leaving the best of the pieces seized by the Stasi to remain proudly on display in a German museum.

27

WHO'S STILL AFRAID?

It was a hot summer afternoon in August 2017 and circumstances promised it would be a big day at the Hohenschönhausen Memorial. Two black Mercedes sedans would be out front in five minutes, the voice on the phone said. Director Knabe was ready. Clicking off his computer, he stood and rushed down the stairs into the courtyard and toward the iron and steel prison gates.

The two vehicles slid up promptly and a small woman stepped out. She had a round face and short hair and was dressed in a green suit. As he motioned for the gates to be opened so that he could greet the German chancellor, Hubertus saw the others standing there. Many former Stasi officers were interspersed with a waiting group. Somehow, they also had gotten the word. As he approached the car for the official greeting and welcome, the group began loudly shouting demands phrased as questions:

'What will you do, Chancellor, to make the government treat the people from East Germany better?'

'We are victims!'

The gathering looked more choreographed than spontaneous: each waited their turn to drown out the welcome with a shouted 'question'.

The chancellor nodded to acknowledge the remarks and quickly followed Hubertus into the prison yard. As he and two victim-witnesses proceeded to show her the dark secrets of the Memorial, Merkel seemed touched.

'Coming here now, just a few days before the anniversary of the day the Wall was erected in 1961, has special meaning for me,' she said to the waiting press. She specifically mentioned the plans underway for the Center for Left-Wing Extremism. 'It's important for Germany to remember its communist past,' she added. Merkel didn't stay long, but offered Hubertus her strong support. He could contact her anytime, she said.

Others later commented cynically that the visit might have been timed to help her politically in the upcoming election. Hubertus chose instead to think the best. Her support for the new center was critical. This seemed to give a huge boost to his funding request to Parliament.

This seems good, he thought.

The presence of former officers around the Memorial that day and other days like it, even more than twenty-five years after the leftist dictatorship in East Germany fell apart, still serves to intimidate many victims and staff alike. They are also vocal in their opposition to any Memorial to the Victims of Communism. Elsewhere, people remain afraid. Not only of confrontations, but also the lingering dread of their own secrets yet to be discovered or leaked. They hope to forget, and they hope that others will also.

There have only been requests from about three million former East Germans to see their files, from a population of seventeen million. So many others are too troubled to want to know for sure if there is a file on them or their family, let alone read the contents.

And what of the missing files – who has those? Or those torn pieces being reassembled? Some politicians in Europe still wonder who will next be unmasked as having been a key informer, or worse.

Throughout Europe, parents still desperately seek children taken by the Stasi in the forced adoptions; others seek the missing artworks and property of their parents. Many remain wary of new information from the Archive coming forth to identify them as having been an informant, or perhaps other compromising information appearing which had been collected by officers for blackmail.

A Dutch professor and expert on the MfS, Willem Melching, noted how being a former Stasi member has now become 'cool' in Europe, in stark contrast to anyone who had a previous association to any right-wing or fascist organizations. At the same time, the former officers and their associations have worked in a highly organized and methodical way to remove access to names of officers in German society. After patiently waiting the first few years in silence, they adapted to the many tools of the privacy laws within the new Germany. Social media, such as Facebook, only made it easier for them.

———

Twenty-six years after the MfS was announced to no longer exist, another careful plan was put in place.

The event at first came and went quietly, passing unrecognized one day in December 2016, months before Chancellor Merkel's visit to Hohenschönhausen. In the rush before the Christmas holidays, the government routinely decided to pass along some noncritical committee vacancies to be filled by other political parties. It's how a coalition government must function. One of these was the innocuous-sounding position of Berlin's cultural senator. That one went to the Left Party to fill, which promptly appointed Klaus Lederer to the job. Turns out Berlin's cultural senator had another lesser-known role – chairman of the Berlin-Hohenschönhausen Memorial Foundation. The overseer of the Memorial. Lederer had lived with his parents in the Berlin-Hohenschönhausen district in 1988. The colonels had been his neighbors.

In effect, by the beginning of 2017 the Left Party, the renamed and merged Communist Party of the GDR, now controlled all Berlin memorials and their management. Then, they waited.

———

Three grim-faced Stasi men filed into a private office near Alexanderplatz and looked down with contempt at the man seated in front of them. He was well known to the Stasi as a GDR dissident and therefore a criminal. The meeting was to be held in secret, kept from almost everyone else in the building. The men had a mission, and a list of demands. The three were high-ranking officers: Lieutenant Colonel Reinhard Grimmer – ZAIG (Central Evaluation and Planning), Colonel Karl Rehbaum, and Lieutenant Colonel Wolfgang Schmidt – Main Department XX (Monitored State, Culture, Churches and Underground). They were important Grey Men.

For added impact that day, the three brought along a fourth man, Hans Bauer, the former deputy attorney general for the GDR, previously in charge of all criminal prosecutions of dissidents.

The door closed, leaving the four staring down at the well-dressed man seated uneasily behind a desk. That the meeting that day would take place there in that office and in secret was unusual. The seated man had been expelled from college due to MfS disapproval when he was twenty-one. The Stasi then later arrested him for displaying a small flag on his bicycle supporting the Polish Solidarity movement. The arrest was a pretense – they targeted him as he had been publicly speaking out against the state. He remained in jail for five months, before being summarily sentenced to twenty-two months' imprisonment. His defense lawyer was later found to be working for the MfS. The young man was then forcibly expelled to West Berlin in 1983 while chained and gagged, his East German citizenship canceled.

Now, he acknowledged the men who stood before him with an uncomfortable nod.

The meeting this day wasn't about any of that, and they weren't there to arrest him again. It was in East Berlin to be sure, but the date was October 23, 2018, and the man seated at the desk was Roland Jahn, the federal commissioner in charge of BStU, the Stasi Archive. The group of men crowded in the room were leaders of The Society of Legal and Humanitarian Support (GRH), the most well-known Stasi advocacy group. They were the most senior Grey Men in Germany at that moment. The men had come secretly to demand that the agency be closed and that the continued reassembling of the remaining 15,000 bags of shredded files be halted.

Jahn looked across the room at them silently. The four men stared back.

'We have a list of… questions,' one of them said as he slid a several-page letter across the desk.

Then the group methodically presented twenty-one demands.

The meeting shocked many people who found out about it later, and some asked why no official record was kept. It was said to be the only time a private meeting between ranking former Stasi members and the head of the Archive had ever taken place since the creation of the agency twenty-eight years before. The fact that the meeting took place at all, and happened there, would only become public knowledge months later, causing the telephones in the BStU press office to ring.

The demanding letter, written by the former officers, reads like a manifesto of historical revisionism. It also cautioned about allowing further 'anti-GDR propaganda'. The GDR was a 'respected member of the UN' and should not be treated like Nazi Germany, it said. The rambling list presented to Roland Jahn that day basically called for the closing of the Archive. *Why treat the Stasi differently with a separate agency? Time to end the reassembly of the torn records as well. Nothing more to be learned there! Transfer the files to the Federal Archives* (where there would be less emphasis on the Stasi, and the records would be not as accessible). *Isn't it time to send the records over to the Federal Archives, where the rest of German history is safely warehoused? Why does your office have such a big budget and so many employees? Isn't it past time to shut it down? Isn't it a fact that you are involved with spreading anti-GDR propaganda?*

The BStU press office, which wasn't invited to the meeting, later issued a statement once they learned about it. The official statement was that it was an exchange of views with the Stasi men.

The meeting would certainly have remained a quiet secret that day had the Stasi organization GRH not released the details and their demands to a left-leaning Berlin newspaper, which promptly published it.

Within weeks of the meeting, the GRH had converted the letter of demands presented to Jahn into a slick green booklet entitled *Truth and Reconciliation*. They distributed it to their members, press, historians, politicians and anyone else who expressed interest, and some who didn't. It was a bold statement that former Stasi officers and their organizations were still there and watching. In effect, they had taken the fight to the enemy once again, twenty-eight years later. And in their view, they had won again.

A few months after that meeting, a career Stasi officer proudly handed me a copy of the green booklet. 'A victory! The meeting alone was a victory,' he added with satisfaction.

28

APATHY AND NOSTALGIA

The confident former Stasi officer sat thinking about the question for a moment. He stared down at his polished thick-soled shoes, and absently brushed a cotton thread off his pants. Then he shook his head and looked up.

'The GDR failed only because the political will was lost. We could have taken care of it.'

Revisionism years later, or maybe not? Had they deployed the resources that the MfS possessed in 1989, including 11,000 heavily armed soldiers and tanks, to carry out the mass arrests planned for Day X, what they called 'democratic socialism' of the GDR might have survived for a time. Repressive regimes rarely go quietly. The man in front of me preferred the term *socialism* over *communism*, and thirty years after the GDR failed he was still a true believer in a firm socialist state. Socialism is the way, he's sure. It's just misunderstood or not implemented correctly. Political will is needed. That view sounded oddly familiar.

Generation Z, the youth of the present in the United States, have a more positive view of socialism now than any previous generation, according to a recent poll. It's even more pronounced in Britain and Central Europe. But do they all really know what has been done under the banner of *socialism* in recent history, or where it came from?

It might be said that an American started it all. And in an unlikely place.

Most people would be as surprised as I was to discover that a Scottish-born immigrant to America first created the word. His name was Robert Dale Owen. In 1825 he excitedly founded a commune in Indiana called *New Harmony*. Karl Marx was just a seven-year-old boy then, playing in the streets of a small town in Germany. Owen put his idea to the test more than twenty years before Marx's most well-known work, *The Communist Manifesto*, was written.

Owen founded his commune intending to demonstrate the superiority of what he at first called 'a social system', and later 'socialism'. It failed after two years, and so did dozens of copycat socialist communes set up in the United States around the same time. They just couldn't work, lacking any sort of coercive force. Perhaps they would have survived longer if they had ruthless secret police as enforcers? Political will. That was the lesson Vladimir Lenin later learned also. He created and ruthlessly perfected the Cheka in 1917, which became the KGB. All totalitarian states after that followed suit. That's what enabled the Ministry for State Security to prop up the GDR for forty years.

But a German created global communism. Karl Marx, with his strong upbringing and elite German education, was the person to encourage widespread attempts on a grand scale to implement government-directed socialism and communism. He referred to it then as 'scientific socialism'. But this isn't ancient history. In September 2018 communist China, self-described as the People's Republic, presented a massive fourteen-foot statue of Marx to the town of Trier, Germany, in celebration of the 200-year anniversary of his birth. It stands in the town square.

While some still celebrate Marx and his failed ideology, others in surprising places found other uses for symbols of violent dictatorships created under the communist banner. After the Wall came down, all over Eastern Europe people got busy knocking down old heavy Soviet statues of all sorts, especially those of Lenin, Stalin and Marx, as they embraced their new freedoms. Today, you would be hard-pressed to locate any of these statues, unless maybe you drive into a remote part of Lithuania as I did one icy day.

After making my way through a rural forested part of the country near the Polish border, I bought a ticket from a silent woman at a kiosk and stepped into Grūtas Park. Really a sculpture garden of failed socialism, it's commonly called Stalin's World by the local people. In 1991, when everyone was desperate to rid their communities of the massive statues, monuments and heavy glaring busts symbolizing totalitarian fear, one man had an idea. He offered to haul them away for free in his large truck. His phone rang for months.

In an ironic twist of a type loved by the millions of souls repressed by communist dictatorships, Grūtas Park has turned out to be a profitable and well-presented capitalist tourist destination, even if it remains unsettling to visitors. Just inside the gate that icy day, with the wind and soft crunch of the fresh snow to accompany me, I paused at a train car with barred windows. It was one of many used to haul people to the Soviet gulag. Men and women who mostly never returned. Usually these cars were drab green or black. The owner of the park, a former mushroom farmer, had painted this one blood red. After a few moments, I turned and made my way down a long path that was lined with hulking communist remnants staring angrily back at me, some now just indignant heads lying on the ground and off their pedestals. Each was carefully labeled, stating precisely where it had originally stood for decades.

As I drove away down the deserted forest road, thoughts of other similar remnants intruded. But besides this display, those found in Russian cemeteries scattered around Eastern Europe – and a ten-foot bust of Lenin that until recently remained embedded in a wall of the Russian Embassy in Berlin for more than twenty years after the Soviet Union fell apart – it's not easy to see the traces. There are few remaining in plain sight anywhere in Eastern Europe. If you had lived under a communist dictatorship for forty years, you would understand why.

Even in Berlin, the Russians later apologized for keeping their Lenin bust. 'It's part of the foundation wall of the embassy complex,' they said. 'The wall would collapse if it were to be removed,' the official statement read. By 2011, it was somehow removed anyway. In London, a smaller white Lenin sculpture sat for years in Holford Square. Lenin had once lived nearby as he plotted the Russian Revolution. Even that one has been removed to a nearby museum following years of it being repeatedly vandalized.

I stopped the car at an unmarked intersection among the tall pine trees to check my map, as a light snowfall resumed. I didn't wish to turn the wrong way and end up in Poland, or Belarus. Turning right, I stepped on the gas, looking for the highway back to Vilnius. It was then that I remembered one other original communist statue that remains prominent today. Years before, I caught a surprising glimpse of it while tracking down a criminal. It's in America.

Looming large in Seattle, mostly unnoticed by tourists, is a sixteen-foot Lenin the Revolutionary statue. Weighing seven tons, it was bought off a scrap pile by an American, in what had been communist Czechoslovakia, and shipped to the United States at great expense. Vladimir Lenin has been on proud display for the past twenty-four years in the city's ultra-left neighborhood of Fremont. It once confronted me through the rain on a dark night as I stopped my car at a street corner while searching for a bank robber. The statue, with its outstretched hands, stands tall in a central location, in what other natives often refer to as the People's Republic of Fremont. It frowns into the distance a mile or two from what Seattle is best known for at the moment, the sprawling headquarters complex of Amazon.

In Germany, where personal experiences of hundreds of thousands of victims of the communist dictatorship still remain as living witnesses, it would be expected that this kind of misinformed fantasy would be rare. Not so – they have a name for it. *Ostalgie. Ost*, the word for East. Nostalgia for East Germany and the GDR. A combination of selective memory, intentional disinformation, uninformed humor and hope to make a leftist dictatorship and communism seem somehow okay. Nothing of the sort exists for the Nazi German dictatorship, which had too much global exposure for its genocide of six million Jews, and the horrors of a destructive world war. The Nazi regime, then and now called National Socialism, was fascist and therefore different, the former Stasi officers, SED apologists and hip Left Party politicians insist. The GDR was *funny* and *harmless*, the proponents of Ostalgie are effectively promoting. It's those fascists who were horrible, those twelve years of Nazi tyranny. The forty years of the communist dictatorship when the citizens were held prisoner and trained to please the state from birth? Simply misunderstood and a product of well-intended mistakes, they say.

For the Stasi and their still-active organizations and other sympathizers in Germany, Europe and the United States, many continue even now to work hard to revise their past and justify the failed leftist socialist state. In Germany, and elsewhere in Central Europe, their strategy has been tilting the scales and helping the Left Party to prop up communism again, once more calling it socialism. The Left Party, official heir of the GDR communist state, is now one of the top five parties in Germany. It's become a serious player in government decision-making. With a parliament that has been fractured, and fractured again, a coalition is essential to get anything done. And it doesn't take much influence to gently place a thumb on the scales of historical clarity.

Their allies are not just apathy, misplaced nostalgia for a 'quaint and fun' East Germany that never existed except for the privileged few – youth who have tired of hearing stories from their parents – but also more direct measures. Few in Europe or the United States would support the Stasi and the communist state they protected if they knew much about what had been done. Without that, more and more appear to support their familiar technique of seeing fascism everywhere, and call once more for a new strong socialist state. Others falsely or naively claim that what the MfS did in crafting a fearsome police state that was above the law is somehow comparable to intelligence collection by the NSA or other US organizations.

The former Stasi officers and their quiet defenders in politics quickly discovered that there is once again value in appearing to be the antifascist protector of society, now also called Antifa in the new Germany.

'It started here you know,' one of the survivors of the Stasi machine whom I sat with weeks before in Chemnitz had whispered to me, as I sat organizing my notes. It wasn't until days later that I realized he was speaking about the way the government claimed to be antifascist in order to repress everyone. He was right, but I had to learn more.

It's just Antifa in the rest of Europe and the United States. A useful tool. It feels good to proclaim you're against fascism, though it's doubtful most who hide their faces, vandalize property and attack others on the streets in its name understand it, or know where the term really came from.

The BfV, the modern German internal intelligence service, certainly knows. Antifa first appeared following the Communist Party Congress in Moscow held in 1923. The Politburo was supporting an attempt to spread communism to Germany, the next logical place after Russia, as was being strongly advocated by the German Communist Party, the KPD. They formed what was called Antifaschistische Aktion (Antifascist Action) for this purpose. That name is still used, but was shortened to Antifa. It's the origin of all groups around the globe that use Antifa today. Its meaning then and now is anti-capitalism and fighting against all those who oppose communism. To the BfV, it's simple to understand:

'Today's Antifa simply believes that capitalism equals fascism, opposing the right wing is just a part of the strategy.'

Bernd Langer, a former member of Germany's original Antifaschistische Aktion, said it himself even clearer. 'Antifascism is a strategy rather than an ideology.'

A right-wing fascist state and a left-wing socialist state – both are eerily similar. Each requires a strong and invasive government, restrictions on personal freedoms and violent action against unapproved speech.

———

'They don't like it at all when we call it the "SED dictatorship" – I must be careful,' Ulrich Mählert confides to me on a hot June afternoon as we sit in his Berlin office on the third floor of a nondescript but sleek office building just down the street from Checkpoint Charlie. The infamous checkpoint between East and West is today a popular tourist destination for visitors to Berlin. Until 1990 it was a deadly serious place, reserved for crossing diplomats and military personnel, on a tense street hosting all sorts of confrontations.

Mählert, a cordial and casually open man, leans over and rapidly cranks the window handle, searching for a nonexistent breeze from the street. I can see he's in a tough spot. He doesn't want to upset politicians on the left, but he has a problem. Calling the SED dictatorship of the GDR something else besides a 'dictatorship' isn't so easy. That's because his business card, which lies in front of me, confirms he's the head of research for the German government agency named the Federal Foundation for the Study of the SED Dictatorship. Hard to change or finesse that.

'Why can't you say the "Study of the Communist Dictatorship" instead? Or just call it Stalinism?' Some have asked him that with exasperation. 'Stalin was the problem, not communism,' they urge. 'Focus on that, not the GDR!'

It's hard for those working to rehabilitate the memory of the communist-ruling SED Party of the GDR, now the Left Party, if the term 'SED' is used again and again in connection with a word that is clear and accurate, if also inconvenient:

Dictatorship.

Mählert has been with the Federal Foundation since 1999, a year after it was formed, and has seen the changes. It's his job to educate society and to study how the communist dictatorship functioned and how it impacted Germany. He describes how the foundation was originally started with part of the millions acquired by the SED in murky circumstances, therefore forfeited at unification in 1990. From the money that could be found, anyway. It started with *their* money. Hence the problem.

'We're now given about five million euros a year by the government to do our work,' he explains. A tiny budget for an important agency. 'In 2018 the German Parliament gave the Left Party five times that amount for their projects.'

Mählert is a historian by training, and the foundation is careful to study mostly things that happened before 1990. 'At least 70 per-cent of our work now is focused on that,' he adds. 'Maybe more.' Before, it was 100 percent. 'Just recently we started to do a few things about other impacts of communism on unified Germany, but very little.'

'So, who does that? Who looks at SED and Stasi influences in the past thirty years?'

'Well…'

'I mean, what they've done since?' I finish my question and notice a new tension in the room.

He looks at me and finally lowers his voice, 'Oh, maybe the news media? We don't want to be involved in politics, or anything controversial.'

'The period of National Socialism,' as he prefers rather than use the word Nazi, 'was worse – they killed more people,' he says. 'We must be careful not to compare the two, because then some East Germans complain.'

'Who does that? Both were totalitarian dictatorships that had oppressive, large governments and limited personal freedoms. Who compares them?'

'Nobody actually. They're kept separate.' He looks away, then back at me. 'I maintain a good relationship with Klaus Lederer, the cultural senator from the Left Party. I can call him anytime,' Mählert volunteers.

I stare out the open window together with him, but I'm thinking about Berlin being called a city of memorials. 'Why isn't there a memorial here for the victims of communism?'

He slowly reaches for his glass, drains it and looks away before responding.

'There's opposition to that. It's not an issue at the moment. Not a funding reason though…' The answer raises more questions.

'Has Germany come to terms with the Stasi and the communist dictatorship?'

'Perhaps. The Stasi was a tool.'

'What of the fact that only one of the more than 100,000 officers over the years served any jail time after unification for any State Security crimes? Is that enough?' Mählert doesn't appear to know that particular number, and sits pouring more water into his glass.

After a full minute of silence with only the sound of traffic from the street, I scratch some notes and we move on.

'How about Antifa?'

'Yes, yes, it's a problem on the left here.'

'Can you offer any advice to those elsewhere in Europe and in the United States who are thinking that socialism or communism is best?'

He sits silently and thinks. 'They must be suspicious of anyone who tells them that there is only one right way, while trying to silence other voices.'

'What's the foundation doing now?'

His face brightens.

'Soon is the anniversary of the fall; maybe there will be some international interest. Next week we sponsor an interesting exhibition about day-to-day GDR life.'

Glancing at the clock at the same time, we see that somehow the afternoon has slipped into evening. He hands me a couple of glossy picture books of photographs of life in East Germany and of the Peaceful Revolution of 1989.

Mählert is somehow candid and careful at the same time.

29

THE FACE OF A TWENTY-FIRST-CENTURY STASI

The timing was perfect!

That thought echoed in the proud chatter in mid-October 2018 up and down the third floor of Franz-Mehring-Platz 1 in Berlin, the home of the Stasi organizations. It was likely a topic of the weekly meeting that was held in the large conference room adjoining the reception room of the GRH. As usual, the Grey Men sat at the long wooden conference table under the huge painting of a stern and glaring Vladimir Lenin.

'*The witch is dead!*' This was the mantra for them and the rest of the German left at that moment. They had all read the article that week in *Spiegel* that used the expression, written by a favored and sympathetic columnist, and considered it very good news. For the organizations, it was a clear win for the cause, and promised to be the highlight of the GRH command meeting that week. Details about how it was done would be the topic of many discussions. A dream come true, an enemy dealt with! And within days of the observance of the sixty-ninth anniversary of the formation of the GDR!

Somehow it also seemed right for them to use that well-known phrase from an American classic story, *The Wizard of Oz*, to celebrate a victory for communism.

The phones had already started ringing off the hook. It would be a very busy day.

Of course, nothing could be proven, and nothing would be admitted. Soon, things would return to normal and they would remain focused on the future, as always. There was no going back to the orderly days of the GDR. But they could continue to use the tools of the present to change the past.

One of the senior former officers sitting in the office that day had no doubts about how the future would have unfolded quite differently if the Stasi had been given a chance in the waning days of 1989. He would make it clear to me months later.

'*We would have adapted. Quite easily, I expect.*'

———

Citizen, present your identity! That demand, which seems like a George Orwell quote, was real and made frequently on the streets and in the doorways of East Germany for nearly forty years. It caused immediate fear and uncertainty. Everyone was required to carry their official identification, the booklet with the blue plastic cover, and present it to the People's Police or the Stasi at any time. No reason for the demand was needed. The requirement didn't originate with the GDR. The Nazis started it in 1938, a dozen years before East Germany existed. The Nazis may have started it, but once again the MfS perfected it as a means of intimidation and control. It became a sensitive subject after the fall, and the old GDR blue booklets were quickly discarded.

Even today, Germans are understandably suspicious of police authority. They are wary of that level of concentrated power. Yet with initial reluctance overcome, all now have the new Federal Republic identification, a plastic card with an RFID chip embedded in it. Meanwhile, about forty million Germans, half the population of the country, have voluntarily given Facebook far more personal access to their homes, lives and friends. More than 2.3 billion other global citizens have done the same. It's common knowledge in US government circles that intelligence and police agencies, as well as employers, media and criminals, routinely use Facebook, and similar sources like LinkedIn, Twitter, Google, Snapchat and Instagram. A blue booklet with a plastic cover is not needed, and had provided far less in comparison.

The Stasi had files on large portions of the population, brown folders filled with paper. In the America of today, with more than 320 million people, 176 million have opened their identities and lives to Facebook, while only a tiny percentage have any national criminal file at all. As nearly all policing in the United States is done at the local level, even having a serious criminal history reported by the local police to the FBI's National Crime Information Center (NCIC) doesn't mean you have an FBI file. As an FBI agent, having a new criminal or terrorist case in front of me in which the person had any previous FBI file was the odd exception rather than the rule. Contrary to the claims of breathless news commentators and bloggers, or some others looking to justify treason, the NSA and the CIA, both intelligence but not law enforcement agencies, are seldom targeting Americans. By statute and careful design they are outwardly focused, with extremely limited roles within the country. But any large or small foreign government, or agenda-driven political group, or market-driven intelligence organization can easily create a digital file for nearly anyone anywhere. Many do just that. Using social media, small or large governments and political groups with otherwise tiny voices easily leverage these tools.

Facebook dominates this world of personal connections for the moment, and has rapidly become a global digital identity document, one that is available to all to review, not just tyrannical governments. There's no need for a late-night knock at the door for millions or billions of residences – Facebook is already inside. Care to share comments on news or other sites? Facebook is used as a tool to scrutinize one's identification first in many instances, before allowing open speech such as posting a comment. Applying for a job? Be prepared to provide your Facebook credentials so your posts and those of your friends can be reviewed. An anonymous Facebook moderator somewhere doesn't approve of your comments? Your credentials are suspended, until you prove yourself to another anonymous person to be real, innocent or misunderstood, or maybe become more politically correct than you should have to be. Younger generations say they have become wary and more interested in content over pseudo-friends whom one never speaks to, and thus prefer Instagram over Facebook. Instagram was bought by Facebook in 2012 for $1 billion.

In a white paper entitled *Libra* and released in 2019, Facebook outlined its intent to set a global digital identification standard, as part of a later worldwide digital currency. Meanwhile, the company with billions of accounts now requires many users to provide official government forms of identification to keep their accounts open, including a birth certificate, driver's license, passport, green card or other documentation. Facebook has at least 15,000 people employed globally to be content moderators – those busy banning things in free societies around the world that the company defines as hate speech. Having an unaccountable private entity deciding what is acceptable speech is arguably as dangerous as a government dictatorship. They also have another 30,000 employees assigned to something called 'safety and security'. Borders and concrete walls have no meaning in digital worlds, but as the Stasi knew well, the control of identity, speech and access do.

The end goal for Facebook is to have one digital identity standard for anyone who wishes to conduct financial transactions, travel, speak anywhere to anyone, be involved in any digital communications or hope to validate themselves and their history of thought to a potential employer. Facebook wants to control that standard and to own that sellable information. But it might turn out to be Google as well, or a company we haven't yet heard of. Is a commercial enterprise that acts for profit or may sometimes go awry blowing with misguided political winds any better than a government dictatorship limited by a border? Physically taking away freedom and jailing people when the law is broken is of course what governments generally do well in free societies, when regulated by the democratic process of checks and balances. Anyone can use information as a weapon and massive collection by commercial entities makes that easier. Regardless, any source for this sought-after control would be a gold mine to the next secret police that would ruthlessly pursue people for political purposes.

To be the Stasi of the twenty-first century all they need are the GDR-style laws that allow them safely to do most anything; the means are far easier now to protect and project a government dictatorship. Laws always lag behind technology. But tyrannical governments that wish to control have another way. By selectively allowing access to economies attractive to those companies that are the most compliant with their regulation and oversight, the next dictatorship can make use of it all. Microsoft, the maker of the only foreign search engine allowed in China, has agreed to concessions to enable its search tool, Bing, to be used there. It censors its search results as required by the Chinese government, to stay in a lucrative market.

Just as former MfS colonel Klaus Eichner referred to the modern surveillance tools of the NSA as a 'dream come true' for the Stasi, and another lieutenant colonel and current leader in the revisionist movement bragged about the technical abilities of the MfS in penetrating computer networks even years ago, there is little doubt what they would have done if given the chance. Today's tools, which are freely available, are much more efficient than a wall to keep citizens in check. The Berlin Wall was erected in plain view, barbed wire at first, followed by bricks and mortar and machine guns. Technology today enables placing an invisible digital wall anywhere a state actor thinks it should be, in minutes.

Stasi in the twenty-first century? How would they have done it? There's little need to speculate.

The MfS were experts at personal destruction and decomposition in countless subtle and not-so-subtle ways. That was possible because they were the grey face of a huge, mysterious and perceived as all-knowing organization that was feared by seventeen million East Germans and millions more outside the GDR. The ruthless efficiency of today's free and unified Germany pursuing Facebook posters with fines and employing more 'content moderators' than anywhere else gives one ominous warning of what a MfS-type program might have included, directed against its own citizens and those abroad who were critical of the communist regime. It's simply much easier and far quicker to destroy a person now than it was for them then. What the Stasi called *Zersetzung*, or decomposition, no longer requires a thick paper file that could be inconveniently found someday. Tech giants provide an undisputed service to the average person as a sideline to their business goals, but are understandably now becoming sensitive about this darker part of their image.

One day recently, Google was on the hunt in Berlin. They needed space for a headquarters complex and had their eyes on the Kreuzberg district, probably since it has a reputation for being a young and hip part of the city. Instead, the district mayor of Lichtenberg from the Left Party made them an interesting and serious offer. How about Google take over dozens of the mostly still empty huge buildings at the centrally located former State Security headquarters? *We'll give you a great price…*

No official response has come from the company, and their hunt in Berlin continues.

Google, with its original company code of conduct that famously included the motto 'Don't be evil', has become a huge global warehouse of personal information. It may have a business model of targeted advertising instead of directly selling information, unlike Facebook, but they collect information about almost everyone on a massive scale. That's of tremendous use to a dictatorship or unfriendly intelligence agency. Google modified their official code of conduct in 2018 to remove the famous motto, but that hardly means that they, Facebook or other technological innovators that drive the internet are evil. As commercial entities they only become easy tools for governments or other organizations that are. If you can't easily live everyday life or speak freely without presenting an identity document to anyone who demands it, your freedom is compromised. If online spaces of expression and speech are patrolled by companies that may be influenced by political views, and looking along the way to sell your information to anyone, bad things will happen.

By 1990, only tiny amounts of speech and expression were controllable in digital spaces; now it's the vast majority. Many of the most prolific users of the digital tools and media are the same people and organizations complaining the loudest about the collection of this information. The officers of the Ministry for State Security were clearly undisputed experts in mass data collection in a pre-digital age. Today, as such collection is inevitable, it should be approached with caution and much close scrutiny, but not fear.

A present-day MfS certainly would make use of any and all tools to protect their communist dictatorship, as they always did. But today they could let commercial social media do much of the work first. In 1989, the technology of the Stasi was limited by what could be bought, stolen or otherwise acquired from the West, copied and improved. The rap on the door by the Grey Men of today could be to demand to know why the resident's social messaging activity was critical of the government, or to discuss why facial recognition cameras had shown them near too many government buildings or foreign embassies, or to talk about their online friends, or their social score. Far-fetched? Hardly. This is all happening now in China.

The Chinese WeChat messaging service – used by a billion people across the globe – is routinely scanned by the Chinese government with keyword search algorithms. As a state actor, it's simple to block entire internet sites and communication applications, forcing people to use others. China is blocking thousands of domains at the moment, perhaps as many as 10,000 sites, including Google, Gmail, Facebook, Instagram and Twitter. In 2017 it was estimated to be spending $197 billion a year on domestic security, and already had installed 176 million security cameras to watch its own citizens. Chinese authorities have announced they are working toward 100 percent digital camera coverage of all key public areas in the near future. And now they have another new project. It's a currently unnamed algorithm that will assign a social score to every person. This score will be based on multiple criteria about how pleased the state is. Score too low? Did you say something critical on WeChat, attend church or visit a foreign embassy? Good luck getting a good job, or a visa to travel. Another Stasi dream come true.

Perhaps the Stasi of the present would also have developed an efficient app to make such things even easier. In 2019, Human Rights Watch managed to reverse engineer a Chinese government app called the Integrated Joint Operations Platform (IJOP). IJOP is currently busy collecting thirty-six categories of personal information on thirteen million Turkic Muslims living in Xinjiang province in northwest China. The app highlights 'suspicious behaviors' for police or security services for investigation – such as if a person isn't using a smartphone, is antisocial with neighbors, or makes political comments without a permit. By tracking phones, vehicles and ID cards, it also has the ability to erect virtual fences that alert police if a person ventures outside their expected routine or normal destinations.

But can the spiraling surveillance state coming from China and its own Ministry for State Security (MSS) really be compared to the East German MfS? What do they have in common? Communism, the need to control speech and a mandate to protect an insecure totalitarian dictatorship that would otherwise become unstable, for one. Total state control of the population and fear as a way to influence and train behavior, for another. In a free capitalist society, the government doesn't have this sort of control over people. Forces more important than the state act daily to provide freedom of choice to most, and to foster free speech and weed out inefficiencies. The government in the United States isn't much of a threat to the individual who is not a criminal, terrorist or spy, regardless of daily shrill claims to the contrary. That's precisely why real capitalism is a threat not only to China, the only communist country of consequence remaining today, but to nonstate actors that seek to employ the same methods to control others. The secret police in China, the MSS, have a mandate far exceeding a combination of the roles of the CIA and FBI, times ten. When consolidated with the two million officers of their primary domestic national police agency, the Ministry of Public Security (MPS), the apparatus is a Stasi on steroids. Except, instead of targeting seventeen million citizens, they target more than a billion.

Leading Chinese officials maintain deep respect for their hero, Karl Marx. In some ways their goals sound much the same as those of the GDR and Cold War USSR.

The world's largest public square rested in complete silence. Found in the middle of a bustling city, it lay nearly empty under a cool overcast sky one early November day. It was nearly twenty-eight years to the day after the fall of the Berlin Wall and the implosion of the GDR dictatorship. A plump, ever-smiling man, who seemed always to wear a dark blue suit, strode confidently to the podium inside an imposing building located just on the western edge of this blood-soaked space in Beijing called Tiananmen Square. His message to all present was clear. The communism of Marx was winning again in the world. Clearing his throat and flashing a slight but confident smile, he began.

'Our party has always adhered to the lofty ideals of communism. Communists, especially leading cadres, should be staunch believers and faithful practitioners of the lofty ideals of communism and the common ideals of socialism with Chinese characteristics. The belief in Marxism, socialism and communism is the political soul of the communists and the spiritual prop of the communists to withstand any test. The party constitution clearly stipulates that the highest ideal and ultimate goal of the party is to realize communism.'

The speaker at the Nineteenth Communist Party Congress that winter day, Chinese president Xi Jinping, paused and looked out at the crowd of thousands of party functionaries seated in the Great Hall of the People. They represented the largest repressive government bureaucracy in the world, at the moment. Xi knew well his role: chairman of the Central Military Commission, general secretary of the Chinese Communist Party, and president of the People's Republic of China, in that precise order.

He stopped for the applause, and went on to praise the German communists once again:

'Facts have repeatedly told us that Marx and Engels' analysis of the basic contradictions in capitalist society is not out of date, nor is their historical materialism view that capitalism must die out and socialism must win.'

The fall of the German Democratic Republic nearly three decades earlier hadn't changed anything.

East Germany was filled for forty years with careful, desperate and risky whispered conversations taking place in private places. In the country controlled by the 91,000 members of the Firm, unapproved public gatherings were prohibited, just as they are now in China. That's normal for any dictatorship, because if people freely exchange ideas, bad things certainly might happen to a repressive regime. With social media, it's increasingly possible for organized groups with a political agenda to make it uncomfortable for digital or physical gatherings in much the same way. The techniques are different, but the goal is the same. To control, shape or prohibit speech. It's no longer necessary to be a state actor to employ Stasi-like digital tools of decomposition against the individual. It's happening every day, especially in America. Anonymous acts of personal decomposition, now called 'doxxing', the publishing of real or false private information, designed to intimidate or destroy, are ever present on social media. It's done by small groups, individuals or foreign government actors pretending to be someone else. The goal is to destroy the person for political gain, in true Stasi fashion.

It's the *Zersetzung* of today.

———

Months after the upbeat speech given at Tiananmen Square, and as the senior former Stasi officers gathered in Berlin on the third floor of Franz-Mehring-Platz 1 one day in late 2018 to celebrate their new victory, the actual story of what happened to bring it about would soon begin to appear.

30

TRUTH AND SOLITUDE

He was sitting on a hard wooden bench late on a winter afternoon in the Charlottenburg district. Just down the street was Tiergarten Park, filled with Berlin's famous linden trees, planted after the war to signify the final restoration of a people and a ravaged city.

I was looking at a thin and tired man who had a careful searching stare. He had been fighting the Ministry for State Security and their supporters for the last forty years – nearly thirty of those after the Wall fell.

Hubertus Knabe greeted me politely. He wore a light black jacket on a cold day and held a small folder. A man in turmoil who appeared calm. It was remarkable considering what had just happened.

'Since they fired me, it's been bad.'

He had been abruptly removed as director of the Hohenschönhausen Memorial, a job he had held for nearly twenty years. It was in all the newspapers. One reporter who caters to The Left wrote in his article, 'Ding-Dong, the Witch Is Dead!' The event had prompted satisfied chatter on the websites and in the newsletters of the Stasi groups, and in the inner circle of their supporters and apologists in the Left Party. The victims' groups stayed oddly silent about it in public.

The allegations had nothing directly to do with him, but were made anonymously against his deputy at the Memorial, Helmuth Frauendorfer. Sexual harassment by the deputy, the anonymous persons said in the anonymous letter, which was never made public. A pattern of inappropriate comments, it claimed. It was styled as a

'MeToo' attack. And then those waiting quickly accused Director Knabe of not moving fast enough to handle it.

September 17, 2018, was the day Hubertus Knabe learned indirectly that there was an anonymous letter making allegations against Deputy Frauendorfer. The next day he called Klaus Lederer, chairman of the Memorial Foundation, who had apparently received the letter, for the details.

'I asked to know who made the allegations, and to see the letter, and it was denied,' Hubertus said. 'How to investigate an anonymous charge?' The privacy of anonymous accusers must be the priority, they recited. He asked again to see it anyway.

'You don't need to see the letter,' Lederer said.

Two days later, after thinking it over, Knabe announced that he was investigating the allegations, and he suspended Frauendorfer. The day after that, Lederer removed him as director. 'Not following up quick enough', he was told. 'To this day, I've never seen that letter, or heard from any accuser,' Hubertus said.

To many in Berlin who spoke privately about it, this didn't even begin to pass the smell test.

'Is this something done by the… organizations?'

He carefully considered my question.

'There are the signs.'

We both waited until two men, both of whom had mobile phones pressed to their ears as they stopped silently next to us, finally moved off.

'But remember, I'm not a victim. Others deserve the attention.'

I nodded. But it's clear that may not be the case. The head of one of the victims' groups in Berlin had made the point to me the previous week.

'Knabe was targeted! It's just like before!'

We briefly stood to get coffee a few steps away. I thought of Knabe's mother, who was pregnant with him when she fled East Berlin in 1959 with her husband and three other children. Eighteen months before the Wall created the biggest prison in the world. Hubertus was born of two East German parents, a West German by birth, thus

spared from being a prisoner with the others. A free man, who chose
to continue fighting.

'And now? What will you do?'

'Take care of my family, try to find something.'

He rocked in frustration on the bench.

'It's worse even. The government approved the center. I had just
learned that Parliament had approved my request to create an official
Center for Left-Wing Extremism at Hohenschönhausen! Just in
August, the Bundestag Budget Committee gave me five million euros
to put it together! I had some ideas on how we could...'

His voice trailed off and he shook his head.

'I doubt now it will be built at all, because of Lederer.'

It had unfolded with precision.

Klaus Lederer, the cultural affairs senator in Berlin, which also conveniently made him chairman of the Memorial Committee. Lederer
was appointed by the Left Party to the position, and promptly led the
push to vote to remove Knabe. Nobody could argue with Knabe's
professional record after eighteen years as the successful creator of
the Memorial, so something else was needed.

It was all over the news. Two others on the Memorial Advisory
Committee resigned in protest because of that decision, the news
said. One of them, a well-known civil rights activist and former Stasi
prisoner, Freya Klier, summed up why when she was asked. This is
'about occupying Hohenschönhausen with a politically more supple
management'.

Knabe and I sat in silence watching the stream of people pass by
until he spoke again. 'The way it all happened was strange.'

'When you...'

'Yes. Yes. I came to work that morning and was presented with a
letter of termination. I wasn't even allowed in the building! Then, a
few days later, I arranged with them to allow me to return to collect
my few personal items from the office. That's when it happened, at
the gates of Hohenschönhausen!'

He zipped his jacket up and shivered.

'I was walking out with my box of a few things. It was just inside the gate, where some staff members and the new interim manager stood. I stopped to greet one of the victim-guides I had hired. I put down my box and stepped up to shake the man's hand. He looked toward the others and his hands hung at his sides. Instead he stepped closer and whispered something to me, there just inside the gates.'

He opened his hand and stared at it before continuing.

'"I won't shake your hand here."' That's what the man said to me as he looked nervously over toward the others.'

Hubertus lowered his head and seemed tired. 'It was as if I was in the GDR again.'

'And then, when I walked out the gate with my box, I saw a man standing on the street corner. There, by the entrance. I recognized him at once.'

'It was… him. Rataizick.'

'The Stasi colonel who had run the prison?'

'Yes. He was there. He just stood there, on the corner, and stared directly at me, but said nothing. He just stared.'

'How did he know to…?'

Hubertus shook his head slowly. 'Good question.'

He focused on a cup of cold coffee.

'I've never been allowed to know who made the accusations against my deputy; their names are kept private. Anonymous accusations, that's all there was. How could I evaluate that? And I wasn't even given the chance!'

A group of university students streamed past, and the winter afternoon shadows were growing longer. Hubertus looked at them and back to me. There was a glimmer. His eyes had the flash of a fighter.

'I called Chancellor Merkel's office. It wasn't so long ago she visited the Memorial and was a strong supporter.'

'You spoke to her?'

'Yes, I managed to speak to her. She said…' He looked away. 'That's the way it has to be, is what she said to me. The way it has to be…' he repeated quietly.

'Is the problem still the Stasi organizations?'

'Yes, but it's much more than that now.' He tensed on the bench. 'It's the rise of the left. They don't want criticism of communism and its millions of victims, only of fascism. So, it's just safer for everyone to talk about only that.'

The hundreds of thousands of victims of GDR communism are being victimized once again.

I thought of the search for the SED's missing billions.

'Do you think they may have access to the missing money even now – the heirs to the SED dictatorship?'

He lowered his voice to just above a whisper.

'Yes, it's possible.'

We stood and I walked with him across the courtyard.

'What are your plans?'

'To take care of my family. I must be careful. There's a saying here. It's far easier to step on a dead dog.'

'Meaning for you…?'

He shrugged. 'I don't know yet.'

We talked a while longer, and finally went our separate ways. After a half-dozen steps, I saw him rushing back to catch me.

'Come, look at this!'

I followed and we retraced our path, stopping at a prominent community bulletin board. He nodded at a freshly tacked-up slick poster advertising a new upcoming event.

Socialism on Stage!

A large and colorful clenched fist covered the poster, which was emblazoned with *Marx, Revolution, The Left, Antifa! Socialism Days! Something better than capitalism.*

He tapped the photo displayed of one the presenters. I recognized the face. It was former State Security officer Andrej Holm, smiling benevolently at the camera.

The false promises of the communists, who had reinvented themselves as Antifa or socialists, were taking hold again. The tired look had returned as he continued to stare at the poster in disbelief. For a flicker he was that young man once again standing at the Palace of Tears, shocked at being refused entry by the Stasi. Then, it was gone. He turned away with hunched shoulders and slowly made his way through the crowd.

During the eighteen years Hubertus Knabe was director of the Hohenschönhausen Memorial in Berlin, the numbers of annual visitors climbed from 7,000 to more than 400,000; half of those who came were young people. The total visitors had just surpassed four million. It had become one of the most visited Cold War memorials in Europe.

Following his termination, the plans for opening a Center for Left-Wing Extremism stalled.

EPILOGUE

COMRADE

Berlin
Saturday

I'm in the back of a darkened taxi. It's late, well past midnight, but the city is still alive with activity from the bars and clubs in Mitte and Kreuzberg. I look up and glance to the right as we stop quickly at a light. It's a street I know well. But today a new, professional-looking and oversized sign is affixed to one of the buildings near the U-Bahn station.

It proclaims with black glossy effect:

Comrade, I'm not ashamed of my communist past.

This is the city as it nears the thirtieth anniversary of the fall of the communist dictatorship.

Several weeks later, I'm in a small café. It's not in Germany or the United States this time, but on the African continent, thousands of miles from either place. I'm here to meet a casual acquaintance, a very accomplished German journalist from Berlin. We'll call her Anika. We find a table and chat in the warm air about both of us living far from home and such. She seems relaxed and excited to share how she adapted to life here and to discuss local job prospects. The conversation warms with the gentle breeze, as we both look outward toward the sea.

'Anika, as you're a journalist, can I ask you something about Germany?'

Smiling, she sits back and nods. 'Well! Planning a vacation?'

I smile also and shake my head. 'Lots to do there for sure, and Berlin is a fantastic city, but no, not at the moment.'

I signal the waiter for refills. 'No, actually it's about the Stasi. Can we talk about them, where they went after? What they did?' The smile fades as she leans forward and stirs her cup, staring intently at it until the waiter leaves. Then, lowering her voice to barely a whisper although we are alone, she looks out the window while carefully speaking.

'Ah, why do you…?'

We had become conspirators.

'It's been nearly thirty years and I'm trying to understand some things about them.'

She rapidly stirs the cup again. 'What things, which…?'

'Do you think they're still influencing Germany?'

She hesitates, checks the time on her phone and reaches for her bag. 'They're still there – some of them not so old even. They're there.'

'In what way?'

'Umm… I don't feel so comfortable…' her voice trails off again. She sits back from the table, and at first says nothing more. I think to change the subject, but decide on silence.

'Yes, Berlin is a great city as you say, but it can be a cruel place,' she finally says softly as she gathers her things, before making excuses and standing to go. We might as well have been sitting in a café in East Berlin in 1988 – instead of on the other side of the world decades later, staring toward a southern sea. Even far from Berlin, the Grey Men are still avoided and not talked about by many of those who should. It will soon be too late.

Later, I remember what Hartmut Richter, a victim I spoke with who nearly drowned during a freezing midnight swim to freedom, said to me. He spoke directly, with a focused and firm voice. Like so many others, he'd had his life altered forever by spending years without a name in a Stasi prison. When I heard his incredible story of survival and what he has done to tell others about it in the decades since, a question surfaced. It needed an answer.

Why did a now seventy-one-year-old man stay so politically active and spend so many hours lecturing to school groups and to anyone who would listen?

When I asked that, he eyed me in surprise and answered at once. 'I'm not going to let those men define history.'

Nobody could argue that the career of the young KGB officer named Vladimir Putin ended in 1990 when he was forced to leave Dresden and drive back to Russia with failure on his mind. His future, and related new threats to global stability, was likely created by that event. Just so, it's foolish to say that the influences of the many thousands of highly committed officers of the Stasi ended. The difference is that it's far easier for their actions, reactions and careful revisionism to be lost in a crowd. Many in that crowd, and those who surround it, have an ongoing interest in promoting doubt and indifference, and hide behind harsh privacy and fear. That's how tyranny is created, sustained and repeated again and again.

Realities are easily shaded by academics or politicians. But having stared in the face of evil and despotism around the world, and spoken with many of those who bore its price, is enough to understand the dangers of allowing clarity to slip away. The ultimate cost of leaving that task only to the quiet historians and their books lying on musty shelves, or to those others simply with the loudest voices and concealed agendas, is unmistakable. The focus on one type of extremism, while quietly ignoring or attempting to normalize even the tyrannies of the other, is a threat to freedom. Adopting the long-used method from the communist playbook of claiming to be against fascism while advocating for other equally harsh actions, seen again in organizations like Antifa and others in Europe and the United States, is simply smoke and mirrors. The future is far too important to be left to any of them to decide.

Street sense accumulated by all in law enforcement and intelligence work says that those who most loudly claim to be one thing are frequently something else. When the perpetrators routinely claim to be the victims, such as with the Stasi and the system they protected, you can be sure they're preparing for it to happen again.

There isn't a good investigator anywhere in the world who fails to remember the victims. The natural human tendency is to want to move on, to declare something won or over. To close a chapter and a door or look away in haste, thinking it's done. That often results in forgetting those who must not be forgotten. In Germany, most recently that's over 400,000 victims of the Stasi and the leftist-communist dictatorship. They're individuals who matter, even if the passage of time means that fewer survivors are now in front of us, and those who remain are mostly silent faces. The ripple effect of the GDR leftist dictatorship, which was only possible because of the Grey Men, passes through generations, touching everywhere in free societies. It must not be brushed aside.

If you look closely, you can find fighters and heroes in unusual places. Hubertus Knabe, the historian in Berlin who was shocked enough by his own experiences and secret police file that he chose not to be quiet but to be something more. His removal from his position and lifelong passion of highlighting victims' issues, for anonymous and murky reasons, has caused yet a new chill that may have silenced others. That's useful for those interested in redefining the Stasi abuses or hiding the history of the new left. In his case, the good news is that it may not have worked. After a brief period of silence following his firing, Knabe responded by creating a new personal platform to continue his work, nearly alone and with even fewer protections. He hasn't been silenced, but the end isn't yet written.

Heroes can be found in many other places. The automotive mechanic and Stasi victim in Atlanta who handles his car repair business by day and spends long nights on the telephone to Germany, desperately hoping to stop the return of those responsible for the leftist dictatorship. The families in Europe and America who continue to fight for the return of property and memories seized by the Stasi. A man who passionately operates a dwindling victims' association from a tiny cramped office in Berlin. Parents who search for what happened to more than 600 missing children. They speak for all of the thousands of young men and women who were arrested, imprisoned or had their lives sidetracked and futures destroyed to protect a failing communist state. They're found also in the lingering voices of the one hundred million murdered victims of Marx-inspired communist dictatorships worldwide.

The current siren calls in Europe and the United States for a return to more government control, with dramatic limits on certain speech, markets and other freedoms, driven by officials, anonymous and nontransparent social media organizations, or others who seek to redefine and control language and thought, have all these people to answer to first. The lessons of the Stasi, the most ruthless, invasive and destructive secret police seen in the last hundred years, and their continued efforts over the last three decades to prosper and rewrite history, continue to speak volumes and warn of future tyranny. The voices of the victims faintly whisper that it could well happen again.

It's up to the rest of us to make sure that we listen closely.

ACKNOWLEDGMENTS

Without any doubt this book would not have even begun without candid comments made by those I many times encountered on the streets of Eastern Europe, in sober memorials, government offices, cafés and small flats, who had endured the unimaginable for half a century. Victims and remnants of communist tyranny are found in all these places, and countless numbers of them in Germany and throughout Europe told me their own extremely personal stories. All of them deserve mention, but that would fill many more pages and, in some cases, needlessly intrude on personal trauma that even now, decades old, is still too recent.

Hugo Diederich, Jörg Drieselmann, Christian Lappe, Hartmut Richter, Lothar Schulz and dozens more in Germany alone went out of their way to describe to a stranger the reality of how the Stasi forever sidetracked their lives and those of their families in ways that words on a page cannot adequately convey.

Many professionals in the intelligence services of the United States, newly freed countries and former German police and security officials also provided insight and guidance. All usually spoke candidly, but for many reasons it's not wise to list them individually or by their true names.

Current caretakers of the memories of the communist dictatorship in Berlin, Leipzig, Potsdam and many smaller places in Germany spent many hours showing me things that matter. The Office of the Federal Commissioner, the BStU, especially the many extra efforts of Dagmar Hovestädt of the press office in Berlin, and Alexander Hartmann in Leipzig, was critical. The victim-witnesses at the Stasi Hohenschönhausen prison who still relive trauma daily make it real to all.

Then there is the young woman who guided me through a Stasi doomsday bunker, which remains buried deep in the woods hundreds of kilometers from Berlin. She didn't wish to be mentioned by name but deserves acknowledgment nonetheless for highlighting the new generation's perspective.

A great deal of attention is certainly owed to those in Germany and others now living elsewhere in Europe and the United States who are quietly, and sometimes boldly, continuing to fight against Stasi and communist revisionism, hoping to preserve clarity for those in the present and the future. Special mention for this is due to Hubertus Knabe, who still says what must be said and to those who must hear it, at continued risk to his livelihood. Knabe is a hero in this effort, and has recently paid a steep price for doing the right thing even though it makes others uncomfortable.

There are several persons who are no longer able to live in Germany, who provided information about former Stasi officers. Although not personally recognized here for good reason, they helped to keep the focus on facts and circumstances that must be remembered. And there were the former officers themselves, who were many times candid and sometimes not.

Jens Gieseke, the most well-known and preeminent German Stasi expert, took the time to sit with me in his office for hours to discuss some basic and many difficult questions that are not being discussed openly. Matthias Judt, the recognized expert on former Stasi officer and elusive moneyman Alexander Schalck-Golodkowski, also graciously spent hours with me adding life and depth to the person who was once the most hated man in Germany. Ulrich Mählert, head of research for the Federal Foundation for the Study of the SED Dictatorship, gave me an afternoon and evening of candid comments and insights.

Several patient translators and researchers in Germany assisted. One of them, Zoe S., merits special mention. She never seemed uncomfortable in odd situations and at strange times and places, and still caught the subtle points, which are many times the most important.

Credit is due to those in the FBI who came before and after me, both in the United States and elsewhere. Agents are found scattered throughout Eastern Europe and the world, often in dangerous and far-flung places, working professionally every day, making the impossible possible. Things I learned from many of them, especially the fellow agents on the streets of America – such as how to ask the right questions at the right time – can never be taught at Quantico.

A deserved nod to John Talbot, a literary agent extraordinaire who was nearly as enthusiastic about this project as I.

The book couldn't have come about at all without Leslie, Ryan and Jason. They inspired this story, and many others.

REFERENCES

The most significant sources for this book remain the personal inter-actions and unwritten trauma that I observed nearly daily in my years working and living in Eastern Europe, the Baltic states, Germany and other formerly Soviet-allied states in Europe, Central Asia and Africa. There's little substitute for walking the streets and talking with those who have witnessed and paid the price, or hearing insights from those in former and current police and security services. Sometimes these contacts took place in odd places and for equally odd and dramatic reasons that still require the location and names to be protected.

Much material comes also from personal interviews conducted in Germany with recognized Stasi experts, victims and former MfS members themselves. The search for answers prompted me to review thousands of pages of official MfS records from the Archive in Berlin. Mention of identification numbers for the Stasi officers refer to the GDR Personal Identification Number (PKZ) used at the time, short-ened to the final six digits.

Interactions with my FBI colleagues, either past or present, and with those in other US intelligence agencies were essential. They're not referenced, or if mentioned in a specific instance, the persons and places are not identified by their true names. Details from NSA or CIA reports refer to once classified documents, all now properly processed for declassification and in my possession. Other significant sources, events or quotations are listed on the following pages.

Preface

Putin in Dresden: Account of Siegfried Dannath, who was in the
crowd at the Dresden KGB office on December 5, 1989, quoted
in 'Vladimir Putin's formative German years', *BBC Magazine*,
March 27, 2015.

Nickname of Putin as 'Stasi' by the St Petersburg KGB: Account by
Putin's German biographer, Boris Reitschuster, quoted in 'Putin's
Stasi Card Discovered After 30 Years' [Putins Stasi-Ausweis nach
30 Jahren entdeckt], *Focus*, December 24, 2018.

MfS identification card carried by Vladimir Putin: Discovered by
others December 2018 in the Dresden MfS offices. The identification card does not mean Putin worked for the Stasi; rather,
it allowed unrestricted access to all facilities and enabled him to
present himself to German citizens as a member of MfS, when
that was useful.

Further accounts of the storming of the Dresden MfS office can
be found in official MfS reports of the incident, in author's
possession.

PART I

1. Personal Destruction as a Fine Art

Anatoly leaned back in the seat: Not his real name.

The statistics of the MfS operations are found within the records
and publications of the Federal Commissioner for Records of the
State Security Service of the former GDR (BStU), specifically
in Münkel, *State Security [Staatssicherheit]*, and Gieseke, *The Full-
Time Employees of the Ministry for State Security [Die hauptamtlichen
Mitarbeiter der Staatssicherheit]*.

600,000 informants: Federal Foundation for the Reappraisal of the
SED Dictatorship.

2. Present and Past

Experiences and activities of Stasi victim Christian Lappe: Various personal interviews with author.

Wilhelm Knabe details: 'A Dark Green – Wilhelm Knabe, Pioneer of the Eco-Party' (radio interview), *Experienced stories*, WDR 5, Germany, October 5, 2003.

Hubertus Knabe, early days: Personal interview with author and Schädlich (ed.), *On the Record [Aktenkundig]*.

3. Awakenings

Stasi investigation of Hubertus Knabe: Extracted from personal account of Knabe written in Schädlich (ed.), *Professional Files*.

'Nobody has the intention of building a wall!': Statement by GDR president Walter Ulbricht, June 15, 1961, quoted in 'The Berlin Wall – the 10 most famous quotes about the barrier', *The Local*, November 9, 2016.

Deaths at the Wall: Berlin Wall Memorial.

4. Enemies of the State

'Worse than the Gestapo!': Simon Wiesenthal, quoted in Koehler, *Stasi: The Untold Story of the East German Secret Police*.

MfS officer dissertation topics: BStU study.

Organization of MfS: Gieseke, *The Full-Time Employees of the MfS*.

At present, former Stasi officers are receiving 350 million euros each year: Author interview with Sabine Kraatz, German Pension Office, 2019.

Stasi murders and abductions: Knabe, *The Perpetrators Are Among Us [Die täter sind unter uns]*.

Hands up!: Author interview with Hugo Diederich, VOS.

'The Birdcage': Author interview with curator, Chemnitz Stasi prison.

5. The Thirty

'*We lived two very different lives*': Author interviews.
Stolen Children of the GDR: 'The Little-Known Tragedy of Forced
    Adoptions in East Germany', *Spiegel*, February 7, 2019.

6. Day X

Directive 1/67: Auerbach, 'Preparing for Day X': BStU study 1/95.
Details about Mielke's offices: Author visits to former Stasi head-
    quarters, Berlin.

7. Chaos, Disbelief and Fear

'*As I said, a new draft travel law…*': Schabowski quote taken from video
    of event, November 9, 1989.
Account at border crossing Bornholmer Strasse, November 9: 'The
    Night of the Wild Boar' [Die Nacht der Wildschweine], *Spiegel*,
    November 2, 2009; Sarotte, *The Collapse*.
the KGB would beat a hasty retreat…: Author conversations with foreign
    intelligence officers.

8. Dissolution, Disappearance and Anger

Runde Ecke: Author's visit to MfS district office in Leipzig and inter-
    view with research assistant Alexander Hartmann and staff.
Nearly 90 percent of these well-trained officers were under the age of fifty:
    Stasilist, in author's possession.
'*I love all people!*': Erich Mielke in an address to the East German
    Parliament, November 13, 1989, video reviewed by author.
Unfortunately, one brown folder looks a lot like another: Actions by the
    HV A to destroy their own personnel files. Interview by author
    with BStU research assistant.

9. Opportunity Hunters

CIA in East Berlin, January 1990: Bearden, *The Main Enemy*.

By December 5, CIA traffic started speculating: 'Developments in Eastern Europe', CIA classified summary, December 5, 1989. Declassified November 12, 2013, copy in author's possession.

Rosenholz Stasi files returned by the CIA in 2003: BStU, Mueller-Enbergs report in possession of author, 'Rosewood, a Source Criticism'.

'Of course, the GDR must be singled out': 'Discussion of the German Question at a Private Meeting in the Office of the CPSU Central Committee General Secretary', January 26, 1990. Wilson Center Digital Archive, copy in author's possession.

Angela Merkel as GDR representative: Account by Ewald König, 'Remembering people, places and myths surrounding the fall of the Berlin Wall', *Euractiv*, November 6, 2014.

10. Follow the Money

'Don't transfer me to detention in the Eastern Sector': '21 Tons of Gold in the Basement' [21 Tonnen Gold im Keller], *Spiegel*, November 29, 1999.

'Please keep silent – my life is in your hands!': Ibid.

Defection of Schalck-Golodkowski: Source interviews by author. As there are two differing accounts of the defection, the most likely was used. Since German intelligence organizations have never released the actual reports, representative dialog has been used for the initial encounter.

'Then they took Peter away.': Account of Rita Garcke, 'No Justice for Victims of Regime's Treasure Hunt', *Spiegel*, July 24, 2014.

PART II

11. The Mission

Removal of computer tapes to military base to create pension
list: Interview with David Crawford, WSJ Germany reporter,
quoted in 'Dealing with the Stasi', johnfeffer.com, June 27,
2014.
Stasilist: Provided by source, in author's possession.
Fictitious curriculum vitae for Stasi officers: Gieseke, *The Full-Time Employees*.
MfS policy directives concerning false employment verifications: In
author's possession.

12. Nobody Really Wants to Know

'*The Stasi ran the place!*': Author interview with Hubertus Knabe.
'*Glue and Annette have become intimate…*': Excerpt from Knabe's MfS
file, quoted in Schädlich, *Professional Files*.

13. Don't Ask

'*One must assume that the foundations for many of these companies…*':
Rainer Engberding, quoted in 'We Stand in the Forecourt of
Hell' [Wir stehen im Vorhof der Hölle], *Spiegel*, November 26,
1990.
'*processing of five outstanding contracts*': dispatch from West German
Embassy, Delhi, September 1990, quoted in 'Under Scrap Value'
[Unter Schrottwert], *Spiegel*, October 22, 1990.

14. The Many

some 700 former officers were practicing as lawyers: Grafe, *German Justice*
[Deutsche Gerechtigkeit].

'*I request the procedure to be terminated immediately!*': quoted in 'DDR Doping Process: Ewald's Defense Plays on Time' [Verteidigung Ewalds spielt auf Zeit], *Spiegel*, June 9, 2000.

just one *was sentenced to prison*: Interview with official of BStU. Also, Herbstritt, 'Law Enforcement for MfS Injustice' [Strafverfolgung wegen MfS-Unrechts], BStU.

'*If the Party had given me the task…*': quoted in 'Erich Mielke, Powerful Head of Stasi, East Germany's Vast Spy Network, Dies at 92', *New York Times*, May 26, 2000.

'*it was necessary to discipline him…*': Quoted in 'Delicate Penalties' [Empfindliche Strafen], *Spiegel*, May 13, 2002.

Sixty-two-year-old Berlin woman fined for 'Sharing' a Facebook post: 'Berliner convicted of incitement on Facebook' [Berlinerin wegen Volksverhetzung auf Facebook verurteilt], *Morgenpost*, May 31, 2017.

15. Surprises in the New Government

One television reporter was skeptical: 'Dossier, Undetected in German Unity – In the Footsteps of a Dictatorship' [Unentdeckt in die deutsche Einheit – Die Stasi-Offiziere im "besonderen Einsatz"] (video), *Contrasts*, Federal Agency for Civic Education, September 11, 1990.

'*I didn't believe it until I heard it on the car radio…*': Interview with author.

16. Uncomfortable Questions

Confidential study titled 'Report on the Employment of former MfS Members…': Provided by source; copy in author's possession.

17. The Last Official Meetings of the Firm

an uninvited and overlooked man: 'Erich Mielke: Who wept for the Lord of Fear?' [Wer weinte um den Herrn der Angst?], Gerald

Praschl EASTblog, originally published in *Superillu Weekly*, June 28, 2000.

they gathered once more: 'East German Spook Reunion', *Spiegel*, November 19, 2007. Also, author interview of attendee Jens Gieseke, 2019.

Dr Hermann Travel was started in 1990 with a single bus: 'One German, two careers' [Ein Deutscher, zwei Karrieren], *Tagesspiegel*, January 16, 2015.

18. Politicians

'By means of a provisional injunction…': Wikipedia.de notice, November 13, 2008. Screenshot in author's possession.

'I oblige to: Use all my strength…': MfS oath, handwritten and signed by Andrej Holm, in possession of author, available from MfS personnel records, BStU.

His hands were seen trembling at the podium: interview with Bärbel Bohley, 'We Were Drifting Away' [Wir waren abgedriftet], *Spiegel*, November 7, 1994.

Gysi was indeed 'Notar': 'Gregor Gysi and the Stasi's Long Shadow', *Die Welt*, February 17, 2013.

19. Kings of the Russian Machine

'What do you want to do if the GDR no longer exists?': Question to Warnig, quoted in 'This German Enjoys Putin's Trust' [Dieser Deutsche genießt Putins Vertrauen], *Die Welt*, August 3, 2014.

'Friendships do not hurt': Warnig motto, ibid.

'Previously, Mr Warnig had several functions…': Quote from online CV for Matthias Warnig, 2019, in author's possession.

Director of Personnel for Gazprom, Hans-Uve Kreher, by his own admission an unofficial employee of the Stasi: 'Toxic Cocktail' [Giftiger Cocktail], *Spiegel*, August 25, 2008.

'[I certify that] I have never been an [official] employee…': Affidavit filed by Felix Strehober, quoted in 'Gazprom Manager in the Sights

of German Justice' [Gazprom-Manager im Visier der deutschen Justiz], *Die Welt*, May 6, 2008.

20. Professor Murder

He had recently returned from visits to Hanoi and Havana: MfS personnel file for Stelzer, reviewed by author.

TOXDAT... 911 pages: 'At Head Height' [In Kopfhöhe ausgerichtet], *Spiegel*, May 17, 1999.

he had a very unusual secret friend: 'Beloved Comrade' [Geliebter Genosse], *Spiegel*, December 17, 1990.

On July 18, 2000, a new company appeared: Goldman, Morgenstern & Partners, LLC, record of incorporation, New York Department of Corporations. Abstract copy in author's possession.

has survived to the present day: 'Visit to Mafia Journalists', Investment Alternatives, March 25, 2013. 'Now You Again!' [Jetzt du wieder!], *Die Zeit*, March 7, 2013. 'The peculiar business of the Gomopa company' [Die eigentümlichen Geschäfte der Firma Gomopa], *Süddeutsche Zeitung*, April 8, 2015.

21. Government Consultants

NSA Codeword document (declassified) reference Eurocrypt: National Security Agency, Declassification & Transparency Section, DOCID: 4009689, April 13, 1994, copy in author's possession.

IM V 55/74 under the code name Victoria: 'A Stasi Debate That Has Not Ended' [Eine Stasi-Debatte, die nicht beendet wurde], *Berliner Zeitung*, April 2, 2003.

22. The Quiet Network

'Hohenschönhausen was really the Dachau of communism': Hubertus Knabe, quoted in 'The New Leader of the Memorial Hohenschönhausen'

[Der neue Leiter über die Gedenkstätte Hohenschönhausen], *Berliner Zeitung*, December 1, 2000.

'Wouldn't that subject him to the death penalty in the US?': Interview with former Stasi colonel Klaus Eichner, '"The Scope of NSA Surveillance Surprised Me"', *Spiegel*, June 18, 2014.

'Moral Issues Do Not Matter': Eichner, quoted in 'Ex-Stasi colonel on BND espionage' [Ex-Stasi-Oberst über BND-Spionage], *Stern*, October 15, 2015.

'It can best be described as the relationship maybe like a father to his children': Former Stasi lieutenant colonel Wolfgang Schmidt in *Stasi: Everyday Life of an Authority [Das Ministerium für Staatssicherheit: Alltag einer Behörde]*, e-Motion Picture, Baden-Baden, 2002.

'Fakes of history!': quoted in 'The Revenge of the Pensioners' [Die Rache der Rentner], *Spiegel*, March 27, 2006.

'for us, this would have been a dream come true': Wolfgang Schmidt to reporter, 'Memories of Stasi color Germans' view of U.S. surveillance programs', *McClatchy*, June 26, 2013.

23. New Organizations

'We work for our members to ensure the proper understanding of history': Author interviews at Stasi organization offices.

Angela Davis receives the Lenin Peace Prize, 1979. 'Russia Davis Prize', AP Archive video.

24. Revisionists

Marco burst in with a wave / So, Vassily was called an SVR officer now: Not their real names.

'more than 800,000 people had visited the Memorial': Seventh Annual Report, Berlin-Hohenschönhausen Memorial, 2015.

'We learn from the past, because the future is not indifferent to us': Joachim Gauck, Stasi victim and former president of Germany, ibid.

'*Not one of them ever complained!*': Peter Pfütze, quoted in '"Red-Painted Fascists"' [Rot lackierte Faschisten], *Spiegel*, April 12, 2006. Also, 'Books by Former GDR Secret Police Officers Spark Outrage': *Deutsche Welle*, April 13, 2006.

'*You will evaporate like water in the sun*': Stasi victim and former inmate of Hohenschönhausen Andreas Möller, quoted in 'The return of the communists in Germany', The Iron Curtain Project, European Commission, 2018.

PART III

25. Desperate Secrets of the Puzzle Keepers

'*We are nine*': Unidentified worker at the Stasi Archives. Interview with author. Berlin, February 2019.

26. The Grey Men Persist

'*I swear…*': excerpt from the Stasi officer oath, BStU, translated by Zoe S.

'*I would like to speak about heroes*': Hubertus Knabe speaking in Vilnius, Lithuania, April 2015, video in author's possession.

'*the Auschwitz of souls*': Jürgen Füchs, quoted in 'Wound for Life' [Wund fürs Leben], *Die Zeit*, April 26, 2012.

Marc Rich and KoKo: Author interview with Matthias Judt, German expert on Schalck-Golodkowski.

'*My power was the money*': quote from Schalck-Golodkowski, *German to German [Deutsch-deutsche Erinnerungen]*.

'*and in the end, we lost*': quoted in 'Former GDR Currency-Procurer is Dead' [Ehemaliger DDR-Devisenbeschaffer ist tot], *Manager Magazine*, June 22, 2015.

27. *Who's Still Afraid?*

the group methodically presented twenty-one demands: meeting between
former Stasi officers and head of the Stasi Archives, 2018. Interview
of Stasi officers by author, and 'Truth and Reconciliation?'
[Wahrheit und Versöhnung?], *Junge Welt*, December 3, 2018.
'A victory!': Interview of former Stasi officer by author, Berlin,
February 2019.

28. *Apathy and Nostalgia*

*'The GDR failed only because the political will was lost. We could have taken
care of it'*: Interview of former Stasi officer by author, Berlin,
February 2019.
'Antifa simply believes that capitalism equals fascism': Report of the BfV,
Germany internal intelligence agency (Office for Protection of the
Constitution), 2017, in author's possession.

29. *The Face of a Twenty-First-Century Stasi*

'The witch is dead!': 'My Evening with Angela Merkel' [Mein Abend
mit Angela Merkel], *Spiegel*, October 12, 2018.
'176 million security cameras': 'China's Surveillance State Should Scare
Everyone', *The Atlantic*, February 2, 2018.
'Our party has always adhered to the lofty ideals of communism': Speech of
Chinese president Xi Jinping to the Nineteenth Communist Party
Congress, Beijing, January 5, 2013.

30. *Truth and Solitude*

I was looking at a thin and tired man who had a careful searching stare:
Hubertus Knabe, interview with author, Berlin, 2019.

SELECT SECONDARY SOURCES

Bearden, M. and Risen, J. (2003) *The Main Enemy: The Inside Story of the CIA's Final Showdown with the KGB*. New York: Ballantine Books.

Bruce, G. (2010) *The Firm: The Inside Story of the Stasi*. New York: Oxford University Press.

Bundestag (2016) *Final report: The expert commission on the future of the authority of the Federal Commissioner for the documents of the State Security Service of the former GDR (BStU) [der Expertenkommission zur Zukunft der Behörde des Bundesbeauftragten für die Unterlagen des Staatssicherheitsdienstes der ehemaligen DDR (BStU)]*. Berlin.

Burnett, S. (2007) *Ghost Strasse: Germany's East Trapped between Past and Present*. Montreal: Black Rose Books.

Central Intelligence Agency (2018) FOIA Reading Room. Washington DC.

Deutschland 86 (2018) *Comrades & Cash*. Berlin: UFA Media.

Federal Agency for Civic Education and RBB (1990) *Dossier: Contrasts — In the Footsteps of a Dictatorship*. Video. Berlin: Bundeszentrale für politische Bildung/bpb, September 11.

Federal Foundation for the Reappraisal of the SED-Dictatorship Berlin (2011) *Coming to Terms: Dealing with the Communist Past in United Germany*. Berlin: Stiftung Aufarbeitung.

Garton Ash, T. (1997) *The File: A Personal History*. New York: Vintage Books.

Gieseke, J. (2000) *The Full-Time Employees of the Ministry for State Security: Personnel Structure and Environment [Die hauptamtlichen*

Mitarbeiter der Staatssicherheit: Personalstruktur und Lebenswelt 1950–1989/90]. Berlin: Ch.Links.

Glaeser, A. (2011) *Political Epistemics: The Secret Police, the Opposition, and the End of East German Socialism*. Chicago and London: University of Chicago Press.

Grafe, R. (2004) *German Justice: Trials Against GDR Border Guards and their Commanders [Deutsche Gerechtigkeit: Prozesse gegen DDR-Grenzschützen und ihre Befehlsgeber]*. Berlin: Siedler.

Hertle, H-H. (2012) *Chronicle of the Fall of the Wall: The Dramatic Events Around 9 November 1989 [Chronik des Mauerfalls: Die dramatischen Ereignisse um den 9. November 1989]*. Berlin: Ch.Links.

Knabe, H. (2007) *The Perpetrators Are Among Us: On the Euphemisation of the SED Dictatorship [Die täter sind unter uns: Über das Schönreden der SED-Diktatur]*. Berlin: Ullstein.

Knabe, H. (2010) *The Truth About the Left [Die Wahrheit über DIE LINKE]*. Berlin: Ullstein.

Koehler, J. O. (1999) *Stasi: The Untold Story of the East German Secret Police*. Boulder: Westview Press.

Ladd, B. (1998) *Ghosts of Berlin: Confronting German History in the Urban Landscape*. Chicago: University of Chicago Press.

Marxen, K. and Werle, G. (eds) (2002) *Criminal Justice and GDR Injustice vol. 3: Abuse of Office and Corruption [Strafjustiz und DDR-Unrecht. Bd. 3: Amtsmissbrauch und Korruption]*. Berlin: De Gruyter.

Marxen, K., Werle, G. and Schäfter, P. (2007) *The Criminal Trials of the GDR: Facts and Figures [Die Strafverfolgung von DDR: Fakten und Zahlen]*. Berlin: Humboldt University.

Miller, B. (1999) *Narratives of Guilt and Compliance*. London: Routledge.

Münkel, D. (ed.) (2016) *State Security: A Reader on the GDR Secret Police [Staatssicherheit: Ein Lesebuch zur DDR-Geheimpolizei]*. Berlin: Federal Commissioner for the Records of the State Security Service of the former German Democratic Republic (BStU).

Muravchik, J. (2003) *Heaven on Earth: The Rise, Fall, and Afterlife of Socialism*. New York: Encounter Books.

Myers, S. L. (2015) *The New Tsar: The Rise and Reign of Vladimir Putin.* New York: Alfred A. Knopf.

National Security Agency (2018) Declassification & Transparency Section. Fort Meade, MD.

National Security Archive. Washington DC: George Washington University, accessed 2018.

Rathmer, M. (2015) *Alexander Schalck-Golodkowski: Pragmatist Between the Fronts [Pragmatiker zwischen den Fronten].* Berlin: Epubli GmbH.

Reitschuster, B. (2018) 'Putin's Stasi Card Discovered After 30 Years' [Putins Stasi-Ausweis nach 30 Jahren entdeckt]. *Focus* (online). Accessed January 2, 2019.

Reitschuster, B. (2018) *Putin's Democracy: What Makes it so Dangerous for the West [Putins Demokratur: Was sie für den Westen so gefährlich macht].* Berlin: Ullstein.

Rosenberg, T. (1996) *The Haunted Land: Facing Europe's Ghosts After Communism.* New York: Vintage Books.

Roth, J. (2012) *Gazprom – The Eerie Empire [Gazprom – Das Unheimliche Imperium].* Frankfurt/Main: Westend.

Sarotte, M. E. (2014) *The Collapse: The Accidental Opening of the Berlin Wall.* New York: Basic Books.

Schädlich, H. J. (ed.) (1993) *On the Record [Aktenkundig].* Berlin: Rowohlt.

Schalck-Golodkowski, A. (2000) *German to German Memories [Deutsch-deutsche Erinnerungen].* Hamburg: Rowohlt.

Schumann, F. and Wuschech, H. (2012) *Schalck-Golodkowski: The Man Who Wanted to Save the GDR [Der Mann, der die DDR retten wollte].* Berlin: Das Neue.

Schissau, R. (2006) *Criminal Proceedings for MfS Injustice: The Criminal Proceedings of German Courts Against Former Employees of the Ministry for State Security of the GDR [Strafverfahren wegen MfS-Unrechts: Die Strafverfahren bundesdeutscher Gerichte gegen ehemalige Mitarbeiter des Ministeriums für Staatssicherheit der DDR].* Berlin: Berliner Wissenschafts.

Spiekermann, U. (ed.) (2014) *The Stasi at Home and Abroad: Domestic Order and Foreign Intelligence*. Washington DC: German Historical Institute.

The Federal Commissioner for the Records of the State Security Service of the former German Democratic Republic (BStU). Berlin, 2018–19.

Wilson Center, Digital Archive. Washington DC: https://digitalarchive.wilsoncenter.org.

Wolf, M. (1997) *The Man Without a Face: The Autobiography of Communism's Greatest Spymaster*. New York: Times Books.

PHOTOS AND ILLUSTRATIONS

Back cover: Stasi Fortieth Anniversary medal issued to officers in 1989, one month before the fall. / Author.

Page viii: Map of the saturation of Stasi offices in East Germany, 1989 / BStU.

Page 42: KGB lieutenant colonel Vladimir Putin's Stasi identification / BStU.

—Guarded main entrance to Stasi headquarters, Berlin 1983 / BStU.

Page 43: Erich Mielke, Stasi minister / Bundesarchiv.

—Erich Mielke, head of the Stasi, at thirty-fifth anniversary, 1984 / Robert Havemann Foundation (RHG).

Page 44: Hohenschönhausen prisoner registration ledgers / Author.

—Stasi disguised prisoner transport truck / Author.

Page 98: Fortieth anniversary of the GDR, October 7, 1989 – weeks before the fall.

—Press conference mistake / Bundesarchiv.

Page 99: Stasi photo of prisoner Hugo Diederich when he was ransomed / H. Diederich.

—Hugo Diederich, Head of Victims' Association (VOS), 2019 / H. Diederich.

Page 100: Part of the remaining 15,000 bags of torn files / Author.

—Hopeless state of reconstruction efforts at BStU in 2019 / Author.

Page 174: Putin/Warnig/Schröder, 2014 / EPA – Anatoly Maltsev.

—Former Stasi officer Matthias Warnig, former German chancellor Gerhard Schröder, then Russian prime minister Dmitry Medvedev, in Moscow at Putin's inauguration, 2018 / TASS – A. Druzhinin.

Page 175: Stasi file with photo, former officer Matthias Warnig / BStU.

—Stasi file with recent photo, former officer Felix Strehober / BStU / DPA – Stephanie Pilick.

Page 236: Lieutenant General Alexander Schalck-Golodkowski / BStU.

—Stasi file with photo, former officer Hans-Ehrenfried Stelzer / BStU.

Page 237: *Rosenholz* files as returned by the CIA in 2003 / BStU.

—*Rosenholz* CD on display at the Stasi Museum / Author.

Page 238: Location of new Stasi headquarters / Organizations in Berlin / Author.

—Proud Stasi officers turned authors / Picture Alliance – Michael Hanschke.

Page 239: Socialism/Antifa event in Berlin with former Stasi officer, 2019 / Author.

INDEX

References to images are in *italics*.

ABOUT THE AUTHOR

Ralph Hope was an FBI agent for more than twenty-five years. Much of that time was spent on the streets of America investigating drug trafficking organizations, violent crimes and terrorism. Following 2001, he served nearly a decade overseas as an FBI representative in the Middle East, Asia, Europe and Africa. He lived for years in Eastern Europe as deputy head of the FBI office in the Baltic states, and in West Africa as head of FBI operations in eleven of those countries. Later, he was selected as liaison representative for the US Department of Justice to United Nations Peacekeeping forces battling Islamic extremists in Mali.